REF 796.48 201

2010 Vancouver Canada

2010

U.S. OLYMPIC TEAM
AT THE XXI OLYMPIC WINTER GAMES

&

U.S. PARALYMPIC TEAM
AT THE X PARALYMPIC WINTER GAMES

Vancouver | Canada

AN OFFICIAL PUBLICATION OF THE UNITED STATES OLYMPIC COMMITTEE

COMMEMORATIVE PUBLICATIONS
SALT LAKE CITY | UTAH

COVER / *The emblem of the Vancouver Games is an inukshuk, stacked rocks in human form created by the Inuit people of Canada's vast Arctic. It was used as a guidepost. Over time, the inukshuk has become a symbol of hope and friendship throughout Canada.* (PHOTO BY STEPHEN MUNDAY/GETTY IMAGES)

PRECEDING PAGE / *Three-time Olympian Lindsey Vonn earned her first Olympic medal—the gold—in the downhill race and the bronze in the super-G.* (PHOTO BY FABRICE COFFRINI /AFP/GETTY IMAGES)

A snowboarder flies through the Olympic rings to kick off the Opening Ceremony of the Vancouver Winter Games. (PHOTO BY SAEED KHAN/AFP/GETTY IMAGES)

PUBLISHER
Mikko Laitinen | Commemorative Publications

MANAGING EDITOR
Lisa Albertson

COPY EDITOR
Jessica Laitinen

PHOTOGRAPHY
Getty Images
Long Photography

ATHLETE PROFILES
Amy Donaldson

PRINTER
O'Neil Printing, Phoenix
Paper: 100# Alpha Gloss Book

PUBLISHED UNDER LICENSE
FROM THE U.S. OLYMPIC COMMITTEE BY:
Commemorative Publications
P.O. Box 711514
Salt Lake City, UT 84171
801.706.2901

Stacey Cook's 11th in the downhill was an inspired comeback. The 25-year-old American was airlifted to the Whistler Polyclinic after a severe crash in the first downhill training run. She was heavily bruised, but nothing was broken, yet returned to complete the last training run and compete in the race. (PHOTO BY ALAIN GROSCLAUDE/AGENCE ZOOM/GETTY IMAGES)

Ten thousand athletes from around the world came to Vancouver, British Columbia, "with glowing hearts" as Canada welcomed competitors from around the world as hosts of their third Olympic Games and second Paralympic Games.

For 27 days, that motto rang true in each and every athlete, official and spectator as the drama, pageantry and spirit representative of the Olympic & Paralympic ideals united us all. Together we mourned the tragic death of Georgian luger Nodar Kumaritashvili, who died trying to live out his Olympic dream, and we rallied behind the spectacular performances of the world's greatest athletes.

Representing true Canadian spirit and determination, the Vancouver Organizing Committee (VANOC) overcame many obstacles to ultimately stage a brilliant Games. Together VANOC, the thousands of volunteers, the Canadian national, provincial and local governments ensured a positive legacy for the 2010 Olympic and Paralympic Games.

Vancouver, with its picturesque backdrop of sea and sky, was already one of the finest cities in the world; but now, the city will be forever recognized for the warmth, passion and joyous celebration on display and for the way the city opened their hearts to the world and let them share in the experience.

On this stage, it was befitting that America's Team would make Olympic Winter Games history by winning the most medals ever by any country and the U.S. Paralympic Team would compete admirably as well. The U.S. Olympic and Paralympic Teams showcased the power of dedication, determination and teamwork as the team came together in pursuit of a common goal to represent themselves, their sport, the U.S. Olympic Committee and their nation, with utmost class and character.

We'll look back fondly on our memories of the 2010 Olympic and Paralympic Winter Games, and be forever grateful that Team USA was able to share in the moment.

L. F. Probst III

Larry Probst III
U.S. Olympic Committee, *Chairman*

The athletes who represented the United States at the 2010 Olympic Winter Games were exceptional in every sense of the word. They won the aggregate medal count in Vancouver with 37 medals. They won more medals than any U.S. Olympic Team in history. And remarkably, they won more medals than any other country in the history of the Olympic Winter Games. As Americans, we were inspired not only by their performance on the field of play, but also by the character and courage they displayed both in and out of competition.

The 13 medals won by U.S. Paralympic athletes placed us fifth in the aggregate medal count. Among our Paralympic athletes were five U.S. military veterans. Sport calls us to be the best we can be. Nowhere can we see that more clearly than in the dedication of our Paralympic athletes.

The success our U.S. Olympic and Paralympic athletes in Vancouver is a testament to their commitment, courage and perseverance. It is also a testament to the excellence of the National Governing Bodies (NGBs) that oversee individual sports in the United States. We are grateful to all of our NGBs for the quality of the programs that they provide to our athletes (Olympic, Paralympic and otherwise).

One of the primary jobs of the U.S. Olympic Committee is to generate financial and in-kind support for our athletes and NGBs. To our broadcast partner NBC, as well as to sponsors, donors and supporters of the U.S. Olympic and Paralympic Teams, we offer a heartfelt thank you. It is your generous support that allows our athletes to achieve their dreams and inspire a nation.

Scott Blackmun
U.S. Olympic Committee, *Chief Executive Officer*

Youth the world over aspire to be just like you ...

"As you, the best Winter Olympic athletes of all time, enter the arena prepared for you here in Canada to compete in the honor and glory of sport—seizing the moment to inspire the youth of the world through your heroic efforts—you carry with you the hopes and the dreams of so many.

You are role models for our children—heroes, giants, human champions—the best ever.

You are living proof that men and women everywhere are capable of doing great good—and that in life as it is in sport—we should always give our best—and never, ever give up."

—John Furlong
CEO | VANOC

Gold medalist Yu-Na Kim of South Korea performs during the 2010 Olympic Winter Games exhibition gala that traditionally follows the end of the figure skating competition. (PHOTO BY VINCENZO PINTO/AFP/GETTY IMAGES)

(Photo by Vincenzo Pinto/AFP/Getty Images)

Table of Contents

Athletes and bibs are left hanging after the cancellation of the second run of the official training for the ladies' Olympic downhill at Whistler Creekside. It's a delay that gave American Lindsey Vonn additional time to heal from a bruised shin. (Photo by Olivier Morin/AFP/Getty Images)

For American Lindsey Jacobellis, Vancouver was supposed to be her gold-medal redemption after losing the gold in Torino after a showboating grab before the finish line went awry. But in the semifinals, Jacobellis came off the first jump and landed off balance and off course after she nicked a gate. She finished fifth in the snowboardcross event. (PHOTO BY ADRIAN DENNIS/AFP/GETTY IMAGES)

With Glowing Hearts

Canadian Rick Hansen carries the Olympic Torch during the Opening Ceremony of the Vancouver 2010 Olympic Winter Games. Paralyzed from the waist down at the age 15, Hansen has traveled the world and raised more than $26 million dollars for spinal cord injuries through his 'Man in Motion Tour.'
(PHOTO BY JASPER JUINEN/GETTY IMAGES)

LUGE
Nodar Kumaritashvili

Nodar Kumaritashvili died in a horrific accident at the Whistler Sliding Center, just hours before the Opening Ceremony of his first Olympic Games. Sadly, the 21-year-old's death came on the very track where he hoped to make his Olympic dreams come true.

Growing up in a family of luge athletes in Bakuriani, Georgia—once a winter sports mecca of the Soviet Union—Kumaritashvili understood and embraced the risks of one of the world's most dangerous sports. The accident that claimed his life altered the luge competition's rules and changed the emotional energy of the Games.

Officials declared him in the hearts of all of those athletes competing in the Games. A monument to him was erected and decorated with flowers, candles and notes in Whistler. A luge track bearing his name will be built in his hometown.

In the end, Georgian president Mikheil Saakashvili said the young man's life — and death—will inspire a new generation of luge athletes.

"Because the Olympic movement is all about perseverance," he said. "It's all about unbroken spirit. It's about the future and strength…and no matter what the tragedy, carrying on. This spirit of humanity is maybe the biggest thing you can take away from the Olympics, more than maybe the medals."

Lindsey VONN

Downhill Thriller

I n the days before Lindsey Vonn became the first American woman to win a gold medal in downhill skiing, it looked like fate was not smiling on Vonn. One of the most accomplished alpine skiers in U.S. history, Vonn, now a three-time Olympian, had yet to ascend the Olympic podium.

The 25-year-old native of Minnesota revealed in an emotional press conference that she had suffered a severely bruised shin in pre-Olympic training and hadn't been able to put on a ski boot for more than a week prior to arriving in Vancouver.

And then the unseasonably warm weather and rain, which wreaked havoc on the ski slopes, bought Vonn time to heal when the super combined race was postponed. Her first race on Feb. 17—the downhill—earned her a thrilling first Olympic medal and the coveted top podium finish.

Julia Mancuso, who finished 0.56 of a second behind Vonn, gave the United States an inspiring 1-2 finish.

Vonn went on to win a bronze medal in her third event —the super-G. She failed to finish the other three races, crashing in her final race, the slalom, and fracturing her pinky.

It might surprise some that a native of the Midwest has turned herself into the world's best alpine skier. But she grew up skiing at famed Buck Hill in Minnesota, which has produced nearly a dozen U.S. Ski Team members. Eventually, she and her family moved to Vail, Colorado, where she currently resides with her husband, Thomas Vonn. He was a member of the 2002 Olympic Ski Team.

Vonn's rise to the top of alpine racing began in earnest during the 2005-06 season, when she started a very specialized training program.

Despite injuries, accidents and the difficulty of trying to excel in every discipline, Vonn's success in Vancouver has made her a testament to dedication and hard work.

Lindsey Vonn overcame a bruised shin injury to win the downhill race in 1:44.19. Vonn is the most decorated downhiller in American history. (PHOTO BY MICHAEL KAPPELER/AFP/GETTY IMAGES)

NORDIC COMBINED
Johnny SPILLANE

Gaining Recognition

Growing up in Steamboat Springs, Colorado, ensured Johnny Spillane would be a skier. His fascination with ski jumping began when he was just a toddler. He watched the ski jumpers at Howelsen Hill and dreamed about launching himself off the jump. He didn't actually jump, however, until he was 11 years old.

Then he spent a couple of years jumping on his alpine skis before he "got serious" at age 13. The oldest of three children, Spillane won the first U.S. World Championship in nordic combined in 2003.

He and his American teammates suffered a devastating blow in the 2002 Olympic Winter Games when they finished fourth on what they considered their home course— Soldier Hollow, in Midway, Utah. He struggled with injuries that hampered his success over the next six years.

An accomplished cook and fly fisherman, Spillane and his teammates came into the 2010 Games hoping to put their sport on the radar of Americans.

The 29-year old, four-time Olympian won the first Olympic medal for the U.S. in nordic combined when he finished second in the 10km normal hill on Feb. 14. He also helped the team earn a silver medal in the 4x5km relay, and he finished his trip to Vancouver with a silver medal in the large hill 10km competition.

"We might not get a ton of recognition," he said after winning the silver medal. "But it was nice that the hard work paid off."

In the team event, consisting of a jump on the large hill (pictured) and a 4x5km relay, the Americans were in second place after jumping, giving Finland a two-second head start in the relay. Johnny Spillane jumped 134 meters on the large hill and helped his teammates claim the silver while upping his medal count to three. (PHOTO BY PHILIPPE MONTIGNY/AGENCE ZOOM/GETTY IMAGES)

OPPOSITE / *Opening Ceremony featured a performance of artists wearing skis and riding snowboards against a backdrop of fabric that projected images of athletes from winter sports.* (PHOTO BY DAVID HECKER/AFP/GETTY IMAGES)

Welcome
to Vancouver

In a dazzling display of color and creativity, Vancouver's Opening Ceremony (below, opposite top), held indoors at the 60,000-seat BC Place, gave a worldwide audience a glimpse into Canada's culture. Meanwhile, at the Games, two of Canada's national pastimes, ice hockey and curling, drew fans from around the world.

(PHOTO BY JAMIE SQUIRE/GETTY IMAGES)

(PHOTO BY SAEED KHAN/AFP/GETTY IMAGES)

(Photo by Sandra Behne/Bongarts/Getty Images)

(Photo by Bruce Bennett/Getty Images)

The USA 1 four-man bobsled team of Steve Mesler (left), Justin Olsen, Curt Tomasevicz (jumping) and Steve Holcomb (helmet) celebrate winning the gold medal. Their bobsled, nicknamed the Night Train, is named after the Harley Davidson motorcycle model known for its relaxed, but powerful ride. (PHOTO BY LEON NEAL/AFP/GETTY IMAGES)

Night TRAIN

One Powerful Ride

They called themselves the Night Train. Officially, however, driver Steve Holcomb, and push athletes Steve Mesler, Justin Olsen and Curt Tomasevicz, were known as USA 1 in the 2010 Olympic Winter Games. And in two glorious days of near-perfect racing, the Night Train put the U.S. on top of four-man bobsled for the first time in 62 years.

It was a moment many years in the making, and one that almost didn't happen for the crew, who boasted both athleticism and chemistry. Holcomb nearly retired from the sport in 2006 because of a degenerative eye disease that left him legally blind.

Instead of allowing him to quit, however, U.S. Bobsled officials helped him find an innovative new procedure that saved his eyesight and the country's best bobsled team.

Interestingly, his coaches felt it may have been his vision problems that helped him instinctively feel the right lines necessary to navigate the Whistler track, which was so difficult a half dozen of the world's best drivers crashed during the two-day competition.

Mesler is a native of Buffalo, New York, who attended the University of Florida as a decathlete. He graduated in Exercise Science with honors and found out about bobsled from the Internet.

Tomasevicz is a native of Shelby, Nebraska, who attended the University of Nebraska, where he played running back and linebacker. He was academic all Big 12 and earned a Bachelor and Master's in Electrical Engineering with a minor in Astronomy.

Justin Olsen is a native of San Antonio, Texas, who attended the U.S. Air Force Academy for a year before trying out for the U.S. Bobsled Team. He played high school and college football.

Holcomb grew up an alpine skier in Park City, Utah. He was attending the Park City Winter Sports School when he found out about bobsled tryouts and earned a spot at a camp in Lake Placid. Just 12 years later, he, and his teammates, would live up to the hype and earn the first U.S. gold in four-man bobsled in more than six decades.

Evan
LYSACEK

Mr. Nice Guy Grabs Gold

Evan Lysacek became the first American to win a gold medal in men's figure skating in 22 years. And he did it by beating one of the world's best, Russian Evgeni Plushenko, the 2006 Olympic gold medalist.

The showdown between Lysacek and Plushenko featured the American's technical proficiency against the Russian's athletic ability (he opened his free skate with a quadruple jump).

In the end, a scoring system that tries to balance the ability to be both athletic and artistic gave Lysacek the gold medal.

A native of Naperville, Ill., the 24-year-old's first pair of skates were purchased by his grandmother. He hoped to be a hockey player, but sandwiched between two sisters, his parents signed him up for figure skating.

It wasn't long, however, before he showed promise. He won the Juvenile title at the Junior Olympics at age 10 and the Junior title at the U.S. Junior Championships at age 14. It was after that success that Lysacek, who played a number of sports as a child, decided to dedicate himself to figure skating. He finished fourth in the 2006 Winter Games and won the World championship in 2009.

He has said figure skating didn't come easily to him. Lysacek said that what he lacked in talent, he made up for with hard work and dedication. His coach, Frank Carroll, has called Lysacek one of the hardest working athletes he's ever trained.

The polite, well-spoken Lysacek is known among other skaters as a persistent competitor who learns from his failures. He is as gracious in defeat as he is in victory.

When Plushenko and the Russian Federation questioned how Lysacek could win the gold without a single quadruple jump, Lysacek simply expressed admiration for Plushenko's ability to win three medals in three different Olympic Games.

Evan Lysacek's hard work paid off handsomely with a gold medal in men's figure skating. In the short program (opposite) Lysacek skated into second place and narrowly edged Russian Evgeni Plushenko in the free skate. (PHOTOS BY YURI KADOBNOV/AFP/GETTY IMAGES)

23

(Photo by Robyn Beck/AFP/Getty Images)

(Photos by Scott Olson/Getty Images)

(PHOTO BY LEON NEAL/AFP/GETTY IMAGES)

(PHOTO BY ADRIAN DENNIS/AFP/GETTY IMAGES)

In the preliminary game between Canada and the United States, goalie Ryan Miller (#39) makes a save as Sidney Crosby (#87) pokes at the puck. (PHOTO BY JULIE JACOBSON-POOL/GETTY IMAGES)

USA underdogs have their own "Miracle on Ice"

The U.S. ice hockey team upset the heavily-favored Canadians in the preliminary round, 5-3. The Americans kept their cool in a tough, emotional and closely fought game that was tied twice. Brian Rafalski scored two goals in the first period and Chris Drury gave the U.S. a 3-2 lead in the second period.

Langenbrunner upped the American lead to 4-2 in the third period, however Sidney Crosby cut Canada's deficit to a single goal with three minutes remaining in the game. With 45 seconds left on the clock, Ryan Kesler's empty-net goal sealed the victory for Team USA and left a stadium stunned.

Alexei Grishin gave his country the first gold medal at the Olympic Winter Games. Shadowed by the team's World Cup star aerialist Anton Kushnir, Grishin wasn't even favored to win. But when Kushnir crashed in the qualifications, the 30-year-old, four-time Olympian found his place in the limelight.

Competing after Jeret Peterson's "Hurricane" trick that put the American in first place, Grishin said to himself, "I have to do it"—and he did.

When the final competitor Kyle Nissen of Canada buckled his landing, Grishin had made Belarussian history. (PHOTO BY MARTIN BUREAU/AFP/GETTY IMAGES)

The Russian-born Slovak biathlete Anastazia Kuzmina broke two bones in her hand one month before the Vancouver Games, but it didn't stop her from winning the gold medal in the 7.5km sprint event (pictured) and the silver in the 10km pursuit. (Photo by Javier Soriano/AFP/Getty Images)

Hannah KEARNEY

Hannah Strikes Gold

Born to parents who believe in the value of athletics, Hannah Kearney was destined for some kind of athletic greatness. She began skiing at age 2, but she was also a varsity soccer and track athlete in high school.

Of course, it was the moguls that became her passion. While she enjoyed early success as a teenager, she suffered a devastating setback in Torino. She finished 22nd in a lackluster performance and said it sent her reeling.

"If I had known I was going to win (in 2010), I wouldn't have cried that hard," she said, admitting it took months to recover from the agony of defeat. She blew her knee out the following year and spent a year recovering.

In the end, that time away from moguls probably helped her shake off any negativity, and she came back ready for the Olympic Games with the kind of confidence and determination that impressed even her competitors.

After winning the first U.S. gold medal of the 2010 Games, she revealed a list of training stats handed to her by one of her coaches before her final run at Cypress. In preparing for the Games she had completed 1,000 water ramp jumps and 14,000 jumps of all types in trying to perfect the two required aerial tricks.

She said it was empowering to conquer her fear of "flipping and twisting" and only made her more determined as she skied bumps faster than any other woman in the world.

The 24-year-old skier from Norwich, Vt., was the first to clinch a spot on the U.S. Freestyle Team with a win at the U.S. Olympic Trials in December. An older but wiser Kearney also chose to march in the Opening Ceremony—something she didn't do in 2006—because, she said, she wanted to enhance her experience as an Olympian.

(PHOTO BY SAEED KHAN/AFP/GETTY IMAGES)

After a lot of hard work and endless training, Hannah Kearney cherishes her gold medal. Judges gave Kearney the highest scores in turns, air and speed, which placed her score .96 ahead of Jennifer Heil of Canada and 1.2 points ahead of teammate and bronze medalist Shannon Bahrke.

Golden dreams

Husband and wife pairs team of Hongbo Zhao and Xue Shen of China captivated the audience and judges alike and ended their Olympic journey with gold.

After skating together for almost two decades the coupled retired from competitive skating after the 2007 Worlds, married and opened a skating school in Shenzhen, China. Favorites for the gold medal in Torino, the Chinese team suffered a setback when Zhao tore his Achilles tendon on a triple toe loop in August 2005. At Torino they settled for the bronze but could never quite give up on their dream of an Olympic gold. In 2009, the couple emerged from retirement and took the Worlds by storm, defeating two-time world champions Aliona Savchenko and Robin Szolkowy of Germany.

Their gold medal ushered in a new era of pairs skating with fellow teammates Qing Pang and Jian Tong (opposite) claiming the silver medal with the best free skate program of the evening. That night marked the first time in 12 Olympic Winter Games that a Soviet Union or Russian team wasn't standing on the top of the Olympic podium.

(Photo by Yuri Kadobnov/AFP/Getty Images)

(Photo by David Hecker/AFP/Getty Images)

(Photo by Yuri Kadobnov/AFP/Getty Images)

And relay bronze makes eight

Apolo Anton Ohno skated to a new record as the most decorated U.S. winter Olympic athlete winning eight medals over the course of three Olympic Games. The 27-year-old shed more than 20 pounds since his Olympic debut in Salt Lake City in 2002. In Torino, he competed at 155 pounds, but in Vancouver, a sleek and fit Ohno showed up at the oval weighing 142 pounds with 2.8 percent body fat.

Reaching speeds of over 30 miles per hour and skating at an aggressive angle require overall body strength from the ankle on up. As part of his "no regrets" motto, Ohno embarked on a rigorous training schedule and stuck to a nutritional program that paid off handsomely in Vancouver. (PHOTO BY MATTHEW STOCKMAN/GETTY IMAGES)

SHORT TRACK SPEEDSKATING

Apolo Anton OHNO

Apolo Eight

Born in Federal Way, Washington, Apolo Anton Ohno came into the Vancouver Games a super-star. A fan favorite and one of the most recognizable winter sports athletes, Ohno already owned five Olympic medals—a gold and silver from the 2002 Games and a gold and two bronze from the Torino Games.

The 27-year-old made history on Feb. 20, 2010, when he went from last place to third on the final lap of the 1000m race. The bronze medal was his seventh and made him the most decorated winter Olympian in U.S. History. Ohno went on to win an eighth medal in the 5000m relay. He is just one of four Americans to win three medals in a single Winter Games—which he did twice, in Vancouver and Torino.

Ohno was raised by his father, Yuki Ohno, after his parents divorced when he was an infant. Because his father, who owned a hair salon, worked long hours, Yuki Ohno got his son involved in athletics—swimming and in-line skating—at a young age to keep him busy.

In 1994, 12-year-old Apolo saw short track speed-skating in the Lillihammer Games and was intrigued.

His father went to work helping his son get access to the best training facilities, and Apolo was admitted to the training program at Lake Placid at just 13 years old. It was his older teammates, however, who helped light the competitive fire that would transform him from a rebellious teen to the country's most successful winter athlete. They nicked named him "Chunky" and chided him for his mediocre effort.

He became much more dedicated to his training and in 1997 he won gold and silver medals in the U.S. Senior Championships. Because of his own struggles as a teen, the young philanthropist heads a foundation that promotes the benefits of a healthy lifestyle.

A sweet victory for Canada

After hosting the Olympic Games for the third time, Canada received its very first gold medal on home soil, courtesy of Alexandre Bilodeau, who took first place in the men's moguls competition held at Cypress Mountain. Appropriately, it was on Valentine's Day. (PHOTO BY ALEXIS BOICHARD/AGENCE ZOOM/GETTY IMAGES)

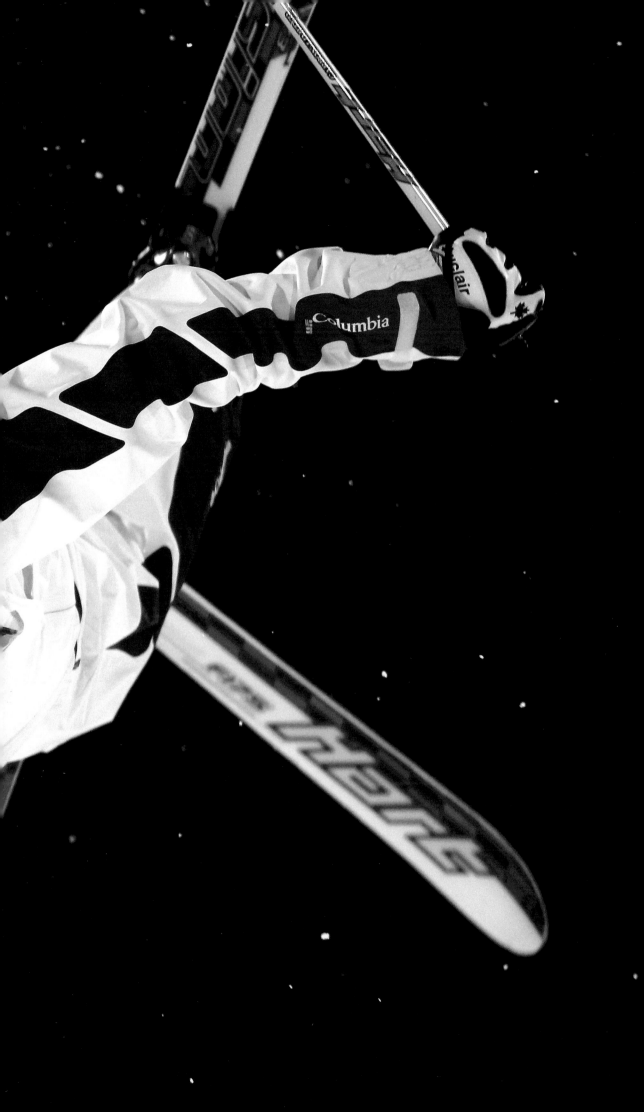

True grit

(PHOTO BY DON EMMERT/AFP/GETTY IMAGES)

    Sprawled on the snow (clockwise from top left) are Anna Olsson of Sweden, Petra Majdic of Slovenia and Marit Bjoergen of Norway after expending every ounce of energy in the individual sprint classic final. The Norwegian claimed the gold. Majdic suffered five broken ribs and a collapsed lung in a training crash. Despite agonizing pain, the Slovenian skier made it through the quarterfinals, semifinals and ultimately won the bronze medal. She had to be helped on stage at Whistler Medals Plaza (above) by a medic that evening to receive her medal. Olsson finished fourth.

(PHOTO BY LARS BARON/BONGARTS/GETTY IMAGES)

ABOVE / China's Mengtao Xu (left) is embraced by teammate Nina Li as gold medalist Lydia Lassila of Australia looks on. (PHOTO BY ROBYN BECK/AFP/GETTY IMAGES)

OPPOSITE / With lights shining through the foggy night, Lydia Lassila sets her eye on gold in the aerials competition. (PHOTO BY ADRIAN DENNIS/AFP/GETTY IMAGES)

Foggy, foggy night

Australia's Lydia Lassila put a damper on Team China's domination of the aerials at Cypress Mountain when she landed in first place with 214.74 points after her second jump. That put Mengtao Xu of China, who, at 19, has an arsenal of triple-flip combinations, in the hot seat. As the last competitor with a chance to secure gold, she attempted a jump with a high degree of difficulty, crashed on her landing and finished sixth. A surprised Lassila, veteran of three Olympic Games, had won gold, leaving Torino silver medalist and three-time defending world champion Nina Li to pick up another silver. Teammate Xinxin Guo earned the bronze.

It was a sweet comeback for the 28-year-old who was forced to withdraw from the qualifying round at the Torino Games when she re-ruptured her ACL on impact.

Shaun WHITE

King of the Halfpipe

T he defending Olympic champion and world's most dominant halfpipe snowboarder didn't even need his much-anticipated McTwist 1260 (later renamed the Tomahawk) to win gold. But being the showman that he is, he thrilled fans when he threw it anyway.

"I came all the way to Vancouver to do something amazing, and I felt like a righteous victory lap was in order," he said after winning gold on Feb. 17, 2010.

The King of the Half Pipe was born in San Diego, Calif. After two surgeries before his first birthday corrected a congenital heart defect, it's been nothing but high-flying, heart-stopping tricks for the 23 year old.

His parents introduced him to snowboarding in an effort to slow him down. Eventually, it was their support—driving him a couple of hours to the mountains and sending videos to sponsors—that enabled him to go pro at the age of 13.

Extremely competitive in both skateboarding (turning pro in that sport at 17) and snowboarding, White became famous for his innovative tricks and quick wit. He took one of his most hurtful disappointments—failing to make the 2002 Olympic team by .30 of a point—and turned it into motivation to leave no doubt about his abilities. He became the first athlete to sweep all of the U.S. Snowboarding Grand Prix events, which are the qualifiers for the U.S. Olympic Team, in 2006.

He won all but one of the Grand Prix events leading up to the 2010 Games. White's list of accomplishments is as stunning as his tricks in the halfpipe. He said the season leading up to the 2010 Winter Olympic Games were his toughest challenge to date.

"I don't think I've ever worked this hard in my life," said White after winning. "I'm glad I had the goods to deliver."

(Photo by Martin Bureau/AFP/Getty Images)

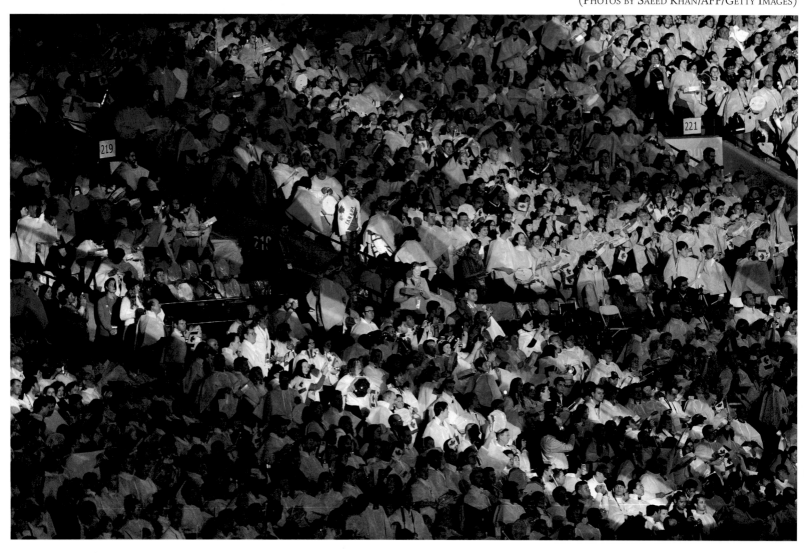

Still reeling from the sudden loss of her mother, Joannie Rochette of Canada gave her own private gesture after she finished her free skate program. Though not perfect, the program was solid and the crowd behind her. The judges' scores kept her in third place for the bronze medal. (PHOTO BY JAMIE SQUIRE/GETTY IMAGES)

Simon says
two more golds

He's no longer the wizard boy look-alike of fictional character "Harry Potter" when he won two gold medals in the 2002 Games in Salt Lake City, but Simon Ammann of Switzerland still has what it takes to dominate the normal and large ski jumping hills. He soared to two more individual gold medals, besting the competition by huge margins. (Photo by Lars Baron/ Bongarts/Getty Images)

vancouver 2010

Bode MILLER

100% Heart

As much an artist as he is an athlete, Bode Miller proved the best way to silence your critics is with a jaw-dropping performance on the slopes. He entered Vancouver the most successful male alpine skier in U.S. history, but also one of the most criticized. Despite struggling with a painful ankle injury that ended his ski season after the Vancouver Games, Miller removed any doubt about his abilities when he won a bronze, a silver and a gold in his fourth Olympic Games. He is the only American to ever win five Olympic medals in alpine skiing, and he did it in four different disciplines.

Miller said for years that it wasn't the outcome that mattered to him, only his effort. In Vancouver, he managed to combine winning with an effort that he felt was the best he had.

"The way I executed, the way I skied, is something I'll be proud of the rest of my life," he said after winning his first Olympic gold in the super combined. "I skied with 100 percent heart. I didn't hold anything back."

Miller won the hearts of skiing fans in 2002 with double silver in Salt Lake City, but missed the medals in 2006. In 2008, he left the U.S. Ski Team, struck out on his own and had success. But before the completion of the 2009 season, he walked away. He said he didn't even think about putting on skis.

At 31, just a few months before the 2010 World Cup season began, he decided the void in his life could only be filled by one thing—skiing. The U.S. Ski Team announced his return in September in a press conference where he said he knew he'd have to earn a spot on the 2010 team. He did that despite an ankle sprain, sustained while playing volleyball in December, which continued to nag him through the Olympic Games.

He said one difference for him in Vancouver was that he embraced the fact that the Olympic Gamess are not just another race.

"The big games are different," he said. "They're more important; there is more stuff to them. There is more energy and that can be positive…You have to accept that it's different. You have to feed off the energy, feed off of the enthusiasm that everyone has here, the inspiration."

In seventh position after the downhill race of the super combined event, Bode Miller posted the third-fastest time in the slalom race to beat Croatia's Ivica Kostelic by 0.33 of a second. With the bronze in the downhill and the silver in the super-G, the American capped his Olympic performance in Vancouver with the gold medal. (PHOTO BY ALAIN GROSCLAUDE/AGENCE ZOOM/ GETTY IMAGES)

Team pursuit upset

Veteran 32-year-old Chad Hedrick (in the lead) teamed with two 19-year-olds, Jonathan Kuck (#3) and Brian Hansen (#1), to eliminate the powerful Dutch team, led by speedskating superstar Sven Kramer, in the semifinals of the team pursuit event. The U.S. team, including 20-year old Trevor Marsicano who skated in the quarterfinals, went on to win the silver medal behind Canada. Holland settled for the bronze. It was Hedrick's fifth Olympic medal in five different speedskating disciplines—he won three medals in the 2006 Torino Games and two in these Games. (Photo by Kevork Djansezian/Getty Images)

A fistful of disappointments

Sven Kramer of the Netherlands is comforted by a team member after the Dutch team took the bronze medal in the men's team pursuit final. Three days earlier, Kramer, who had won the gold in the 5000m race, was disqualified from the 10,000m race. Kramer had handily won the race but a miscommunication regarding lane change between his coach and him had cost Kramer the gold. (Photo by Robyn Beck/AFP/Getty Images)

Photo finish

It was a race to the finish line in the men's individual sprint classic cross-country event as Nikita Kriukov (left) of Russia slid ahead of teammate Alexander Panzhinskiy for gold. Norwegian Petter Northug, 9.2 seconds behind, won the bronze medal. (Photo by Lars Baron/Bongarts/Getty Images)

SPEEDSKATING

Shani DAVIS

Fast, Focused and Fired Up

Shattering barriers is something this native of Chicago, Illinois, has been doing since he was a toddler. The 27-year-old found his way into speedskating thanks to attorney Fred Benjamin. His mother worked for Benjamin and suggested he might like it better than roller skating.

Not only did he like it, he was immediately competitive. His mom, Cherie Davis, woke him up early to help him train and eventually moved so he could be closer to the track in Evanston, Illinois, when he was 10.

Davis entered the Vancouver Games, already the owner of two medals. He'd won a gold and silver in Torino, and he was favored to win in the same events—the 1000 and 1500m races.

He won the gold in the 1000m but finished second in the 1500.

"That's just the way of sport," said Davis after the race. "On any given day, anyone can go out and achieve great-ness. Even though I'm a heavy favorite, I try not to see myself as a favorite. I try not to get too far ahead of myself no matter what I've accomplished. I like to have the underdog approach. I was really fired up, hoping I could cap these Olympics off with a gold, but that's just the luck of the draw. I did the best I could, and I just wasn't strong enough."

Despite falling short of his own goals, he still owns four Olympic medals and nine world records (including the 1500m). Davis was the first African American to win an individual gold at the Winter Games when he won the 1000m in Torino. He is still considered one of the best technicians in the sport and proved his prowess in the 1000m and 1500m by winning the 2010 World Cup title one month after the Vancouver Games.

OPPOSITE / *Shani Davis of the U.S. skates to gold in the 1000m speedskating event at the Olympic Oval in Richmond, outside Vancouver.* (PHOTO BY VINCENZO PINTO/AFP/GETTY IMAGES)

From debuts to matchups, the Vancouver Games did not disappoint

In a classic men's figure skating showdown, American Evan Lysacek (opposite, top) battled Evgeni Plushenko of Russia for gold and was nice enough to sign autographs for adoring fans.

Serbia made its debut in the Olympic Winter Games. It was the first time the nation had participated in the Winter Games after competing as Serbia and Montenegro in previous Games. It fielded athletes in alpine skiing, biathlon, cross-country skiing and bobsled (opposite, bottom).

Canadian fans (below) celebrated before the preliminary game between its home country and the United States but would leave stunned when the American underdogs upset the host nation team, 5-3.

American ex-gymnasts Lacy Schnoor, Emily Cook and Ashley Caldwell found a new passion in aerials. Schnoor and Caldwell made their Olympic debut.

(Photo by Streeter Lecka/Getty Images)

(Photo by Bruce Bennett/Getty Images)

Jeret PETERSON

The Hurricane

If there was one moment of Olympic glory that also signified redemption, it was when Jeret "Speedy" Peterson landed the toughest trick in aerial skiing—the Hurricane. The triple flip with five twists, which he named, has haunted and heralded Peterson's tumultuous ski career.

"I don't know that I can really put it into words," he said of winning the silver medal. It was a moment that even brought tears to the eyes of his coaches because of Peterson's personal struggles.

The native of Boise, Idaho, was introduced to aerials when a neighbor invited him to a camp in Lake Placid, N.Y. The adrenaline junkie was immediately hooked on the high-flying sport.

For the 28-year-old, the idea of twisting and flipping through the air on skis has always been less troubling than the idea of dealing with the demons that tortured his life away from sport.

Overcoming depression and other obstacles that have often hampered his development in the sport, Peterson's victory in Vancouver helped him prove something to himself. After attempting the Hurricane in 2006 and failing to land it perfectly, some thought he should abandon it for easier tricks. He finished seventh in Torino and afterward said he had to take a couple of years off from the sport to get his life and priorities in order. He never considered abandoning skiing, however, because he said he loves it so much.

He returned to the sport, determined to work harder and maintain balance in his life that would allow him to finally earn the success he deserved.

In the weeks leading up to Vancouver, Peterson said he was grateful to those who'd supported and guided him, and he was proud of himself for finding his way to a better life.

"This Olympics is very special for me," he said during training in Park City. " So many things in my life have been very difficult and challenging. For me to be able to overcome those and still end up on top really means a lot to me. I do give myself a pat on the back for being able to realize my dreams one more time. And it's something that hasn't really come easily."

Vancouver

Sportin' the Olympic Ideal

By Amy Donaldson

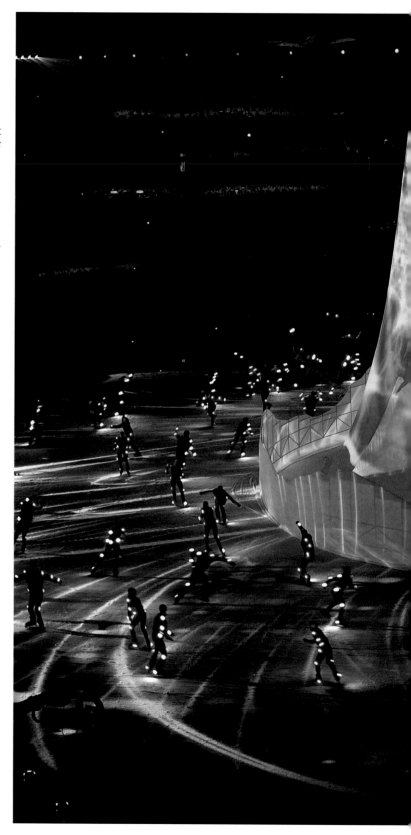

I f the Olympic spirit took a living, breathing form, it would look, sound and smile like the people of Vancouver, Canada. Controversy could have consumed the 2010 Olympic Winter Games, and at times did. The tragic death of Nodar Kumaritashvili just hours before the Opening Ceremony cast a pall over what is normally a celebration of the world's ability to set aside politics and prejudices and celebrate the strength of the human spirit.

Instead, because of the way the athletes, fans and officials handled the situation, it gave the Games more meaning. The decision of the Georgian team to stay in Vancouver and compete with Nodar in their hearts epitomized the very ideals Olympians champion every day—persevere despite pain, honor life with love.

Even changing weather conditions that postponed races, cost organizers millions of dollars in canceled tickets and challenged course workers didn't deter VANOC (Vancouver Olympic Organizing Committee) one bit. Be it snow one day, rain the next, followed by sunshine and warm wind, VANOC rolled up its sleeves and responded.

Using chemicals, straw, creativity and good, old-fashioned round-the-clock elbow grease, the volunteer course workers earned those iconic blue coats.

Every day organizers dealt with issues that, in some cities, would have sullied the Games. But not in Vancouver.

The reason was the relentless cheerfulness of a host city willing to walk, ride a bike or take a bus rather than inconvenience its guests with traffic jams. Their ability to embrace the thorns with the roses made it impossible not to catch their enthusiasm and unfettered affection for everything Olympic.

And the 2010 Games featured some of the most dynamic competitions in history.

Probably the most memorable to North Americans were the two showdowns on ice at Canada Hockey Place. The Canadians and Americans met in the preliminary rounds, where the U.S. defeated the heavily favored Canadians, 5-3. But the Canadians would have the best revenge when they defeated the U.S. in overtime to earn the gold medal.

Acrobatic skiers and skaters wearing LED lights perform during Vancouver's Opening Ceremony. (PHOTO BY CRIS BOURONCLE/AFP/GETTY IMAGES)

(Photo by Michael Kappeler/AFP/Getty Images)

(Photo by Adrian Dennis/AFP/Getty Images)

(Photo by Martin Bureau/AFP/Getty Images)

(Photo by Luis Acosta/AFP/Getty Images)

While the U.S. won the most overall medals with 37, Canada found a silver lining in earning the most gold medals of any country—14. The Canadians curse of not winning gold on home soil ended when Alexandre Bilodeau of Montreal surprised everyone when he won gold on the second day of the Games in men's moguls. He did not win a single World Cup before besting defending Olympic gold medalist (and former Vancouverite) Dale Begg-Smith, Australia, for the country's first-ever Olympic gold in Canada. He quickly became known as "Alexandre the Great."

The XXI Olympic Winter Games will be known for its stories as much as medal counts.

And for the United States, the stories of overcoming odds, team work, determination and, above all, perseverance would prove to be so inspiring, refreshing and thrilling there would be no room in the hearts of spectators for negativity.

When the Vancouver Organizing Committee chose the theme, "With Glowing Hearts," organizers couldn't have foreseen how prophetic it would be. The warmth of the welcome, or as they say in some parts of Canada, *Bienvenue*, was heartfelt and heartwarming and, in the end, redeeming.

ABOVE / *The Opening Ceremony started with a tribute to fallen luge athlete Nodar Kumaritashvili of Georgia and ended with fireworks and in between, the well-kept secret of the final torchbearer was revealed, though this time there were four: ice hockey legend Wayne Gretzky (bottom, left), NBA all-star Steve Nash, skier Nancy Greene and speedskater Catriona Le May Doan (top, right), who saluted the crowd with her torch when one of the four cauldron lifts failed.*

Native Canadian performers dance during the Opening Ceremony of the Vancouver Games. (Photo by Jasper Juinen/Getty Images)

Oh Canada!

At every Games, athletes from veterans to first-time Olympians, officials, spectators and performers are all swept into the magic of the Opening Ceremony, and Vancouver was no different as it served up its Friday night special. There were welcome poles representing each of the Four Host First Nations and a giant bear studded with LED lights.

Twenty-five hundred plus athletes from 82 nations paraded into the stadium. Five-time Olympian luge athlete Mark Grimmette carried the U.S. flag and led his teammates during the parade of athletes.

Seven nations—the Cayman Islands, Colombia, Ghana, Montenegro, Pakistan, Peru and Serbia—made their Olympic Winter Games debut. And 60,000 people, most wearing red and white and waving maple leaf flags, filled the seats of the indoor stadium to witness the three-hour long spectacle that ended in fireworks.

(PHOTO BY ROBYN BECK/AFP/GETTY IMAGES)

(PHOTO BY KEVORK DJANSEZIAN/GETTY IMAGES)

▲ (Photo by Leon Neal/AFP/Getty Images)

(Photo by Alex Livesey/Getty Images)

Alpine Skiing

Inspired Comebacks

Story Contributors: Doug Haney & Amy Donaldson

(Photo by Fabrice Coffrini/AFP/Getty Images)

The U.S. Alpine Ski Team produced a historic eight medal haul at Whistler Creekside. But its Vancouver story wasn't about records. It was one of skiing with inspiration and embracing every ounce of what makes the Olympic Games special. Its story is one of Bode Miller, Lindsey Vonn, Julia Mancuso and young Andrew Weibrecht competing with unmatched passion that produced a pride and excitement for alpine skiing that reverberated throughout America.

The U.S. men started the Games with Miller's galvanizing race in the downhill, where he earned the bronze medal, the first of his three medals. The weather was so wet and windy, many weren't sure the race could be held.

"Everyone was a little bit shocked at how it looked this morning," said Miller, who came into the Games with two silver medals from the 2002 Salt Lake Games. "There were a lot of changes (weather-wise) and maybe that helped build a little of the anxiety and the excitement, and then everyone starts to get it." Switzerland's Didier Defago won the gold medal, while the silver went to Norway's Aksel Lund Svindal.

Miller returned to the podium four days later—this time winning the silver in the super-G. He finished .28 of a second behind Norway's Aksel Lund Svindal, who capped a remarkable comeback after a horrific crash in 2007. Svindal lost control during a training run in Beaver Creek, Colo., in 2007 and broke a number of bones in his face and suffered a deep gash in his leg, as well as lower abdominal injuries. He lost more than 30 pounds and spent five months recovering. In 2009, he was back on top, winning the overall World Cup title.

The surprise for the U.S. was young Andrew Weibrecht who claimed the bronze medal, skiing just .31 of a second slower than Miller. The previous top international result for Lake Placid's Weibrecht was on a World Cup circuit downhill race in 2007 where he finished 10th from the 53rd start position.

On Sunday, Feb. 21, Miller won his first ever Olympic gold medal in the super combined, starting the slalom, the second race of this demanding event, in seventh position.

1-2 finish

Pre-race favorite Lindsey Vonn (#16) of the U.S. set aside the struggles with her shin injury and showed the world what she's made of. She crossed the finish line in 1:44.19, .56 of a second ahead of teammate Julia Mancuso (#10).

"I knew what I had to do, I knew what type of run I needed to take. I had to attack and I did that," said Vonn. "I made it down. It's awesome, it's all I ever wanted."

Vonn was trailing Mancuso in the early part of the course that starts out gently, but accelerated through the steep and fast middle section to claim her first Olympic gold medal.

Steep and deep

The downhill, the premier event in Olympic skiing, featured an incredibly tight and deep field skiing a course that was unlike the training conditions. Favorite Didier Cuche of Switzerland bowed out in sixth place. It was his teammate Didier Defago (center), three-time Olympian, who threw down a blistering run to claim the coveted gold. Bode Miller (right), skiing the eighth run of the day, set the early pace, which was fast enough to earn the bronze medal. Only .02 of a second ahead was Norway's Aksel Lund Svindal who took the silver. It was the tightest podium finish in men's downhill history.

(Photo by Clive Mason/Getty Images)

(Photo by Francois Xavier Marit/AFP/Getty Images)

Starting in seventh place after the downhill, Bode Miller of the U.S. posts a 51.04 slalom time in super combined event to win his first Olympic gold medal. (PHOTO BY OLIVIER MORIN/AFP/GETTY IMAGES)

"The super combined—it was really one of those things—I'll remember that feeling and my place in the whole picture really clearly for a long time," he said, winning the race with the third fastest run of slalom behind teammates Ted Ligety and Will Brandenburg. "I used to race very similar to that, with that kind of heart and intensity all the time when I was younger and then to have that come back and be inspired at these Games was incredible."

Brandenburg, who suffered a serious downhill training crash the day before the super combined event, put together an amazing race, posting the second fastest slalom time to finish 10th overall. Before Vancouver, he had never scored in a World Cup race.

WOMEN

The first alpine competitions for women were held on Wednesday, Feb. 17—three days after the women's downhill was originally scheduled. It was worth the wait for the U.S. skiers as Lindsey Vonn battled through a painful shin bruise to win her first Olympic gold medal, while teammate Julia Mancuso returned to the Olympic podium with silver.

Bode's gold

The men's super combined came down to another match-up between Aksel Lund Svindal of Norway, the super-G champion, and Bode Miller, the super-G silver medalist. Miller's time of 2:44.92 was the one to beat. Svindal, the last man down the slope with a chance of knocking the American off the top of the podium, led Miller by .76 of a second going into the slalom. In the end, Svindal missed a gate near the last of the run and failed to finish.

Asked about Miller, Svindal said: "I'm not surprised, but I am impressed."

Maria Riesch of Germany claims her second gold of the Games by winning the slalom in a total time of 1:42:89. Her other gold came in the super combined. (PHOTO BY CLIVE MASON/GETTY IMAGES)

Team spirit

"How unusual it is now, how unique it is to find that kind of energy to go above and beyond what you could normally achieve on your own because you're a part of something else."

Bode Miller, four-time Olympian who captured his third, fourth and fifth Olympic medals at Whistler Creekside

Mancuso came down the Creekside run first and was the leader with a time of 1:44.75. Vonn, skiing a few racers later, knew she'd have to be nearly perfect to beat her teammate.

"I saw my name number one and I was completely overwhelmed," said Vonn, who skied into the finish area, looked at the leader board and then threw her hands into the air. She screamed "Yes! Yes!" and fell to the ground. Afterward she talked about how tough those weeks leading up to Olympic competition had been—physically and mentally.

"It's been a really tough couple of weeks," she said after a flower ceremony in the finish area in front of throngs of screaming fans. "Since my injury, pretty much having your Olympic dreams crushed, and then fighting back from it, doing therapy and getting healthy."

It was Mancuso's first podium in two years, and she became the most decorated female alpine Olympian in American history when she won the silver medal in the super combined the following day. She now owns a total of three Olympic medals.

Austria's Elisabeth Goergl won the downhill bronze with a time of 1:45.65. American Stacey Cook finished 11th with a time of 1:46.98.

Vonn, who raced in every discipline, won her second medal of the Games, a bronze, in the super-G. Austria's Andrea Fischbacher won gold and Slovakia's Tina Maze picked up her first of two silver medals in these Games. Falls and missed gates disqualified Vonn from the super combined, giant slalom and slalom events. Instead it was Vonn's best friend and rival on the slopes, Maria Riesch of Germany who claimed the gold medals in the super combined and slalom events.

In all, the U.S. Ski Team not only posted its best Olympic results, it also had the most medals of any country in alpine skiing in Vancouver.

Miller summed up the secret to the team's success in Vancouver: "I'm really proud of our team. We went after it this time. We weren't scared. We stomped on it. From Lindsey on down, we were always aggressive."

Julia Mancuso

A successful and popular skier from Olympic Valley, Calif., Julia Mancuso won the gold medal in the giant slalom in Torino 2006.

Plagued by nagging back problems in 2009, Mancuso focused on regaining her form in hopes of defending her title in her best event.

A week before the giant slalom race, Mancuso burst back into the spotlight when she won the first of two silver medals at Whistler—one in the downhill, the other in the super combined. With her performances in Vancouver, she became the most decorated American Olympic female alpine skier.

"When I realized that I got another medal, it's that moment that you wait for as an athlete," said Mancuso. "I couldn't have asked for anything more. I mean I haven't been on the podium for two years and then to come in here and take two silver medals is incredible and then to be a part of a team that had an amazing Olympics is special."

Weather conditions plagued the women's giant slalom event. Race officials, trying to squeeze a race in between the snow and fog, started the skiers in intervals—with racers 16 through 30 leaving every minute. Mancuso, No. 18, was already on the course when teammate Lindsey Vonn skied off course. Flagged by officials, Mancuso had to restart her first run in 31st position and ultimately finished a heroic eighth place on a deteriorating course. (PHOTO BY OLIVIER MORIN/AFP/GETTY IMAGES)

"The Olympics are something
special for Americans,
but this is how we ski all year.
We're always pushing it,
always hammering,
and always looking for speed.
We love skiing."

—Andrew Weibrecht,
bronze medalist, super-G

Andrew Weibrecht

Growing up in Lake Placid, participating in winter sports is almost mandatory. Andrew Weibrecht was the fourth of five children and spent his childhood trying to keep up with his older brother on the same slopes that hosted the 1980 Olympic Games.

The U.S. Ski Team coaches saw potential in the 24-year-old almost a decade before he won the bronze medal in the super-G in the Vancouver Games.

Despite racing with a shoulder that needed surgery, the fearless Weibrecht raced as he always does—for the win—and came up big in Vancouver.

Known for finding speed where most athletes wouldn't think it possible, Weibrecht was able to make up for a small mistake at the top of the hill. Before that third-place finish, he had never finished higher than 10th in a World Cup race.

American Andrew Weibrecht, here racing the slalom portion of the super combined, finished 11th in the competition at Whistler Creekside. (Photo by Olivier Morin/AFP/Getty Images)

Ted Ligety finished a stunning fifth in the super combined with the fastest run of the slalom. In the giant slalom event (pictured), the 28-year-old American posted a ninth-place finish. (PHOTO CREDIT BY FABRICE COFFRINI /AFP/GETTY IMAGES)

Sarah Schleper, sporting a bandage on her chin, received stitches between competition runs after knocking her chin on a gate during warm-up. Her 16th-place finish was the best U.S. result in the slalom event. Schleper is a mother of a two-year-old son and the first-ever four-time Olympian among U.S. female alpine skiers. (PHOTO BY CLIVE MASON/GETTY IMAGES)

Biathlon

Racing Against the Weather

Story Contributor: Viktoria Franke

For the first time ever in biathlon the yellow bib of the World Cup leader was handed over to a U.S. athlete—Tim Burke. The 28-year-old Burke, who grew up around Lake Placid, experimented with a lot of different Olympic sports when he was young. Once he tried biathlon, he never looked back.

With Burke leading the circuit in a sport dominated by Europeans and solid results posted by all the U.S. men, expectations were high entering the Vancouver Games.

In the first men's race, the 10km sprint, where competitors start at 30-second intervals and race against the clock, Burke placed 47th in the event won by France's Vincent Jay. Weather conditions played a factor in the results, seriously upsetting the racers starting in the middle of the pack, like Burke, wearing bib number 29.

The only American to benefit from the weather was Jeremy Teela. He started 13th and finished ninth. When the race started the conditions were still fair with some rain that soon turned into a heavy snowstorm, making the track soft and slow. The results later showed that all but one of the Top 10 finishers had been in the first start group up to bib number 15.

"I still had rain when I was racing and our skis were prepared for rain. But the ones in the middle or the end of the field, they had a real disadvantage," Teela analyzed after the race. Teammates Lowell Bailey placed 36th and Jay Hakkinen 54th.

"The first guys had a complete ice rink out there," added Hakkinen. "Once that snowstorm came out, the times dropped off so fast, there was no chance." But that is the sport of biathlon, where anything can happen.

Bad luck followed the men's team into the 12.5km pursuit race. Teela, who was to start 1:13.9 minutes behind the Frenchman, was sent out 22 seconds too early. The mishap with start times affected quite a few racers and their performances, including the women's races. Seeing a star at the result board next to his name, Teela wondered what competition rule he had broken along the way.

America's best biathlete Tim Burke (#47), Norway's Lars Berger (#46) and Estonia's Kauri Koiv (#48) compete in the 12.5km pursuit event. The race was won by 31-year-old Bjorn Ferry of Sweden. Burke, still recovering from the 10km sprint event hit by a mid-race snowstorm two days earlier, finished in 46th place. (PHOTO BY FRANCK FIFE/AFP/GETTY IMAGES)

Teela finished 24th in the end. Bailey (36th), Burke, (46th), and Hakkinen, (57th), weren't able to post better results starting too far back from Jay, who claimed the bronze. Bjorn Ferry, starting 1:12 behind, won the gold.

After those two races the U.S. men had trouble recovering, leading to another disappointing result in the 20km individual competition with Burke posting a 45th place finish.

In the last individual biathlon race, the 15km mass start, Burke and Teela both posted solid results. Burke, skiing comfortably in the lead group, missed three targets at the third shooting stage and fell to 24th place. With strong skiing and just one penalty in the last stage, Burke moved up to 18th place at the finish line. Teela, dealing with sinus problems before the race, ended in 29th place after four penalties.

Ranked third in the world, Russian Evgeny Ustyugov took the lead with clean shooting and solid skiing to outpace France's Martin Fourcade by 10.5 seconds for the gold medal.

The men's relay team with Bailey, Hakkinen, Burke and Teela finished 13th—6:20.2 minutes behind the Norwegians, who took the gold medal. With four penalty loops overall, the U.S. relay was the only team with more than two penalties that still managed to finish in the Top 15.

And they're off! Two-time Olympian Lowell Bailey (#10) skies the first leg of the men's 4x7.5km relay. The U.S. finished in 13th place. The Norwegians claimed the gold. (PHOTO BY PHILIPPE MONTIGNY/AGENCE ZOOM/GETTY IMAGES)

He's dubbed the "Biathlon King." At 36-years-old Ole Einar Bjoerndalen marked his fifth Olympic appearance in Vancouver and collected his sixth gold medal in the 4x7.5km relay. Bjoerndalen also picked up the silver in the 20km individual race, won by teammate Emil Hegle Svendsen. His total Olympic medal haul is 11. (Photo by Philippe Montigny/Agence Zoom/Getty Images)

WOMEN

The biathlon competition opened with the ladies 7.5km sprint, a race skied over a three-lap distance and two stops at the firing range, 10 shots total, five prone and five standing. For each miss, the biathlete skis a penalty loop of 150m. Slovakian Anastazia Kuzmina upset the odds-on favorite Germany Magdalena Neuner to win the gold medal. Kuzmina's win allowed her to start first in the 10km pursuit, held three days later. This time, Neuner, starting 1.5 seconds behind, proved unbeatable and won 12.3 seconds ahead of the Russian-born Slovak.

American Sara Studebaker posted a final time of 22:05.3 to place 45th in the sprint, qualifying for the pursuit competition where she finished 46th, 4:44.1 minutes behind the dominating German.

"It was the first international pursuit I raced this year so that was quite exciting. The crowd was amazingly loud and I just loved to be able to compete here," Studebaker stated after her first two races. The other U.S. women were not able to finish the sprint in the top 60 and did not qualify for the pursuit event.

The women showed an unexpected solid team result over the 15km individual with Lanny Barnes of Durango, Colo., finishing 23rd. With a clean shooting and a finish time of 43:31.8 minutes, she posted the best Olympic result of the US women's biathlon team since Joan Smith and Joan Guetschow back in Lillehammer 1994. Sara Studebaker finished her race with one penalty in 34th place. With two penalties, Laura Spector (Lenox, Mass.) finished 0.1 of a second ahead of Haley Johnson (Lake Placid, N.Y.) for 65th place. Johnson missed four targets.

The US quartet of Studebaker, Barnes, Johnson and Spector placed 17th in the women's 4x6km relay on February 23rd. They had a final time of 1:15:47.5, more than six minutes off the pace of the Russian team, which took the gold medal ahead of France and Germany.

American Sara Studebaker finished 34th in the 15km individual race. (PHOTO BY ALEXANDER HASSENSTEIN/ BONGARTS/GETTY IMAGES)

Lanny Barnes had the best U.S. finish in the 15km individual race coming in 23rd out of 87 racers. (PHOTO BY AL BELLO/GETTY IMAGES)

*With a ninth-place finish in the 10km sprint, Jeremy Teela posted the best finish among the U.S. men in the biathlon events. In 15km mass star, pictured here, Teela finished 29th. (*PHOTO BY LARS BARON/BONGARTS/GETTY IMAGES*)*

*Jay Hakkinen competes on the second leg in the 4x7.5km biathlon relay. The U.S. team finished in 13th place. (*PHOTO BY ALEXANDER HASSENSTEIN/ BONGARTS/ GETTY IMAGES*)*

Bobsled

50-50
Pays Off

Story Contributor: Amanda Bird

American Steven Holcomb navigated his matte black four-man BoDyn bobsled, the "Night Train," at 95 mph down the most demanding and treacherous track in the world at the Whistler Sliding Center to solidify his dominance in the sport on February 27, 2010. Greeted with train whistles and "USA" chants from the crowd, Holcomb and his push team of Justin Olsen, Steve Mesler and Curt Tomasevicz made history by winning the Olympic gold medal, breaking a 62-year gold-medal drought for the U.S. In a sport that's won by hundredths of a second, team USA I was victorious by 0.38 of a second after sliding a four-run combined time of 3:24.46.

Andre Lange from Germany finished second in the four-man competition, and immediately embraced team USA I in celebration after the crew crossed the finish. Lange has long dominated the sport since beginning competition in 1998. His sliding resume includes five Olympic medals and eight World Championship titles. Lange announced his retirement at the 2010 Olympic and grasped Holcomb's hand in salute, as if passing over the torch.

The U.S. qualified the maximum number of sleds, three, for both two- and four-man races. Mike Kohn teamed with Jamie Moriarty, Bill Schuffenhauer and Nick Cunningham as USA III to finish 13th in the four-man competition. Kohn and Schuffenhauer were members of the bronze and silver medal winning teams that broke a 46-year medal drought for the U.S. at the 2002 Olympic Winter Games in Salt Lake City. Both athletes announced their retirement following the 2010 Olympic race.

Up-and-coming U.S. pilot John Napier made a mistake in the difficult 11-12-13 curve combination on the track on the first day, which resulted in a crash. Napier and his team of Steve Langton, Chuck Berkeley and Chris Fogt were not seriously injured, but were unable to compete in the final two runs due to muscle strains.

In the two-man bobsled event, Lange, partnering with brakeman Kevin Kuske, added his fourth Olympic gold medal to his sliding resume, while German teammate Thomas Florschuetz claimed silver and Russian Alexsandr

It was pilot Steven Holcomb of USA 1 who dubbed curve 13, the "50-50" curve, describing the odds of coming safely through this unlucky curve. After four fast heats, USA 1 claimed the gold and the honor of breaking a 62-year gold-medal drought for the U.S.
(PHOTO BY MARK RALSTON/AFP/GETTY IMAGES)

Steve Mesler of USA 1 celebrates after winning the gold medal in the four-man bobsled. (PHOTO BY CLIVE MASON/GETTY IMAGES)

Zubkov slid a bronze medal performance. Holcomb and Tomasevicz slid a four-run combined time of 3:27.94 seconds, good enough for sixth place.

Napier, who burst onto the scene this season after winning gold in the Lake Placid, N.Y. two-man bobsled World Cup competition, teamed with Langton to finish tenth, while Kohn and Cunningham crossed the finish in 12th place.

WOMEN

For the women, it was a North America sweep of the podium. Canada captured its first-ever Olympic medals in women's bobsled on their home track. Kaillie Humphries and Heather Moyse took gold with a four-run combined time of 3:32.28, 0.85 of a second ahead of their compatriots Helen Upperton and Shelley-Ann Brown.

Despite nursing a strained hamstring suffered during training, Erin Pac teamed with Elana Meyers to navigate her "Pinky" BoDyn sled on the notoriously difficult track. The U.S. duo's combined time of 3:33.40 earned them the bronze.

Four years ago Pac was just learning how to drive a bobsled after moving up from the back of the sled as a push athlete, and Meyers was wrapping up her collegiate softball career at George Washington University. Pac and Meyers didn't cross paths until 2007, when Meyers made the World Cup team her rookie season. Little did they know that three years later they would be celebrating their Olympic debut success together.

Out of 21 teams competing, the three U.S. teams placed in the top six slots. Bree Schaaf, a skeleton athlete turned bobsled pilot, paired with Emily Azevedo for fifth place with a total time of 3:34.05. Shauna Rohbock, the 2006 Olympic silver medalist, returned to the track with Michelle Rzepka for her Olympic debut. They finished sixth with a combined time of 3:34.06, just one-hundredth of a second slower than their teammates.

OPPOSITE / *Mike Kohn, Jamie Moriarty, Bill Schuffenhauer and Nick Cunningham of the Unites States finished 13th in the four-man bobsled competition.* (PHOTO BY RICHARD HEATHCOTE/ GETTY IMAGES)

Elana Meyers (left) and Erin Pac raise their arms in victory and strike a pose with the Canadian gold and silver medalists.

BOBSLED

Erin & Elana PAC & MEYERS

Underdogs Prevail

E lana Meyers dreamed of representing the United States in the Olympic Games as a softball player. But when the sport was dropped from the Olympic line-up, she took her parents' suggestion to give bobsled a try.

"They had seen it in the 2002 Winter Games and they suggested I try it," she said. "They knew bobsledders were big and powerful athletes like those in softball."

An email to a U.S. team coach earned her a tryout and her performance earned her a spot on the national team in 2007.

The graduate of George Washington University, where she played shortstop and pitcher, was immediately successful.

Like many bobsled and skeleton athletes, Pac got her start in track and field. She was competing for Springfield College in Massachusetts when her coach told her that the U.S. Bobsled Federation was looking for new recruits. After a tryout, she was hooked.

Pac began her career as a bobsled brakeman in 2002. She decided to make the switch to driving when she failed to make the 2006 Olympic team as a brakeman.

"I think it's such a thrill to go down the hill every time," said Pac. "I mean, you're scared and nervous and once you get to the bottom, it's such a rush that you were able to accomplish completing the ride."

Pac and Meyers were not favored to win a medal in Vancouver, which made their bronze medal performance on one of the world's fastest tracks even more impressive.

"It has been a lot more intense than people really know," said Meyers, who is now training to be a driver. "We've had our ups and downs as a team, and we've been together on and off for three years. It's just been a really big struggle the whole time and to be able to come together and win on the world's biggest stage is amazing."

Pilot John Napier, Charles Berkeley, Steven Langton and Christopher Fogt compete in USA 2 during heat 1 of the four-man bobsled. A crash on the second run ended their Olympic dreams. (PHOTO BY RICHARD HEATHCOTE/GETTY IMAGES)

Shauna Rohbock and Michelle Rzepka in sled USA1 posted a time of 53.73 in heat 1 of the women's bobsled competition. Their subsequent three runs were all faster and the duo finished in sixth place. (Photo by Richard Heathcote/Getty Images)

Cross-Country Skiing

Through Snow, Wind, Rain and Sun

Story Contributor: Amy Donaldson

When Alaska's Kikkan Randall won a silver medal at the World Championships in 2009, she became the first American woman to reach the podium in a cross-country World Championships.

The success of the three-time Olympian gave the U.S. hope that she might lead one of the country's most promising young squads to an Olympic podium for the first time in more than eight decades.

Six first-time Olympians—Morgan Arritola, Holly Brooks, Caitlin Compton, Simi Hamilton, Garott Kuzzy, and Liz Stephen, and five veterans—Kris Freeman, Torin Koos, Andy Newell, Randall and James Southam—made up the 11-member U.S. Cross-Country Ski Team.

And while the Americans found varying degrees of success, no athlete was able to earn a medal in a sport that is traditionally dominated by Europeans.

While the failure to earn a medal might be viewed as a disappointment by some, Randall's eighth-place finish in the sprint event was the best ever for an American woman in an Olympic cross-country ski race. Randall also paired up with Minnesota's Compton to finish sixth in the team sprint free technique race.

The native of Anchorage also finished 23rd in the 30km mass start, one of the most exciting races of the Games.

The 90-minute, women's 30km race came down to 0.3 of a second. Poland's Justyna Kowalczyk beat Marit Bjoergen, Norway, in one of the most thrilling finishes of the cross-country competition. It was the first-ever Polish gold in cross-country, and Bjoergen's silver was her fifth medal in the 2010 Games.

On the men's side, the best finish was that of Koos and Newell, who finished ninth in the men's team sprint free on Feb. 22. Southam was the top finisher in the men's 15km free with a 48th-place finish and in the 30km pursuit with a 34th-place finish.

American Torin Koos (#13) paired with Andy Newell in the team sprint free competition that requires both endurance and speed. Competitors skate six laps each and must physically touch their teammate without interfering or obstructing another team for the exchange to be legal. Norway's Oeystein Pettersen (#2), who replaced reigning world champion Ola Vigen Hattestad after he withdrew on the morning of the race with a sore throat, teamed with Petter Northug to win the gold. The Americans finished ninth. (Photo by Franck Fife/AFP/Getty Images)

The American men (Newell, Koos, Kuzzy and Hamilton) finished 13th in the men's 4x10km relay.

The cross-country races in the 2010 Games were filled with drama, and the sprints, in particular, were popular as spectators only had to wait a few minutes for the race-car like action to return to view in the stadium. In the sprints, competitors raced around a 1.6km loop with the top 30 finishers moving onto five quarterfinal heats. Only the two fastest from each heat move on to the semifinals as well as the two remaining fastest skiers in all of the heats combined.

Slovenian skier Petra Majdic slid off of a bridge and into a gully during a training run. The 30-year-old broke both poles and suffered abdominal injures and broken ribs. She refused to withdraw from the upcoming individual sprint class race and instead took pain medication. She ended up winning the bronze medal. She was presented with Slovenia's Golden Order of Services award "for exceptional performance under difficult odds" by Slovenian president Danilo Tuerk.

The weather was an issue for cross-country athletes more because the wax an athlete chose in the morning might not be the best option a couple of hours—and a couple of snow, rain or wind storms later. None of the events were postponed because of weather issues as athletes just skied through wet, windy conditions and sometimes sunshine to earn their Olympic glory.

OPPOSITE (TOP) / *Caitlin Compton of the United States finished 42nd in the 15km pursuit race.* (PHOTO BY AL BELLO/ GETTY IMAGES)

(BOTTOM) / *Kikkan Randall of the United States finished 10th in the individual sprint classic qualification (pictured) and advanced through the quarterfinals earning a slot as a "lucky loser." The top two skiers of each heat advance to the semifinals as well as the two remaining fastest skiers in all of the heats combined. Randall was eliminated in the semifinals but her eighth-place finish was the best record for an American female cross-country skier in the Olympic Games.* (PHOTO BY LARS BARON/ BONGARTS/GETTY IMAGES)

ABOVE / *Three-time Olympian Kris Freeman, battling equipment issues, finished the 15km free race (pictured) 59th. He also raced in the 30km pursuit, held on a 52-degree day, finishing in 45th place—but that was after this elite 29-year-old American, who was diagnosed with Type 1 diabetes at age 21, laid down on the snow, his blood sugar level crashing. A coach from the German team noticed Freeman and rushed over a bottle of Gatorade and an energy gel. Some two and a half minutes later, Freeman rose and completed the race. "I don't identify myself as a diabetic, I identify myself as a cross-country skier," says Freeman, who nonetheless inspires diabetic kids at summer camps with his Olympian feats.* (PHOTO BY ALEXANDER HASSENSTEIN/GETTY IMAGES)

Fifty-five athletes competed in the 50km mass start classic, held on the final day of the Olympic Winter Games, where the temperature averaged 32 degrees F. American James Southam (#44) finished 28th in the race. (PHOTO BY SHAUN BOTTERILL/ GETTY IMAGES)

Andy Newell skied the second classic leg of the 4x10km relay for the U.S. team, which finished 13th. Sweden won the gold, Norway took silver and the Czech Republic earned the bronze medal. (PHOTO BY ALBERTO PIZZOLI/AFP/GETTY IMAGES)

Mass starts

ABOVE / *It was a chase to the finish in the men's 50km mass start as Swiss Dario Cologna fell in the final straightaway. Norway's Petter Northug (#1) and Germany's Axel Teichmann (right) battled for the gold, but the strong Norwegian overtook Teichmann by 0.30 of a second to bag his second gold of the Games. With Cologna down, Sweden's Johan Olsson claimed his second bronze.* (PHOTO BY DON EMMERT/AFP/GETTY IMAGES)

LEFT / *Justyna Kowalczyk (#1) won Poland's first Olympic gold, finishing first in the women's 30km mass start classic and denying Norway's Marit Bjoergen her fourth Vancouver gold. The 27-year-old Norwegian collected a full set of medals at these Games, also winning silver in the individual sprint and bronze in the 15km pursuit.* (PHOTO BY DON EMMERT/ AFP/GETTY IMAGES)

The Europeans

ABOVE / *Evi Sachenbacher-Stehle of Germany (#3), Riitta-Liisa Roponen of Finland and Magda Genuin of Italy (1) compete during the team sprint semifinals. Sachenbacher-Stehle and her teammate Claudia Nystad won the event with Sweden's Charlotte Kalla and Anna Haag taking silver and Russia's Irina Khazova and Natalia Korosteleva claiming the bronze medal.* (PHOTO BY ALEXANDER HASSENSTEIN/BONGARTS/GETTY IMAGES)

OPPOSITE (TOP) / *Charlotte Kalla of Sweden gives a victory roar after winning the 10km free event.* (PHOTO BY FRANCK FIFE/AFP/GETTY IMAGES)

OPPOSITE (BOTTOM) / *Sweden's Anders Soedergren, Marcus Hellner, Johan Olsson and Daniel Richardsson celebrate their gold medal in the 4x10km relay besting its rival Norway by almost 16 seconds. Sweden's cross-country team left the Vancouver Games with seven medals while its Nordic neighbor was the winningest team with a total of nine cross-country medals.* (PHOTO BY FRANCK FIFE/AFP/GETTY IMAGES)

Curling

Curling Finds Its Voice

Story Contributor: Terry Kolesar

Canadians are obsessed with two sports—ice hockey and curling—and in the Vancouver Games, they expected nothing less than the gold medal. Home to more than 700,000 of the 1.1 million curlers around the world, curling is a Canadian pastime and nowhere since its re-introduction to the Olympic Winter Games in Nagano in 1998 has curling found a more appreciative and knowledgeable fan base.

Capacity crowds of 5,600 filled the Vancouver Olympic Center, rowdily cheering its home team. Curling etiquette normally calls for quiet during the shots. However, the boisterous, foot-stomping home crowd brought the Danish skip Madeleine Dupont to tears after she missed two crucial shots that ended with Canada winning the match, 5-4, in the extra end.

Canada went on to play Sweden in the women's final but even the noise-deafening crowd couldn't shake the rock-solid Swedish team, who capitalized on Canada's mistakes to defend their Olympic gold medal. When Canadian skip Cheryl Bernard missed a double takeout with her final stone, Sweden celebrated a dramatic extra end win over Canada, 7-6.

In the bronze-medal game, China capitalized on a big miss by the Swiss to earn the nation's first Olympic medal in curling in just their first appearance on the Olympic stage.

As the defending Olympic champion, the men's Canadian team breezed through the round-robin tournament with a perfect record and faced Norway for the gold-medal game. The Norwegians had drawn a lot of attention with their crazy diamond-patterned pants in a sport where black pants are the norm. Pants aside, it was skip Kevin Martin's night as Canada got off to an early lead by virtue of steals and held off Norway for the 6-3 win. At the final of end 10 the capacity crowd serenaded its home team with the national anthem 'O Canada.'

In the bronze medal match, Switzerland defeated Sweden, 5-4, on the last rock to make the podium.

The gold-medal match-up between Norway and Canada pitted skips Thomas Ulsrud (top, center) and Kevin Martin (below, center). Martin, who had lost to the Norwegians in 2002 by one shot, found redemption in gold at the Vancouver Games. (PHOTOS BY TOSHIFUMI KITAMURA/ AFP/GETTY IMAGES)

American Jeff Isaacson (center) checks the direction while his teammates, sweepers Chris Plys (left) and John Benton (right), guide the 40-plus pound stone down the ice to its target, the house, in a match against China. The U.S. team lost, 11-5. (PHOTO BY TOSHIFUMI KITAMURA/AFP/GETTY IMAGES)

U.S. MEN

On the heels of the historic bronze medal won in Torino in 2006, the USA men's curling team led by John Shuster came into the 2010 Olympic Winter Games ranked No. 5 in the world but couldn't put enough wins together to make a run at the podium. Plagued by inconsistent play, the American team of Shuster, Jason Smith, Jeff Isaacson, John Benton and Chris Plys stumbled out to a 0-4 start, losing three of the first four on the final rock in extra ends. The coaching staff elected to make a lineup change after the slow start to try to do whatever it took to get a win. The switch helped as the U.S. earned back-to-back wins over France and Sweden but the momentum would be short-lived as the American men would not win again thereafter.

U.S. WOMEN

Debbie McCormick's team came into the 2010 Olympic Winter Games with high expectations based on the team's experience at the international level as a result of having won the past four straight U.S. National Championships. But McCormick and teammates Allison Pottinger, Nicole Joraanstad, Natalie Nicholson and Tracy Sachtjen were outshot and finished the round robin well out of playoff contention, earning just two wins.

The U.S. got off to a rocky 0-3 start before picking up a 6-4 win over the Russian Federation. Much like their counterparts, they'd earn a second victory right away—6-5 over Great Britain—but would remain winless after. The U.S. ladies also struggled to string together consistent play at all four positions throughout their matches, finishing a disappointing last in the 10-team field.

Allison Pottinger (left) and Natalie Nicholson of the U.S. sweep the ice during the round-robin match against Russia. Their goal is to melt a very thin layer of ice to help the stone go farther and straighter, without touching the stone, which would take it out of play. The Americans won this match, 6-4. (PHOTO BY ALEX LIVESEY/GETTY IMAGES)

ABOVE / *With her eye on the target, skip Debbie McCormick releases a stone as her teammates Nicole Joraanstad (left) and Natalie Nicholson (right) sweep during a match against Canada. The U.S. woman lost, 9-2.* (PHOTO BY SAEED KHAN/AFP/GETTY IMAGES)

OPPOSITE (BOTTOM) / *Skips Anette Norberg of Sweden (fourth from left) and Cheryl Bernard of Canada (second from left) take a moment to regroup during the dramatic gold-medal match. Sweden triumphed over Canada, 7-6, in an extra end.* (PHOTOS BY ALEX LIVESEY/GETTY IMAGES)

Skip exchanges

After losing the first four matches, skip John Shuster (left), who was the lead for the U.S. team that won the bronze medal in Torino, was replaced by Jason Smith (top, right). Smith led the team to a victory over France.

Back in the line-up the next day—and helping call the shots against France—Shuster, who has been curling since 1993, made some crucial shots against Sweden, giving the Americans their second win of the round-robin tournament. (PHOTO BY CAMERON SPENCER/GETTY IMAGES)

Figure Skating

Upsets, Heartbreak & Golden Moments

Story Contributor: Scottie Bibb

Figure skating embodies all the action-packed elements of a Hollywood production—artistry, costumes, choreography, dazzling perform-ances and an all-star cast. There's passion, heartbreak, drama and the inevitable contro-versy. Figure skating combines sheer athletics with grace under fire that makes it all look effortless. And at the Vancouver Games, figure skating did not disappoint.

American Evan Lysacek's hard-fought victory over reigning Olympic champion Evgeni Plushenko of Russia was the most compelling upset of the competition. Cana-dian Joannie Rochette's heartbreak was felt around the world as she stepped on the ice just two days after her mother died. Prior to these Games, the ice dancing compe-tition had always belonged to European teams, but not in Vancouver. Three North American teams placed in the top four, with two of those hailing from the United States. And 36-year-old Hongbo Zhao and his wife and partner Xue Shen, 31, came out of retirement to capture China's first gold in the pairs competition.

TOP TO BOTTOM / *The famous "Kiss and Cry" area, where skaters await their scores with their coaches, elicits a range of responses from some of the American competitors: surprise (Mirai Nagasu), disappointment (Jeremy Abbott) and joy (Rachael Flatt).*

OPPOSITE (BOTTOM) / *Men's figure skating gold medalist Evan Lysacek of the U.S. drinks in the moment with silver medalist Evgeni Plushenko of Russia and bronze medalist Daisuke Takahashi.*

(PHOTO BY YURI KADOBNOV /AFP/GETTY IMAGES)

(PHOTO BY MATTHEW STOCKMAN/GETTY IMAGES)

(PHOTO BY MATTHEW STOCKMAN/GETTY IMAGES)

Nineteen-year-old Yu-Na Kim of South Korea, gold medalist in ladies figure skating, is flanked by Mao Asada (left) of Japan, silver, and Joannie Rochette of Canada, bronze. (PHOTO BY CAMERON SPENCER/GETTY IMAGES)

Tanith Belbin and Ben Agosto of the U.S., silver medalists in the Torino Games, finished just out of the medals in fourth place in the ice dancing competition. (PHOTO BY MATTHEW STOCKMAN/GETTY IMAGES)

AN END TO A GOLD-MEDAL DROUGHT

These Games belonged to Lysacek, who willed his way to two clean performances, using well-rounded skills, an expert knowledge of the international judging system and superior choreography to edge the Russian legend by 1.31 points. Daisuke Takahashi took the bronze, the first-ever Olympic figure skating medal for a Japanese man.

The two-time U.S. champion became the first American man to win Olympic gold since Brian Boitano in 1988, and the first reigning World champion to grab the honor since Scott Hamilton in 1984. The Naperville, Ill., native also is the first men's champion from somewhere other than Russia or the Unified Team in six Olympic Games.

Lysacek served notice with an inspired short program to Stravinsky's "Firebird" that had solid jumps—including a triple Lutz-triple toe loop combination—as well as the second-highest program components scores of the event. He earned a personal best 90.30 points and entered the free skate just .55 points behind the Russian.

"I had a little bit of a monkey on my back from my short program in Torino," Lysacek said. "That was one of the worst short programs of my life; now, this is one of the best."

Plushenko, too, was impressive, landing a quad toe-triple toe and a sterling triple Axel.

In the free skate, Lysacek silenced most—although not all—of his doubters, out-dueling Plushenko with a strong battery of jumps and other elements, wrapped up in a commanding performance to Rimsky-Korsakov's "Scheherazade." He earned 167.37 points, giving him a total score of 257.67 points.

Plushenko began his tango program with a quadruple toe-triple toe but had to fight for the landings of several other jumps. While the two skaters were judged equal in program components, the Russian did not do as many jump elements in the second half of his program, allowing the American to edge him in the technical elements score.

American Johnny Weir placed sixth in the free skate and sixth overall after an inspired free skate to "Fallen Angels." He hit two clean triple Axels and executed two jump combinations after the program's halfway point. Two-time and reigning U.S. champion Jeremy Abbott took himself out of the running by placing 15th in the short program and climbed to ninth overall after landing two triple Axel combinations and five other triples.

CHANGING OF THE GUARD IN ICE DANCING

North Americans did more than arrive in Vancouver—they dominated. For just the third time since ice dancing became an Olympic sport in 1976, a Russian, Unified Team or Soviet couple failed to win gold, and for the first time the winners were not from Europe.

The top two couples—Canadians Tessa Virtue and Scott Moir, and Americans Meryl Davis and Charlie White—train together in Canton, Mich., sharing coaches and choreographers Igor Shpilband and Marina Zoueva.

Reigning World champions Oksana Domnina and Maxim Shabalin of Russia, who generated a lot of controversy for their original dance to an Aboriginal theme, took bronze. Americans Tanith Belbin and Ben Agosto, the 2006 Olympic silver medalists, finished fourth.

For the free dance, the Canadians mesmerized, floating across the ice to Gustav Mahler's haunting "Adagietto," while the Americans grabbed fans with a thrill-packed rendition of "The Phantom of the Opera."

Virtue and Moir's 110.42 points brought their overall total to 221.57, shattering their previous personal best of 204.38.

"We knew it was in us, but to get out there on the Olympic ice and to perform and to execute like that was a feeling that I've never had," Moir said, referring to their personal-best score

Davis and White, too, set a new personal best in the free dance—107.19 points—despite a one-point deduction for an extended lift. They ended with a score of 215.74 points, nearly 14 points above their previous record.

Americans Emily Samuelson and Evan Bates gained strength during the competition, placing 14th in the compulsory, 11th in the original dance and 11th in the free dance.

MILLION-DOLLAR GOLD

In the ladies competition, it was all about grace under pressure. World champion Yu-Na Kim of Korea had millions of dollars of sponsorships riding on the gold while Canada's Joannie Rochette was dealt a traumatic blow when her mother suddenly died of a heart attack. In the wings was 2008 World champion Mao Asada of Japan hoping to steal the limelight from Kim.

From the moment Kim set foot on the ice for her "James Bond" short program to the time she finished her final combination spin in her free skate, she was explosive. She brought down the house, earning a world-record overall score of 228.56 points, a whopping 23.06 points ahead of Asada.

Asada didn't let up on Kim, landing a total of three triple Axels in the two programs and becoming the first woman to land two in the free skate. But she made other errors, most notably popping a planned triple toe, and she settled for silver.

Rochette claimed the bronze—and many hearts —as the reigning World silver medalist skated a solid short program and maintained her third-place ranking with a courageous free skate.

At every Olympic Games since 1968, at least one U.S. female figure skater had landed on the podium. In Vancouver, with only two U.S. women in the field and only one World Championships appearance between them (Rachael Flatt finished fifth at the event in 2009), the odds were against the teenage skaters. That didn't stop Mirai Nagasu, in the days leading up to the Olympic Games, from issuing this warning: "It's 'Bring it on. All or nothing.'"

The 16-year-old from Arcadia, Calif., delivered on her promise, performing a thrilling free skate that electrified the crowd at Pacific Coliseum. Finishing in fourth, Nagasu acknowledged, "I think my best years are to come."

A relaxed and smiling Flatt genuinely seemed to enjoy herself on the Olympic stage. Flatt thought she had skated a clean program, but the judges downgraded both her triple flips and the high school senior placed a respectable seventh.

THE BEGINNING OF A NEW DYNASTY

In the pairs competition, skating in their fourth Olympic Games, Xue Shen and Hongbo Zhao of China were the sentimental favorites. After 18 years of skating together, Shen and Zhao finally reached the top of the podium in Vancouver. The Chinese team ended a run of 12 Olympic gold-medal pairs performances by the Soviet Union/Russian skating dynasty. Their country mates, Qing Pang and Jian Tong, grabbed the silver after putting down a first-place free skate, while the bronze went to Germans Aliona Savchenko and Robin Szolkowy.

Sixteen-year-old Mirai Nagasu of the U.S. enchanted the crowd with her grace and athleticism on the ice. She finished fourth with a promise that her best years are to come. (Photo by Yuri Kadobnov/AFP/Getty Images)

Meryl & Charlie
DAVIS & WHITE

LEFT / *Meryl Davis and Charlie White's performance to "The Phantom of the Opera" was big and bold and gave them their personal-best score of 107.19 points in the free dance as well as the silver medal.* (PHOTO BY MATTHEW STOCKMAN/GETTY IMAGES)

13-year Partnership Yields Silver

No U.S. ice dancing couple has been together as long—13 years—as Meryl Davis and Charlie White have been. That commitment to each other and their sport paid off in Vancouver, where they won a silver medal.

Davis and White were paired up by their coach when they were just 10 years old. White, a Bloomfield Hills, Mich., native who began skating at age 3, split his time between ice dancing and hockey, and won a state championship in hockey as a youth. He and Davis actually missed the 2005 State Farm U.S. Figure Skating Championships because White broke his ankle while playing hockey in the fall of 2004. He is a student at the University of Michigan.

Davis, who began skating at age 5, is a native of West Bloomfield, Mich. She is studying anthropology at the University of Michigan.

The duo had almost instant success, but it was a disappointment at the 2009 World Figure Skating Championships that gave them the motivation they needed to medal at the Olympic Games. They finished .04 away from being on the podium at those World Championships and have said repeatedly that being that close to a podium finish helped keep them energized and hungry for success.

White and Davis became somewhat of an Internet sensation with their original dance, which depicts an Indian wedding ceremony. One of the pair's coaches, Marina Zoueva, was inspired for the theme while looking through a clothing catalog featuring a Hermes scarf with Indian dancers.

The folk dance, a crowd favorite, was especially well received in India, a country that has virtually no connection to the popular winter sport. In addition to the silver medal they won in Vancouver, they won the U.S. championship in 2009 and 2010.

OPPOSITE / *The assigned theme for the original dance was country folk, and Davis and White's Bollywood dance became a YouTube sensation. To learn how to move their arms and bodies in true Indian dance style, the two spent months working with a former professional performer from India.* (PHOTO BY DIMITAR DILKOFF/AFP/GETTING IMAGES)

While finishing on the podium at the Olympic Games is the ultimate prize, the *experience* of being there is the real reward for the vast majority of athletes.

Amanda Evora's bubbliness embodied the "just-happy-to-be-there" attitude of the U.S. pairs teams in Vancouver. Both teams knew a medal was a near impossibility.

"Our goal was to make the (Olympic) team," Evora's partner Mark Ladwig said. "Now (our goal) is to beat our personal best and show the world what we can do."

Americans Emily Samuelson and Evan Bates, competing together for eight years, skated their free dance to the music Canto Della Terra *sung by Sarah Brightman and Andrea Bocelli. The duo worked hard to perfect their lifts, spin faster and master the intricate footwork of all the required dances. They finished in 11th place.* (PHOTO BY MATTHEW STOCKMAN/GETTY IMAGES)

Evora and Ladwig met their stated goal, posting personal bests in both programs to place 10th overall, while U.S. champions Caydee Denney and Jeremy Barrett, partnered for only two years, finished 13th.

Pairs figure skaters Amanda Evora, 25, and Mark Ladwig, 29, skated to 10th place overall with a personal-best score at their first world-class competition. By placing second at the U.S. Championships, the duo qualified for the Olympic Games and the World Championships that followed. (PHOTO BY ALEX LIVESEY/ GETTY IMAGES)

Like most teenagers, Rachael Flatt, 17, knows how to have a good time, and she managed to do just that in her Olympic debut, finishing in seventh place in ladies figure skating. (PHOTO BY MATTHEW STOCKMAN/GETTY IMAGES)

Caydee Denney, 16, and Jeremy Barrett, 25, of the United States placed 13th in the pairs competition. (PHOTO BY MATTHEW STOCKMAN/ GETTY IMAGES)

With perfect expression, Tessa Virtue, 20, and Scott Moir, 22, skated flawlessly to Mahler's Symphony No. 5 in their free dance. The couple, partnered on ice for 14 years, won Canada's first gold in ice dance. (PHOTO BY KEVORK DJANSEZIAN/ GETTY IMAGES)

Freestyle Skiing

Trailblazers Shine

Story Contributors: Amy Donaldson & Lindsey Sine

If there was one sport that epitomized the defiant attitude athletes and fans exhibited throughout the Olympic Games when it came to the whims of Mother Nature raining on the much-anticipated athletic parade of the world's best athletes, it was freestyle skiing.

The sport has long been home to trailblazers, rebels and adventurers and 2010's athletes were no different.

From the first Olympic gold medalist for the United States' Hannah Kearney to the last, and maybe most emotional, silver medalist Jeret "Speedy" Peterson, the competitions were electric and the performances enduring.

MOGULS

Kearney won her medal in the midst of fog, rain, sleet and bone-chilling winds. The visibility was so poor, fans couldn't always see the competitor standing on the mountainside at Cypress before judges signaled them to navigate the course of bumps and two required jumps.

All four U.S. women made the finals, with Kearney qualifying first, just in front of home country favorite and World Cup champion Jennifer Heil. The gracious, well-liked Heil was long expected to be the first Canadian to win gold at an Olympic Games hosted in Canada. Many in the crowd endured the horrific weather conditions in hopes of seeing Canadian history. She was, after all, the defending Olympic gold medalist.

But it was not to be.

Three-time Olympian Shannon Bahrke stayed in the top spot until Heil laid down what looked like the winning run.

"I heard the roar of the crowd," said Kearney. "I heard Jen's score. I knew I was going to have to ski the run of my life."

She did just that earning the highest score of her very accomplished career—26.63. Heil's silver medal score was 25.69, while Bahrke earned the bronze.

In women's moguls, it was Hannah Kearney (center) of the United States who captured the gold medal bumping Canadian Jennifer Heil (left) into second place. Kearney's teammate, Shannon Bahrke (right), earned the bronze. (PHOTO BY ALEX LIVESEY/GETTY IMAGES)

On the couch

While Alexandre Bilodeau of Canada—sitting in first—and Dale Begg-Smith of Australia (center)—reclining in second—knew they had secured a medal, Bryon Wilson of United States (right) anxiously awaited the score of the last moguls skier, Guilbaut Colas. The Frenchman scored 25.74, good enough for sixth place and great news for Wilson, who claimed the bronze. (PHOTO BY JAMIE SQUIRE/GETTY IMAGES)

The next night, in similar conditions, Montana native Bryon Wilson continued his Cinderella season by earning the bronze medal. Wilson started the season without a spot on the World Cup circuit. His hope at the beginning was to gain experience for the future. Two great races in Finland got it all started and he skied the rest of the season like a veteran.

Canada would get a gold in moguls, it just wasn't the skier they expected. Instead of Heil, Alexandre Bilodeau won the gold in moguls with a score of 26.75. He edged Australia's Dale Begg-Smith, who ironically was born and raised in Vancouver. Begg-Smith had been so dominant on the World Cup circuit, many considered him a lock for the gold.

Bilodeau's gold caused Vancouver Olympic Organizing Committee's (VANOC) CEO to publicly thank him and declare, "Alex, You're the man."

AERIALS

The U.S. was back in the spotlight in the aerials competition. While none of the U.S. women earned a medal, three of them made the finals, including 16-year-old Ashley Caldwell. She was recruited into aerials through a new program that hopes to lure more gymnasts into the high-flying, heart-stopping sport.

Lacy Schnoor, Draper, Utah, finished ninth, and two-time Olympian Emily Cook was 11th.

Australia's Lydia Lassila won the event with a score of 214.74. Her victory gave the Australians the most winter Olympic gold medals—two—in the country's history.

China continued to show its dominance with Nina Li finishing second and Xinxin Guo in third.

On the men's side, the favorite for gold, Anton Kushnir of Belarus, fell on his second jump and didn't qualify for the finals. He had won four of the World Cup competitions in 2009-10 and was ranked number one.

On a cold, clear Thursday night, Jeret "Speedy" Peterson thrilled fans from all countries when he landed his famous "Hurricane." The toughest trick in the sport, it only earned him the silver because of the deep compression on his landing.

Still, for the three-time Olympian, it was a victory on many levels.

"I don't know that I can really put it into words," he said.

Kushnir's teammate, Alexei Grishin, won the gold medal with a score of 248.41. Peterson's score was 247.21. China's Zhongqing Liu was third with a score of 242.53.

MOGULS
Shannon BAHRKE

High Energy Style

Known for her constant smile, pink-streaked hair and high energy style, three-time Olympian Shannon Bahrke cemented her place as one of the best female moguls skiers with a bronze medal in Vancouver.

It was a momentous accomplishment for the native of Tahoe City, Calif., who said before the Games that she would retire at the end of the season. She planned to get married and pursue business opportunities, as well as finish her education at the University of Utah.

Bahrke might be known for her near-constant smile, but she also knows a lot about overcoming adversity.

In 2000 she began to suffer flu-like symptoms that turned out to be a staph infection in her spine. As the days turned into weeks, doctors began telling her she wouldn't ski again and that she should focus on just saving her life. She recovered and defied predictions by returning to the slopes.

She won the first U.S. medal in the 2002 Games—a silver—but then struggled with injuries, including a broken jaw and several knee injuries. She recovered from a 2005 injury to make the 2006 Olympic Team, but finished a disappointing 10th place.

She blew her knee out during the 2007-08 season, and spent a year in rehab, going to school and starting a business—Silver Bean Coffee. The company, which she runs with her fiancé, Matt Happe (pronounced Happy), offers ski-theme blends, as well as blends named for other skiers like Julia Mancuso and Billy Demong. A portion of the proceeds are donated to the charities supported by those athletes. Bahrke also has a Best Friends Blend, which benefits Best Friends Animal Society, a no-kill animal shelter in Kanab, Utah.

Bahrke has a younger brother, Scotty, who coached his sister and competed in aerials in these Games.

"The moment I stepped out onto the moguls course I tumbled all the way to the bottom and immediately fell in love with the sport," writes Shannon Bahrke on her web site. As an athletic kid, freestyle skiing was a good fit for this 12-year-old skier, who described herself as "an unruly child and just a little crazy." The 29-year-old American claimed the bronze in moguls. (PHOTO BY ADRIAN DENNIS/AFP/GETTY IMAGES)

Nathan Roberts of the United States flew through qualifications but failed to place in the finals of the moguls competition. (Photo by Streeter Lecka/ Getty Images)

SKI CROSS

The Olympic debut of men's ski cross took center stage, but it wasn't the Americans who stole the spotlight. It was Michael Schmid of Switzerland who earned the gold while 37-year-old Casey Puckett, a five-time Olympian (1992, 1994, 1998, 2002 and 2010), and 36-year-old Daron Rahlves, a four-time Olympian (1998, 2002, 2006, 2010), were eliminated in the first round of the finals. Both had been former members of the U.S. alpine team.

Errol Kerr, who is from Truckee, Calif., and represented Jamaica in ski cross, described the unpredictable sport.

"You're putting four guys at a time—that gives you eight poles, 12 edges and guys are racing down a course with huge jumps up to 100 feet through the air, and guys are going 60 miles per hour and the first guy to the bottom wins," said Kerr.

The U.S. did not have a woman compete in women's ski cross, but Ashleigh McIvor, Canada, thrilled the host country winning the gold medal.

High-flying tricks

ABOVE / *Ryan St. Onge twists and turns in the night sky qualifying for the 12-skier final in the men's aerials. The 27-year-old, who first made the U.S. Ski Team when he was only 14 years old, placed fourth, just shy of the podium.* (PHOTO BY MARTIN BUREAU/ AFP/GETTY IMAGES)

OPPOSITE / *Jeret "Speedy" Peterson, a three-time Olympian from Boise, Idaho, said he jumped "horribly" in training. "I just told myself, look, you need to start having fun, because this is what this is all about," said Peterson. The result was "The Hurricane" and the silver medal in the men's aerials.* (PHOTO BY MARTIN BUREAU/AFP/GETTY IMAGES)

"It was cool for me to come in and get a medal after Hannah won yesterday and Shannon got the bronze."

"I watched Hannah's run and I decided that's what I wanted to do."

Bryon Wilson, bronze medalist, moguls

Bryon Wilson

The 21-year-old was one of the feel-good stories of the Vancouver Games. He wasn't even competing on the World Cup circuit when a teammate's injury offered him the chance to ski in Finland. He finished second in two races during that competition and earned himself a spot on the U.S. Olympic Team.

Originally from Butte, Montana, he moved to Utah in 2006 to pursue a ski career. He was an accomplished gymnast and baseball player before dedicating himself to moguls skiing.

Ice Hockey

Silver Linings

Story Contributors: Amy Donaldson, Christy Jeffries,
Harry Thompson & Dave Fischer

The gold-medal showdown between the U.S. and Canada in men's hockey was, quite simply, the Clash of the Titans in the birthplace of the game itself. No sport is more important to Canadians than hockey. And no gold medal was more coveted than the men's and women's hockey gold. Most Canadians wouldn't even consider, let alone discuss, the possibility of silver.

As Canadian athletes struggled with the pressure to "Own the Podium" because the Olympic Games were on home turf, the Americans were leading the overall medal count.

Then the young American men's hockey team, which wasn't expected to win gold in Vancouver, stunned the mighty Canadians by beating them at their own game, 5-3, in pool play.

The loss only enhanced the frenzy that surrounded the eventual gold-medal game—which turned out to be a rematch—of the North American powers. The Canadians changed goalies—benching legendary goalie Martin Brodeur in favor of the local boy, Roberto Luongo— and fought through some tough elimination-round games to get their re-match.

Ranked fifth coming into the tournament, the U.S. team exceeded all expectations with a silver-medal finish.

Team USA swept through the preliminary round, defeating Switzerland, Norway and Canada. The U.S. logged a tournament-best plus-nine goal differential through its first three games and earned the tournament's number one seed heading into the playoff round.

After blanking Switzerland, 2-0, in the quarterfinals, Team USA stormed Finland in the semifinals, scoring six first-period goals en route to a 6-1 victory and a rematch against Canada for gold.

The gold-medal matchup featured some of the game's best players including Ryan Miller of the United States and Sidney Crosby from Canada.

The U.S. fell behind, 2-0, in the game, but some late-game heroics would send the contest into sudden death overtime. Zach Parise scored the game-tying goal with just 24 seconds left in regulation time.

The U.S. men's hockey team was ranked fifth coming into the Olympic tournament and finished in an impressive second place. Even so, the loss to Canada in the gold-medal game took its toll on the players. (Photo by Harry How/Getty Images)

But in the overtime it was 22-year-old Sidney Crosby who scored the game-winning goal off a pass from Jarome Iginla. He is one of the few hockey players to win the Stanley Cup and an Olympic gold medal in the same year.

Ryan Miller was named the tournament's most valuable player and best goaltender, while fellow American Brian Rafalski was named the tournament's best defenseman. Miller, Rafalski and Parise were all named to the media's all-tournament team.

"I couldn't be more proud of this group," said Ron Wilson, head coach of Team USA. "They did everything we asked and represented our country in an outstanding manner both on and off the ice."

MINING FOR GOLD

The 2010 U.S. Olympic women's ice hockey team went to Vancouver with one goal in mind. Gold.

After a pair of world championships in the years leading up to the Games, the No. 1-ranked U.S. squad appeared to be poised to return to the top of the medal podium for the first time since its inaugural Olympic victory in 1998.

While just two members remained from that historic gold medal-winning squad of yesteryear and only four others had any Olympic experience, the core group had spent the last four years rebuilding the program. Putting everything they had into becoming a cohesive, disciplined, strong and skilled team, the Americans got a taste of victory at the 2008 and 2009 world championships.

The gritty determination and passion that garnered them back-to-back world titles was evident throughout the 2010 edition of the once-every-four-year dream-come-true for female hockey players. And it was especially evident once the 21 players got a crack at their archrival Canadian counterparts in the gold-medal game.

The U.S. team left it all on the ice that Thursday afternoon, but came up a little short against a talented and composed Canadian team that rode two first-period goals from 18-year-old phenom Marie-Philip Poulin and a 28-save effort from goaltender Shannon Szabados to win its third straight Olympic gold medal, 2-0.

"As I told the players before the game, make sure you have no excuses, no regrets and no alibis at the end of the night," said Mark Johnson, head coach for Team USA.

"We were able to walk out of the arena with our heads held high. It was a three and a half year process to get there and expectations were very high. I am very proud of my team. I thought they competed for 60 minutes and came up a little bit short."

The biggest crowd to ever watch a women's hockey game was treated to perhaps one of the greatest women's hockey games of all time. The end-to-end action kept the fans on the edge of their seats as the teams battled it out. Every inch of ice was fought for, every shot was contested, every scoring chance earned.

Zach Parise (#9) of the U.S. scored the equalizer against Canada in the men's dramatic gold-medal game. Canada went on to win, 3-2, in overtime. (PHOTO BY CRIS BOURONCLE /AFP/GETTY IMAGES)

Defensemen Brian Rafalski (#28) and Ryan Suter (#20) of the U.S. shut down Sidney Crosby (#87) of Canada. Canada defeated the United States, 3-2, in overtime to win the gold medal. (PHOTO BY HARRY HOW/GETTY IMAGES)

ABOVE / Gillian Apps of Canada collides with American defenseman Caitlin Cahow (#8) during the women's gold-medal game between Canada and the U.S. Canada won 2-0. (PHOTO BY BRUCE BENNETT/GETTY IMAGES)

RIGHT / While bitter rivals, American and Canadian fans display sportsmanship at its finest, walking side-by-side down the streets of Vancouver. (PHOTO BY MARK RALSTON/ AFP/GETTY IMAGES)

Vetter makes a save

Jessie Vetter (#31) of the United States makes a save from Marie-Philip Poulin (#29) of Canada during the women's gold-medal game. Poulin would later score two goals in the first period. Vetter kept the United States in the game with 26 saves but Canada went on to win, 2-0. The stellar goalie gave up three goals during the entire tournament. (PHOTO BY HARRY HOW/GETTY IMAGES)

"We had two great teams going head-to-head with a lot of passion and a lot of commitment that we put in along the way. It was guaranteed to be a great game and it was," said forward Julie Chu, who was competing in her third Games.

"You can get the mentality of just packing it in and just giving up but we played hard and fought to the buzzer. We can be proud of that."

The U.S. came into the final game outscoring its opponents 40-2, with dominating 12-1, 13-0, 6-0 and 9-1 wins along the way. The Americans had not allowed a first-period goal and had outshot the opposition by a staggering 183-49 margin. When Poulin scored for Canada in the first period of the gold-medal game, it sent the near capacity raucous home crowd of 16,805 into a frenzy. It was only the second goal that U.S. netminder Jessie Vetter had surrendered all tournament.

Even the crowd acknowledged afterward that they witnessed a game between two champions as they joined with U.S. fans in a rousing chant of U-S-A as the medals were handed out.

"It's great for our sport to be able to play in front of a crowd like that," said defenseman Caitlin Cahow. "What a long way we've come. I was just proud to be a part of it."

"A lot of people put a lot of time and energy into this process. I think we're a lot better off than we were three and half years ago. Our young players have experienced success at world championships and then faced a little stinger at the Olympics. Hopefully they grow from that," said Johnson.

"We walked away with a silver medal. That's not a bad thing."

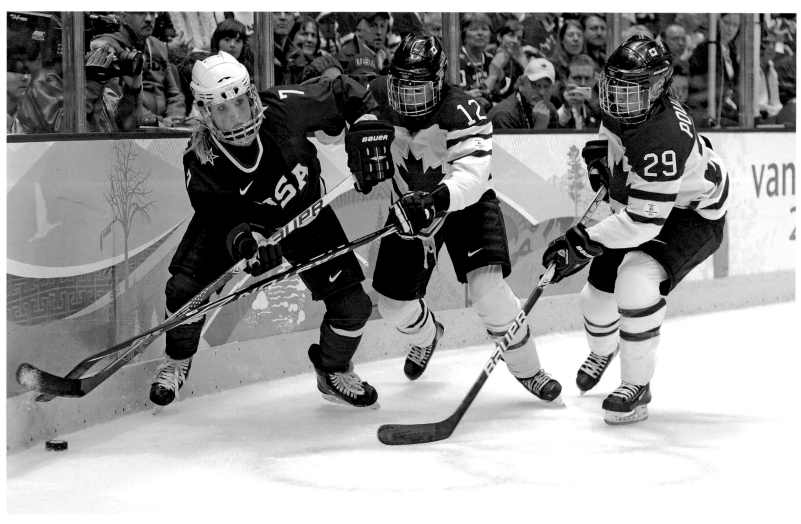

Monique Lamoureux (#7) of the United States is pursued by Meaghan Mikkelson (#12) and Marie-Philip Poulin (#29) of Canada during the women's gold-medal game. (PHOTO BY HARRY HOW/GETTY IMAGES)

Kacey Bellamy (#22) maneuvers past Haley Irwin (#21) of Canada during the gold-medal game. (PHOTO BY HARRY HOW/GETTY IMAGES)

Jenny Potter's (#12) shot on goal is saved by Shannon Szabados (#1) of Canada during the gold-medal game. (Photo by Harry How/Getty Images)

With the loss to Canada still fresh, U.S. players accept their silver medals. (Photo by Alex Livesey/Getty Images)

Luge

Sliding into History

Story Contributor: Sandy Caligiore

(Photo by Peter Parks/AFP/Getty Images)

The Whistler Sliding Center had lugers talking about this new venue long before the 2010 Olympic Winter Games began. The luge competitions were ready to live up to their billing. The events were to be among the most closely watched during the Games for one very good reason: speed. When you walked near the track, the buzz was palpable.

This is saying something in a sport where speed is the element. Competitors hitting 80 miles per hour usually do not draw much commentary. But when a track was designed to reach approximately 85 miles per hour and the racers bulleted down at 95 MPH, it became cause for concern.

The steepest—a nearly 50-story decent from top to bottom—and consequently, the fastest, track in the world elicited varied opinions.

"Too fast."

"Very challenging."

"I like it."

"I have concerns."

"It's right up my alley."

Germans on Top

The Germans dominated luge collecting four medals in the men's and women's single events and one in the doubles.

OPPOSITE / *Lugers get an abbreviated training session to prepare themselves and their sled for the new start.*

RIGHT (TOP) / *Tatjana Huefner gives Germany another gold in women's singles.* (PHOTO BY LEON NEAL/AFP/GETTY IMAGES)

RIGHT (BOTTOM) / *Felix Loch of Germany jumps for joy as the gold medalist in men's luge.* (PHOTO BY LEON NEAL/AFP/GETTY IMAGES)

Two years of preparation on the part of the teams, VANOC and the International Luge Federation (FIL) became a moot point on the afternoon of February 12. Just a few hours prior to the Opening Ceremony in Vancouver, a crash occurred during men's training that brought the Olympic Games to its knees and delivered deadly news around the world.

Nodar Kumaritashvili, a 21-year-old athlete from the Republic of Georgia, did not negotiate a clean line through the course's 16th and final curve. Kumaritashvili hit a wall and careened out of the track, striking an unprotected metal stanchion that supports the roof of the course.

The Olympic Broadcasting Service, as is the norm with such high-profile sporting events, was using those practice runs to rehearse their race-day coverage for a global audience. As luck would have it, the fatal run was shown on venue video screens and monitors for all to see. At that instant, the music and the joviality associated with an Olympic celebration came to an immediate halt. The mood was somber. A pall had been cast over the Whistler Sliding Center as the news eventually circulated about the fate of the Georgian.

With training now canceled for the balance of the day, the luge racers were sent back to the Athlete's Village to prepare for the two-hour journey from Whistler to Vancouver for the Opening Ceremony.

In the meantime, event organizers and venue operators, chief among them the FIL, painstakingly discussed next steps in meetings that extended beyond the Ceremony and the moment of silence that was observed in the stadium for Kumaritashvili.

U.S. sliders

Christian Niccum (top) and Dan Joye, seen here on a training run, posted a sixth-place finish in the doubles finals. (PHOTO BY LEON NEAL/AFP/GETTY IMAGES)

Tony Benshoof finished in eighth place in the men's competition. (PHOTO BY OLIVER LANG/AFP/GETTY IMAGES)

It was after 10 p.m. local time when the FIL announced that training would resume the next morning, and that all competitions were going to drop to the next lowest start so as to reduce speed. The men competed from the women's start; the women and doubles competed from the junior start.

When the men's start was dropped to the flatter women's start ramp, it favored the best starters in the world and the Germans rose to the top of the podium. Felix Loch won the gold with a four-run combined time of 3:13.085, setting a track record on his first run. At 20, Loch became the youngest Olympic champion in luge history. His teammate, David Moeller, finished 0.679 of a second behind to claim the silver. Armin Zoeggeler of Italy, two-time Olympic gold medalist and the best slider leading up to the Olympic Games, took the bronze with a combined run time of 3:14.375.

American Tony Benshoof nursing a bad back all season had planned to use the steep men's start to accelerate and mitigate his back issues. The Minnesotan's considerable driving skills could put him in the medal hunt. But Benshoof couldn't generate the kind of early momentum needed to contend and he finished eighth with a combined time of 3:15.128.

WOMEN'S SINGLES EVENT

When the ladies began training from the junior start, just ahead of curve six, it became clear that whoever negotiated the very first turn would have the advantage. Too much steering and the sled dove into the lower wall; too little steering and the sled climbed the curve, essentially sending the athlete uphill in a downhill sport.

Loch's teammate Tatjana Huefner, winner of five of the eight World Cup stops during the winter and bronze medalist in Torino, figured out the revised start and had changes made to her sled to accommodate the first turn. With a flawless fourth run, Huefner clocked a top speed of 83 mph (134.1 kph) and posted a combined time of 2:46.524 to clinch the gold. Austria's Nina Reithmayer, .490 of a second behind, slid into silver-medal position and German teammate Natalie Geisenberger took the bronze, .577 of a second off the pace. Reithmayer's silver ended the Germans' complete domination of the Olympic podium since 2002.

American Erin Hamlin came into the competition relaxed and confident in her driving ability in Whistler's high-speed environment. With a 2009 World Championship win in Lake Placid and three World Cup bronze medals in the months prior to Whistler, Hamlin was determined to upset the German applecart. At the start of training before Nodar's accident, Hamlin's times placed her firmly among the contenders. But America's best hope for a medal failed to master the new start and finished 16th.

One last Olympic slide

For 14 years Mark Grimmette and Brian Martin competed on the luge circuit,
initially funding their races because they believed they could contend with the Europeans.
Grimmette was the U.S. flagbearer in the Opening Ceremony,
making his fifth Olympic appearance. It was Martin's fourth Olympic Games.
Together they won 65 international medals.
One month after the Games, the duo announced their retirement.

*In 1996, Americans Mark Grimmette (on top) and Brian Martin became a team and raced together in Nagano in 1998, where they won the bronze medal. In 2002, they claimed the silver medal in Salt Lake City. In Vancouver, the best doubles team in U.S. luge history had hoped to add another doubles medal to their collection, but it didn't work out. The duo finished 13th. (P*HOTO BY M*ARK* R*ALSTON*/ AFP/G*ETTY* I*MAGES*)*

DOUBLES EVENT

In the doubles, the competition centered on Austria's Linger brothers, Andreas and Wolfgang, the defending Olympic champions and the strong German teams.

But it was another set of brothers, Latvia's Andris and Juris Sics, who surprised the field and slipped in between Austria and Germany to take the silver medal with a combined time of 1:22.969. The Linger brothers claimed their second gold .254 of a second ahead of the Latvians. The bronze went to Germany's Patric Leitner and Alexander Resch, whose smoking second run pulled them from fifth place to third.

The U.S. doubles effort also struggled with curve six. Christian Niccum and Dan Joye, supported by their wives and children in the audience, finished in sixth place. Ironically, Olympic silver and bronze medalists Mark Grimmette and Brian Martin ended training with excellent starts and finish times to match. It was, however, a different story the next night in the two-heat event as the best sled in U.S. history finished 13th.

"We figured it out in training, but just didn't get it done tonight," stated Martin, who along with Grimmette raced their last Olympic run in their storied 14-year career together.

America's best hope for a medal in the ladies' luge singles event, Erin Hamlin, finished 16th. (PHOTO BY SHAUN BOTTERILL/ GETTY IMAGES)

Nordic Combined

A Historic Medal Haul for Team USA

Story Contributors: Amy Donaldson and Tom Kelly

Thirty-three-year-old Todd Lodwick came out of retirement to finish what he'd started with Billy Demong and Johnny Spillane in a sport that most Americans know nothing about—nordic combined.

The three skiers had been among the world's best for a decade and a half, but they had been unable to earn that elusive Olympic medal. In fact, no American had ever won a medal—of any color—in the sport which combines ski jumping and cross-country racing.

Vancouver, they said, was different.

They entered the Games with a sense of destiny, confident they could vanquish the nightmarish memories of a fourth-place finish in 2002 and a mediocre performance in 2006. All they needed was one more skier who would dedicate his life to training year-round for one moment of glory.

In the end, two-time Olympian and Park City, Utah, native Brett Camerota would be their fourth. The result was a team that earned four medals—three second-place finishes and one gold medal.

The strength of the Americans was working as a team—each athlete helping the other. That became vividly clear in the opening event. After the individual competition jump on the normal hill, veteran Todd Lodwick was second and Johnny Spillane fourth—both in serious contention for a medal.

The Americans knew they would have to set a torrid pace in cross-country skiing to secure a medal. Starting second, Lodwick went out full speed, sucking the wind out of the field while Spillane was able to sit back and pick a point for his move. Meanwhile, starting 24th after a bad jump, Billy Demong was sprinting through the field. Suddenly, the three American World Champions were all battling for medals.

Silver medalists (from left to right) Brett Camerota, Todd Lodwick, Johnny Spillane and Billy Demong show off their Olympic bling. The four are the first Americans to win an Olympic medal in the nordic combined team event. (PHOTO BY MICHAEL KAPPELER/ AFP/GETTY IMAGES)

One-two finish: American Billy Demong (#6) approaches the finish line with teammate Johnny Spillane (#2) following close behind in the nordic combined 10km large hill event. Demong won the gold medal four seconds ahead of Spillane. Austrian Bernhard Gruber earned the bronze medal. (PHOTO BY FRANCK FIFE/AFP/GETTY IMAGES)

At the finish, it was Spillane who made history with the silver—much as he had with the breakthrough World Championship win in 2003. Lodwick, who sacrificed himself for the team, was fourth and Demong an amazing sixth. And while it was Spillane who took to the medals stage that evening in Whistler, it was an entire team that shared the medal.

The team would get another chance at making history nine days later in the team event.

Again, it was Lodwick who set the stage on the jumps. He was beaming and pumping his fist after a massive jump on the large hill that put the Americans into second behind Finland heading into the cross-country portion with arguably the best skiers in the field.

As the athletes were warming up for the afternoon relay, temperatures were dancing as a storm moved in on the Whistler Olympic Park. It was a clear track for the opening leg, with Brett Camerota doing his job to simply keeping Finland in check. He skied brilliantly, even taking the lead, before turning it over to Lodwick.

Finland would drop away and the battle began between Austria and America as snow began to fall. The worst of it hit for Spillane on the third leg as he struggled to maintain as Austria took control. On the anchor leg, Demong continually kept himself in position, but just didn't have the ski power to overtake Austria as the Americans took silver.

There was a brief, fleeting moment at the finish where a feeling of heartbreak in missing gold overshadowed the silver. But then it sunk in—four Americans had just combined to win yet another historic medal for Team USA. And this one was for the team!

With four athletes with medals, there was little pressure and more opportunity in the final individual large hill event. On a morning of challenging wind, Spillane jumped to second with Demong sixth. Bizarre jumping conditions left top skiers scattered through the field. Spillane and Demong, though, were in a great spot—pushing immediately to the front to control the race, while Lodwick closed the back door to keep the challengers at bay.

As the Americans came into the stadium a final time, it was clear more history would be made. Demong sprinted ahead—his fitness shining through—to take the first American gold, while Spillane collected an unprecedented third silver medal.

"To me, this program has always been about the team," Demong said. "This Olympics has shown that, even to ourselves, more than ever."

Billy Demong crosses the finish line to win the individual 10km large hill event in another historic win for the United States. Johnny Spillane finished second and collected his third medal of these Games. (Photo by Lars Baron/Bongarts/Getty Images)

Billy DEMONG

Golden Opportunity

Billy Demong relied on time, training and a positive perspective to turn what appeared to be misfortune into one of his life's greatest gifts. Suffering a severe head injury the summer after his worst disappointment as an athlete gave Billy Demong the time he needed to avoid burnout in the grueling sport of nordic combined.

"In the summer of 2002, I dove into a swimming pool and hit my head on the bottom," Demong said in a press conference after he and his teammates won the silver medal in the team event in the 2010 Olympic Games. A fractured skull meant no skiing, no training.

"I basically mentally quit," he said. He went to school and worked construction and that gave him a whole new perspective on the demands of his sport, which combines ski jumping with cross-country ski racing.

"When I came back, it took me three years before I ever even scored a World Cup top 10 again, but I had a really good time every day along the way," he said. "That was one of the changes we made (as a team). Going forward, we had the ability to get better but take ourselves less seriously."

At 29, Demong's dedication to training for nearly 15 years helped him earn the first gold medal for the United States in any nordic event.

The same day he won his gold medal, Feb. 25, he was chosen to carry the American flag in the Closing Ceremony and he proposed to his girlfriend, Katie Koczynski.

The native of Vermontville, N.Y., and Koczynski returned to Park City, Utah, after the Olympic Games where he planned to continue training and she planned to attend graduate school.

Teamwork

After the ski jumping portion of the team event, the U.S. team was in second place behind Finland. Todd Lodwick (green bib) had the biggest jump for the Americans at 136.5 meters and the judges' highest score for a total of 132.2 points, followed by Johnny Spillane (yellow bib), 127.5, Billy Demong (blue bib), 123.8, and Brett Camerota (red bib), 122.3. Their total points put the Americans two seconds behind Finland in the cross-country start.

For the first two legs, the Americans held the lead, but on the third leg, Austria, starting 34 seconds after the Americans, had caught up. Felix Gottwald, who became Austria's most successful Winter Olympian by claiming his third gold at a Winter Games and his seventh overall, took the lead and anchor Mario Stecher managed to hold onto it for the win.

Stecher, who had the faster skis, stayed in control of the race on the final curve to give his team the gold medal. The Americans took the silver medal and Germany earned bronze. (PHOTO BY CLIVE MASON/GETTY IMAGES)

OPPOSITE / The U.S. nordic combined team's success centered around teamwork. Veteran Todd Lodwick came out of retirement to help win an unprecedented silver medal for the United States in the team event. Lodwick, leading a pack of skiers in the 10km cross-country portion of the normal hill event, gave his teammate Johnny Spillane an opportunity to sit back and make his move. Spillane earned the silver medal, the first-ever Olympic medal in nordic combined for the United States. Lodwick finished fourth. (PHOTO BY CLIVE MASON/GETTY IMAGES)

Short Track Speedskating

Thrills and Spills

Story Contributors: Linda Jager and Amy Donaldson

One of the most exciting sports for spectators, short track athletes skated in front of a full arena with loud, raucous crowds prepared for thrills and spills, as well as potentially historic moments. They were not disappointed.

On the final night of competition, 27-year-old Apolo Anton Ohno proved himself to be in a class by himself helping Team USA earn the bronze medal in the men's 5000m relay. It was his eighth medal.

In short track competition, skaters must advance through several rounds in each distance to reach the Olympic A final, which is the medal event. Team USA did well placing participants in seven of the eight Olympic A finals. The team had a record medal haul for short track—six total, two silver and four bronze.

The U.S. was the only country that medaled in both relays and used a different combination of four of its five skaters in the Olympic semifinal, which resulted in all 10 short track Olympians returning home with Olympic medals—an athlete has to skate in at least one relay race to receive a relay medal.

Individually, Apolo Anton Ohno brought home a silver in the 1500m and a bronze in the 1000m, Katherine Reutter won a silver in 1000m, and J.R. Celski earned a bronze in the 1500m.

RIGHT (TOP) / *Travis Jayner of the United States congratulates Canadian Francois-Louis Tremblay, who won the gold in the men's 5000m relay.* (PHOTO BY JAMIE SQUIRE/GETTY IMAGES)

RIGHT (BOTTOM) / *Bronze medalist Apolo Anton Ohno (right) of the United States enjoys the moment with teammates (from left) J.R. Celski, Simon Cho, Travis Jayner and Jordan Malone after winning the bronze medal in the 5000m relay.* (PHOTO BY STREETER LECKA/GETTY IMAGES)

Apolo Anton Ohno charges ahead of Canada's Francois-Louis Tremblay in the men's 500m short track semifinals. Ohno was later disqualified in the finals for impeding. Tremblay won the bronze. (PHOTO BY YURI KADOBNOV/GETTY IMAGES)

1500m ...
the final curve

The first night of short track upheld the sport's exciting and unpredictable reputation. Coming into the final curve of the 1500m race (above), teammates Jung-Su Lee (#243), Si-Bak Sung (#244) and Ho-Suk Lee (#242) of South Korea lead Americans Apolo Anton Ohno and J.R. Celski. It looked to be no medal for the favorite Ohno. (PHOTO BY CAMERON SPENCER/ GETTY IMAGES)

Then, suddenly and inexplicably, Si-bak Sung and Ho-suk Lee collide (left) and slam into the barriers, handing Ohno the silver medal and Celski his first Olympic medal, bronze. (PHOTO BY DIMITAR DILKOFF /AFP/ GETTY IMAGES)

Ohno tied four-time Olympic speedskater Bonnie Blair as the most decorated U.S. Winter Olympian when he captured the silver medal in the 1500m to increase his Olympic medal total to six. Ohno returned days later to break that record with his seventh Olympic medal, a bronze in the 1000m, making him the most decorated U.S. Winter Olympian in history. His eighth medal came as a member of the bronze medal 5000m relay team on the final night of competition.

The ladies 1000m featured a strong performance by Olympic rookie Reutter, starting off with a win in her heat with an Olympic Record time. She also won her quarterfinal and semifinal races and went on to win the silver medal in the final.

"I didn't know if I'd won," said Reutter following the race. "I looked at my coach and said, 'what position was I?' He held up the number two, and that's when I said, 'Really?' And then every emotion I've ever had, all the work I've put into this, came out. I started screaming. At that moment, I've never been more proud to be an American, to be from the Unites States of America, to finally have my flag. And I couldn't wait to see it raised."

In the semifinal of the ladies 3000m relay, the U.S. squad—Kimberly Derrick, Alyson Dudek, Lana Gehring and Reutter—finished second to qualify for the A final. In the A final, the team (Allison Baver, Dudek, Gehring and Reutter) struggled and finished fourth. When the Korean team was disqualified for bumping a Chinese skater on a pass on the final curve, Team USA went from consolation prize to winning the bronze medal and the first women's Olympic short track medal since 1992.

"This is like a dream," said three-time Olympian Baver. "To be at the Olympics is one thing. To come out with a medal, not very many people have the opportunity to do that. I'm very proud to bring home the bronze to the U.S."

The men's 1500m had Ohno and first-time Olympian Celski both advancing through the heats and semifinals to an exciting A Final. This distance marked Celski's return to international competition, just five months after a devastating leg injury at the Olympic Trials. Both athletes skated

PHOTO SEQUENCE / *On the last corner of the 500m final, Apolo Ohno ran up on Francois-Louis Tremblay and put his hand up so as not to run into him.*

"There was no space," said Ohno.

Just before the Canadian slipped and slid into the padding, South Korea's Si-Bak Sung went down, changing the face of the race. Charles Hamelin stayed upright in the chaos and charged for the finish line with the American closely following. Ohno celebrated his silver medal finish only to have it taken away as officials ruled the contact illegal. With Ohno disqualified, the silver and bronze medals went to Sung and Tremblay, respectively.

(PHOTO BY JASPER JUINEN/GETTY IMAGES)

(PHOTO BY YURI KADOBNOV/AFP/GETTY IMAGES)

(PHOTO CREDIT BY ROBYN BECK/AFP/GETTY IMAGES)

j.r. CELSKI

A Cut Above

J.R. Celski was just 14 years old when he found himself standing on the ice with his idol, Apolo Anton Ohno, trying to figure out how to beat him in a race. "I'm not going to lie," said Celski. "It was pretty intimidating. To think of trying to beat him, it was daunting. But ultimately, I want to beat everybody. I want to be the best I can be."

That attitude propelled the 19-year-old from gawking admirer to legitimate competitor—and teammate to the very man who convinced him to enter the sport just five years ago.

"It was watching Apolo Ohno that made me want to do it," he said of making the transition from in-line skating to speedskating."

The youngest of three boys, Celski began in-line skating when he was 3 years old. He and his father both won national titles in the sport. Then he saw Ohno win gold in the 2002 Games, and the course of Celski's life changed.

He took up speedskating and he excelled at it. At 14, he decided to move to California to get the best coaching and moved in with his older brother, Chris.

Celski wasn't sure he'd skate again, let alone represent the U.S. at the Vancouver Games, when he suffered a crash five months earlier during the U.S. Nationals in which his skate cut a six-inch gash in his left thigh.

"It was kind of like, 'This is the end of my career'," he said. "My leg was split open."

Not only did he recover, but his great start at the beginning of the season secured him a spot on the U.S. team.

Celski earned bronze medals in the 1500m race and the 5000m relay in Vancouver.

"When I was laying on that ice, I was in defeat at first," said J.R. Celski about his U.S. National accident five months before the Vancouver Games. "I thought my whole career was over. But I guess in those moments is where we truly define ourselves." The introspective 19-year-old recovered from a lacerated quadricep muscle and turned his thoughts into action winning two bronze medals in these Games. (PHOTO BY MATTHEW STOCKMAN/GETTY IMAGES)

Meng Wang (#112) of China, Seung-Hi Park (#141) of South Korea, Yang Zhou (#114) of China and Katherine Reutter (#157) of the United States compete in the ladies 1000m final. Reutter passed both Park and Zhou but lost out to Wang in a furious dash to the finish. Park finished third and Zhou was disqualified. (PHOTO BY JASPER JUINEN/GETTY IMAGES)

strong in a great tactical race. While it looked like they would finish fourth (Ohno) and fifth (Celski), two of the Korean skaters tangled and fell at the last turn and Ohno and Celski crossed the line in silver and bronze positions, respectfully. This was the first time the U.S. had two male medalists in the same Olympic race.

"I can't describe the emotions that went through my head these last five months," said Celski after winning his bronze medal. "I stayed confident in myself and never had any doubts in myself."

In the women's 1500m race, China's Yang Zhou won the gold with Korea's Een-Byul Lee and Seung-Hi Park claiming second and third, respectively.

Katherine Reutter finished fourth. The Illinois native who moved to Utah to train at the Utah Olympic Oval said she didn't grow up dreaming of being an Olympian.

"I grew up wanting to be the best speedskater," she said after winning the 1000m silver medal. "It brought me to

the Olympics."

In the men's 1000m, Ohno skated another strong series and was in great position in the A final. In the last few laps of the race he got tangled up and dropped back to fifth, but made a huge outside pass in the last turn to capture the bronze, his historic seventh medal, making him the most decorated U.S. Winter Olympian in history.

"It means a lot to me, especially in a sport like this," said three-time Olympian Ohno following his historic win. "There's not many athletes that come to back-to-back Olympic Games and medal. Very, very few. For me to do it in three Games. I'm very happy. I'm very blessed."

The men's 5000m relay semifinal saw the defending World Champions (Ohno, Simon Cho, Celski and Travis Jayner) skate a solid race to advance to the A final. In the A final, the squad (Ohno, Celski, Jayner and Jordan Malone) faced off against a crowded field of five teams on the ice. Team USA passed China in the last turn of the 45-lap race

OPPOSITE (BOTTOM) / *Ha-Ri Cho of South Korea (blue) and Yang Zhou of China battle it out in the ladies 3000m relay finals with the Canadians in third and the Americans nearly a half lap behind. Cho crossed the finish line first but was disqualified for bumping Zhou and throwing her off her skate line. With South Korea out, China claimed the gold medal and the Canadians and Americans were promoted to silver and bronze medals, respectively.* (PHOTO BY JAMIE SQUIRE/GETTY IMAGES)

ABOVE / *The South Korean short track powerhouse of Si-Bak Sung (#244), Jung-Su Lee (#243), Ho-Suk Lee (#242), Seoung-Il Kim (240), and Yoon-Gy Kwak (#241) give thanks for the silver medal in the 5000m relay. Sung (#244) won the silver in the 500m; Jung-Su Lee (#243) won gold in the 1000m and 1500m; and Ho-Suk Lee (#242) won silver in the 1000m.* (PHOTO BY JASPER JUINEN/GETTY IMAGES)

Americans (from left to right) Allison Baver, Kimberly Derrick, Alyson Dudek, Lana Gehring and Katherine Reutter celebrate the thrills of short track speedskating, which propelled them into bronze medal position after the South Korean team was disqualified in the 3000m relay. (PHOTO BY VINCENZO PINTO/ AFP/GETTY IMAGES)

Watching the Olympic Games

to win the bronze behind Canada and Korea, with less than 0.28 of a second separating the top three teams.

The success of Team USA in Vancouver will serve to inspire a new generation of speedskating athletes.

"A lot of our guys—I was one of them—started the sport because we saw some kind of inspiration from something that sparked us watching the Olympic Games on TV," said Ohno.

"That's when I first learned about short track and the beauty of the sport and what it's all about. Then the journey began with buying my first pair of skates and learning how to skate. So hopefully, back home in the Northwest, or anywhere in the United States, someone can seek some kind of inspiration from what we've done and what we stood for as Olympians."

Apolo Anton Ohno

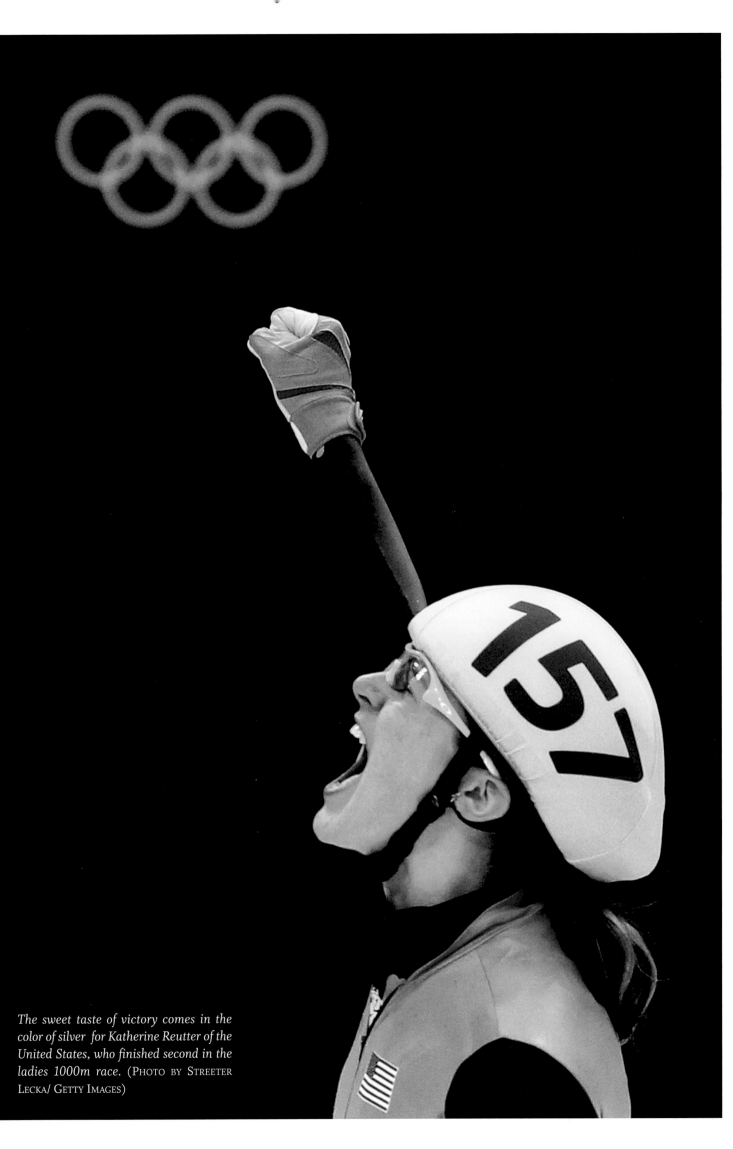

The sweet taste of victory comes in the color of silver for Katherine Reutter of the United States, who finished second in the ladies 1000m race. (Photo by Streeter Lecka/ Getty Images)

Skeleton

Split Seconds Determine Color of Medal

Story Contributor: Amanda Bird

ABOVE / *Canadian Jon Montgomery blazed down the track reaching a top speed of 90.5 mph on his third heat, setting a new track record of 52.20 and putting him in position to battle for the gold medal. His fourth blistering run cinched the deal.* (PHOTO BY MARK RALSTON/AFP/GETTY IMAGES)

Racing head first down an icy track looks dangerous but bobsledder turned skeleton racer Michelle Kelly of Canada says that skeleton is "actually the safest of the three sliding sports." Good to know. Fast and technical described the track at Whistler Sliding Center as skeleton racers navigated 16 turns reaching up to 90 mph. A strong running start and impeccable driving skills, which boil down to a delicate art of manipulating the friction to find the fastest line down the 1450 meters of track, mean the difference of hundreds of seconds and the color of a medal.

Back in the Olympic lineup since the 2002 Olympic Games in Salt Lake City, the men's skeleton race was up for grabs. Strong contenders from Canada, the United States and Germany were poised to challenge Martins Dukurs of Latvia, the World Cup Champion and the favorite going into the race.

In the end, it was Jon Montgomery who won the gold for the host nation in an exciting contest. Montgomery was more than two-tenths of a second behind Dukurs entering the final heats, but was able to slide the fastest runs of the competition to claim the coveted Olympic gold medal by only 0.07 of a second. Montgomery won the competition with a total time of 3:29.73.

In his final run, Dukurs posted a solid start but his lead crumbled in the latter half of track. The Latvian, hoping to win his country's first-ever gold medal in the Olympic Winter Games, finished second with a combined time of 3:29.80. In third was Russian Alexander Tretyakov with a total time of 3:30.75.

RIGHT / *At age 30, Eric Bernotas took his first trip down a skeleton track in 2002. In his Olympic debut in Torino, Bernotas placed sixth, the best U.S. men's finish. In Vancouver, the 38-year-old put together four runs—53.23, 53.55, 53.33 and 53.16 seconds—to finish 14th in the competition.* (PHOTO BY CLIVE MASON/GETTY IMAGES)

Zach Lund likes to fly, be it feet-first or head-first down a track or in the sky. Lund, who switched from luge to skeleton in 1999, finished fifth in the men's skeleton event. Off the track, the 30-year-old American is pursuing studies in aviation. (PHOTO BY SHAUN BOTTERILL/ GETTY IMAGES)

On the American side, Zach Lund finished fifth just 0.42 of a second from the medals.

Four years ago, Lund was the medal favorite going into the 2006 Olympic Winter Games. Lund, heartbreakingly, ended up watching the race from the sidelines after he tested positive for finasteride, a substance found in the anti-balding medication he was taking. It has since been removed from the banned list and a bald-headed Lund (see picture on page 264) reported to the 2010 Games.

Eric Bernotas finished 14th with a combined time of 3:33.27 in his second Olympic Games.

John Daly, who made his World Cup debut just four months before the Olympic Games, finished 17th with a combined time of 3:34.01. "A seventeenth at the Olympics is better than watching it from my couch at home," quipped Daly.

WOMEN'S EVENT

Amy Williams put Great Britain back on the map for winter sports after posting three of the four fastest runs to claim the women's gold medal with a combined time of 3:35.64. Williams obliterated the track record by nearly two-tenths of a second with a third run of 53.68 seconds.

Kerstin Szymkowiak from Germany took the silver with a total time of 3:36.20, while German teammate and 2008 World Champion, Anja Huber, snuck up to grab the

As a youngster, American John Daly was a BMX racer but after a brutal crash that left both his wrists broken, the 15-year-old looked around for other sports. Already an avid track & field athlete, Daly was introduced to sledding and found a new driving force in the sport of skeleton. In his Olympic debut, the 24-year-old finished 17th. (Photo by Leon Neal/AFP/Getty Images)

(PHOTO BY RICHARD HEATHCOTE/GETTY IMAGES)

For 25-year-old Katie Uhlaender, the Opening Ceremony marked the one-year anniversary of her father's death, and just five months ago, the American was still on crutches after several surgeries to repair a shattered kneecap.

"I was faster in training, but coming back from what I've been through, I don't think I could have been more proud to be here and more honored to compete in the Olympics," said Uhlaender, who finished 11th in the skeleton event.

LEFT / Katie Uhlaender congratulates Amy Williams of Great Britain, who won the gold medal in the women's skeleton.
(PHOTO BY SHAUN BOTTERILL/GETTY IMAGES)

bronze medal after crossing the finish with a total time of 3:36.36, just one-tenth of a second ahead of American Noelle Pikus-Pace.

With red, white and blue streaked hair and an American flag painted on her cheek, Pikus-Pace slid across the finish line for the last time of her career. Competing at the Olympic Games was the moment Pikus-Pace had dreamed about for the last four years. She was the 2005 World Cup Champion and medal favorite going into the Torino Games before a freak accident that broke her leg knocked her out of contention. Pikus-Pace finished her career with 12 World Cup medals, a World Cup title, and gold and silver World Championship trophies.

Fellow American Katie Uhlaender literally crutched her way into the Olympic season, recovering from several surgeries to repair a shattered kneecap. The two-time World Cup Champion and 2006 Olympic bronze medalist capped her season with an 11th-place finish after sliding a four-run total of 3:37.93.

Amy Williams of Great Britain hit a top speed of 89 mph on her way to the gold medal in the skeleton event. (PHOTO BY RICHARD HEATHCOTE/GETTY IMAGES)

The last race of Pikus-Pace

"*What an incredible experience it was to represent the United States at the Olympics,*" *said Noelle Pikus-Pace, who raced to fourth place while husband Janson and daughter Jacee watched. "I am so grateful for the support I had to get there. My family, friends and coaches, especially Greg Sand and Martin Rettl, helped me achieve my dream. I am going to miss them, our team, and the sport, but I am looking forward to being with my family and beginning a new adventure as well.*"

Competing in Vancouver was the moment Pikus-Pace had dreamed about for the last four years. She was the 2005 World Cup champion and medal favorite going into the 2006 Olympic Winter Games before a freak accident in October 2005 broke her leg, 114 days before Torino, and knocked her out of contention. The U.S. failed to qualify a second sled for the games, leaving Pikus-Pace to watch from the sidelines.

Ski Jumping

Soaring to New Heights

Story Contributor: Lindsey Sine

In the 2002 Olympic Winter Games, at 20 years old, he was the ebullient ski jumping phenom and double gold medalist who was affectionately remembered for his likeness to popular fictional character Harry Potter. Now 28—and no longer a double for the boy wizard—Swiss ski jumper Simon Ammann repeated his double gold-medal haul with a decisive victory in both the normal (106 meters) and large (140 meters) hill events at Whistler Olympic Park.

"I'm back at the top of the world," enthused Ammann, who became the first two-time Olympic champion on both the normal and large hills and equaled the "Flying Finn"

Matti Nykanen's record of four Olympic gold medals. At the Torino Games in 2006, where his best individual effort had been 15th place in the normal hill, Ammann struggled to regain his 2002 form and consistency. But he bounced back coming into the Vancouver Games ranked No. 1 in the World Cup standings.

In the normal hill, Amman soared 108 meters on his second jump for a commanding lead and a total score of 276.5 points. Polish veteran Adam Malysz, who lost to Ammann in Salt Lake City, took the silver with 269.5 points, and Olympian newcomer 20-year-old Gregor Schlierenzauer from Austria earned the bronze.

One week later, this trio found themselves back on the podium in the same gold, silver and bronze medal positions in the individual large hill event. Simon Ammann (center) of Switzerland, Poland's Adam Malysz (left), and Austria's Gregor Schlierenzauer celebrate their second medals of the Games. Two days later, Schlierenzauer would add a gold to his Olympic medal haul in the team event. (PHOTO BY MICHAEL KAPPELER/AFP/GETTY IMAGES)

At 16-years-old Anders Johnson competed in his first Olympic Games in Torino. Four years later, he arrived at Vancouver as part of a young team determined to change the face of U.S. ski jumping. Johnson, 20, who finished 49th in the normal hill event, has his sights set on Sochi 2014. (PHOTO BY AL BELLO/GETTY IMAGES)

One week later, Amman, Malysz and Schlierenzauer repeated their 1-2-3 standings in the large hill event. Amman won the competition by a huge 14.2-point margin.

In the team event, Austria, the reigning Olympic champion, demonstrated its prowess on the large hill. True to their nickname "the Eagles," the four-man team of Wolfgang Loitzl, Andreas Kofler, Thomas Morgenstern and Schlierenzauer soared to an impressive victory over second-place Germany and third-place Norway. Their score of 1107.9 points was the highest in Olympic team history with Schlierenzauer contributing two huge jumps of 140.5 meters and 146.5 meters. The victory gave Morgenstern, the 2006 Olympic champion, his third gold medal in his Olympic career.

For three determined American ski jumpers, Peter Frenette, 17, Nick Alexander, 21, and Anders Johnson, 20, Vancouver was an opportunity to help bring recognition to the sport of ski jumping. Traveling and competing much of the time at their own expense, the three have made huge sacrifices to dedicate their lives to the sport they love. Qualifications for the normal hill competition were held the same day as the Opening Ceremony, two hours away in Whistler. All three jumpers qualified and gladly missed the

ABOVE / *Peter Frenette embarked on a journey that most 17-year-old athletes can only dream of—making the most of his first appearance at an Olympic Winter Games. As the U.S. Olympic Team's youngest male, Frenette is part of program to turn around the sport of U.S. ski jumping, which hasn't brought home a medal since 1924. His selection to the U.S. Olympic Team was a surprise, even to his parents, as the Frenettes had their eyes on 2014. Frenette placed 32nd in the large hill event, pictured here.* (PHOTO BY ALEXANDER HASSENSTEIN/ BONGARTS/ GETTY IMAGES)

OPPOSITE (BOTTOM) / *Since the age of 10, Nick Alexander, now 21, has devoted his life to the sport of ski jumping with the goal of helping to pioneer the U.S. into a powerful ski jumping nation. In Vancouver, his Olympic debut, Alexander finished 40th in the large hill event and tied teammate Frenette for 41st in the normal hill event.* (PHOTO BY AL BELLO/GETTY IMAGES)

Opening Ceremony to have the opportunity to compete in the medal rounds the next day. Frenette and Alexander also qualified on the large hill, finishing 32nd and 40th, respectively. With the loan of one of the nordic combined jumpers, Taylor Fletcher, the three were able to compete in the four-man team event, finishing 11th out of 12 teams.

OPPOSITE (TOP) /*Austrians Thomas Morgenstern (yellow bib), Andreas Kofler and Wolfgang Loitzl (red bib) hugged teammate Gregor Schlierenzauer (blue bib), whose huge jump maintained their gold-medal position in the ski jumping team event.* (PHOTO BY AL BELLO/GETTY IMAGES)

Snowboarding

Repeat Golds

Story Contributors: Amy Donaldson and Lindsey Sine

No event at the Vancouver Games was more anticipated by U.S. fans than the men's halfpipe. With reigning gold medalist Shaun White promising to throw his jaw-dropping McTwist 1260 in the Olympic competition, the ticket to watch—even in the bitter cold—was a hot item. VANOC reported the highest television ratings came on the night White landed his trick, which he later renamed the Tomahawk, even though he didn't even need it to take home the gold.

"I came all the way to Vancouver to do something amazing, and I felt like a righteous victory lap was in order," said White after he earned his second gold medal in the halfpipe competition with a score of 48.4. Peetu Piiroinen of Finland won the silver with 45 points.

White's teammate Scotty Lago won the bronze with a score of 42.8. A thrilled Lago catalogued his journey to the Olympic Winter Games—"Twenty one broken bones. Multiple concussions. Not going out at home," and concluded, "It's awesome."

The event was a show-stopper with reporters from nearly 100 media outlets waiting to speak with White for more than an hour after his gold-medal performance.

"I feel great," said White afterward. "I can't even describe it. It's one of those things where, I can't even begin to tell you, or begin to describe how many times I've gone over this run in my mind, gone over this competition in my head, imagined what it would be like. I can finally go to sleep now."

Twenty-three-year-old Shaun White, who began snowboarding at 6 and went pro at 13, defended his Olympic gold medal in the halfpipe competition. Off the slopes, White, a diehard rock-n-roll fan, likes to shred on his guitars. (PHOTO BY ADRIAN DENNIS/AFP/GETTY IMAGES)

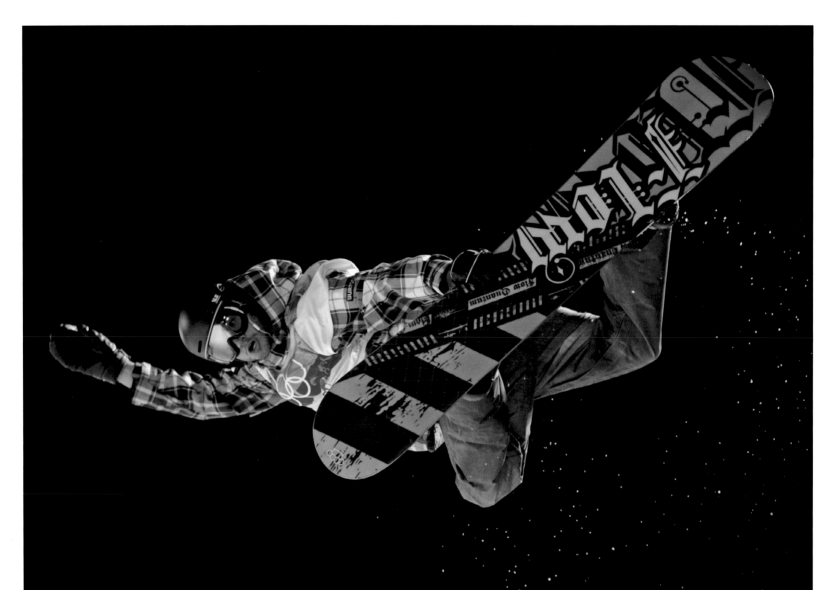

After scoring 42.8 to claim the bronze medal in the men's halfpipe event, Scotty Lago celebrates with gold medalist Shaun White. (PHOTO BY MARTIN BUREAU/AFP/GETTY IMAGES)

INSET | (PHOTO BY STREETER LECKA/GETTY IMAGES)

Scotty Lago

The 22-year-old Seabrook, N.H., resident couldn't contain himself as he bounced up and down after winning the bronze medal at Cypress Mountain. He called it one of his proudest moments, and he dedicated his run to two friends who might very well have been competing at the Games instead of him were it not for injuries—Danny Davis and Kevin Pearce.

Scotty Lago earned his spot on the U.S. Olympic Team after a second-place finish in the season's final Grand Prix in Park City, Utah. He is a member of "Frends," a group of snowboarders that includes Pearce and Davis, among others. They deliberately dropped the "I" in friends to show their commitment to the group, rather than themselves.

ABOVE / Team USA men's snowboard team member Louie Vito consoles Gretchen Bleiler during the women's snowboard halfpipe final. Bleiler, a Midwest-born girl transplanted to the mountains of Colorado at age 10, was the halfpipe silver medalist in Torino. Coming to Vancouver as a medal contender, the 30-year-old Bleiler finished 11th after falling on both of her runs.

Vito, also from the Midwest, made his big splash on the halfpipe scene at age 17. The first-time Olympian finished fifth in the men's competition.

Bleiler and Vito, both known for their charismatic personalities, teamed up to do a public service announcement for AskLearnListen.com to promote a healthy lifestyle and say "no" to underage drinking. (PHOTO BY STREETER LECKA/GETTY IMAGES)

Hannah TETER

Carving a Life

Hannah Teter is known as much for her generosity as she is for her snowboarding ability. The 23-year-old American came into the 2010 Olympic Winter Games as the reigning Olympic champion in halfpipe.

The youngest of five children, she grew up in Belmont, Vermont. She began snowboarding because her older brothers did it, and she was just 19 when she won the gold medal in Torino.

After winning she dedicated herself to charity work. In 2008, she founded the charity "Hannah's Gold" that raises money from the sales of Vermont maple syrup to support the Kenyan village of Kirindon. In 2009, she donated all of her prize money to the Kirindon program, and after the devastating earthquakes in Haiti, she began raising money for charity efforts there.

Most of her sponsorship deals are linked with some kind of charity work, including a Ben & Jerry's ice cream flavor named after her—Hannah Teter's Maple Blondie.

Teter earned her place on the U.S. Olympic Team with two second-place finishes in Grand Prix events in Park City, Utah, on Jan. 22 and 23 and then she donated her winnings from that weekend to relief efforts in Haiti.

Teter went on to win the silver medal at Cypress, and then said she planned to rededicate herself to charity and to attempt to live "off the grid." Thanks to her sponsors, and her success at the Games, she managed to raise about $50,000 for charity while she was competing in the 2010 Games.

A composed Hannah Teter of the United States grabbed the silver medal in the ladies' halfpipe competition. (Photo by Alex Livesey/Getty Images)

Unbeknownst to her, Torah Bright's parents flew from Australia to Vancouver to watch their daughter compete. After a fall on the first run, Bright pulled off a massive do-or-die second run to beat American Hannah Teter for the gold. The Australian native, who lives in Utah, didn't want her parents to fly twice to North America for her June wedding. (PHOTO BY STREETER LECKA/ GETTY IMAGES)

Kelly Clark of the U.S. laid down two solid runs to earn the bronze medal in the halfpipe competition. (PHOTO BY ADRIAN DENNIS/AFP/GETTY IMAGES)

WOMEN'S HALFPIPE

One night later, the stands were once again packed at Cypress Mountain to witness the women's halfpipe finals competition. Australia's Torah Bright won the gold medal with an impressive second run. She qualified in first place but fell on the first run of the finals. That meant she had to hustle to the top and lay down that gold-medal performance as the first rider of the second finals run.

She won her country's first gold medal of the Games, and first in snowboarding, with a switch backside 720, a trick no other woman performs. She suffered with a concussion after a fall at the X Games, but never considered not competing in Vancouver.

Americans Hannah Teter and Kelly Clark finished second and third, respectively.

Kelly Clark

For some, a third-place finish would be a disappointment, especially for an athlete who already owns an Olympic gold medal (2002). Consider also that Clark won all but one of the Grand Prix events in qualifying for the 2010 U.S. Olympic Team.

But Clark said missing the podium in the 2006 Games was so devastating that earning the bronze medal at Cypress felt like the amazing accomplishment it was. She said it was especially satisfying because she landed the very trick that caused her to miss the podium in Torino.

(PHOTO BY JAMIE SQUIRE/GETTY IMAGES)

Seth Wescott (#17) and teammate Nate Holland represented the United States in men's snowboardcross big final. Coming from behind, Wescott defended his Olympic gold passing home crowd favorite Mike Robertson (#3) on the small jump leading into the final big turn. He beat the Canadian to the finish line by about the length of a snowboard. Holland spun out in a turn and finished fourth.

(Photo by Alexis Boichard/Agence/Zoom/Getty Images)

Seth WESCOTT

Tapping into Gold

Thirty-three-year-old Seth Wescott knew there was a special kind of energy at the Olympic Games. He knew it because it had helped him win the first-ever snowboardcross gold medal in 2006 in his Olympic debut.

"In Torino, I really keyed into this other sense of energy you get on that day, and I had really been looking forward to experiencing that again," he said. "And it happened again."

So even though he'd struggled with injuries in the months leading up to the Vancouver Games, Wescott knew he had a chance to defend that gold medal.

"I got pretty banged up in December," he said. "January was kind of a tough month mentally…so to be able to overcome that at the X Games and finally be healthy again, I kind of felt that things were going to go well [at the Winter Games]."

He was so confident that he packed the same American flag he carried after winning the gold in 2006. It is a flag that draped the casket of his grandfather, who served in World War II.

Because snowboardcross has only been included in two Olympic Winter Games, Wescott is the only man to win gold in the event. He co-owns a restaurant near Sugarloaf, Maine, and is the only resident of the state to win a gold medal in the Olympic Winter Games.

He competed in halfpipe when he was younger and just missed making the 1998 Olympic Team. He was dealing with knee surgery in 2002, and said that by then, he felt he was probably past his prime in halfpipe, a sport dominated by teens and those in their early 20s.

"It's a harsh learning curve," he said of halfpipe. "You get to a point where you've punished your body so much with that discipline, you want to stop progressing. I definitely hit that point mentally with my halfpipe riding."

When it was announced that snowboardcross would be part of the 2006 Olympic Winter Games, he said it was "an easy decision at that point" because he still loved snowboarding so much.

SNOWBOARDCROSS

White might have been the most anticipated American snowboarder, and the most easily recognized, but it was Maine's Seth Wescott who earned the country's first gold medal in snowboarding at the Vancouver Games.

Wescott, who earned a gold medal in the snowboard-cross debut as an Olympic sport in 2006, had struggled with injuries and consistency leading up to the 2010 Games. But he was confident in his abilities, even asking someone to hold the same flag he carried in the 2006 Games before the races started.

Snowboardcross has been referred to as NASCAR on snow. Riders—four at a time—lay down a qualifying run that determines seeding for a series of races that include jumps, bumps and crashes.

Wescott, 33, edged hometown favorite, Mike Robertson for the gold medal. France's Tony Ramoin, 21, earned the bronze medal.

On the women's side of snowboardcross, it was Canada's Maelle Ricker who thrilled the standing room only crowd. The day was foggy and rainy, but a native of Vancouver, Ricker said she woke up, realized it was "just another west coast day" and upset the world's top snow-boardcross athlete, American Lindsey Jacobellis.

Jacobellis finished fifth, barely missing the big final.

Deborah Anthonioz of France earned the silver medal, while Oliva Nobs of Switzerland claimed the bronze medal.

Two other American women entered the competition with 17-year-old Faye Gulini and 21-year-old Callan Chythlook-Sifsof finishing 12th and 21st, respectively, in the final rankings.

PARALLEL GIANT SLALOM

On the final days of snowboarding in the Games, the rain poured down on Cypress Mountain where the parallel giant slalom team of Chris Klug, Michelle Gorgone and Tyler Jewell fought their way up, each making finals to compete on the sport's grand stage for America.

Gorgone finished 14th in the final rankings for the women. Nicolien Sauerbreij of Netherlands earned the gold medal while Ekaterina Ilyukhina of Russia finished second for silver and Austria's Marion Kreiner claimed the bronze medal.

In the men's competition, Klug finished seventh, giving the U.S. its highest finish in the parallel giant slalom. Canada's Jasey Jay Anderson defeated Karl Benjamin of Austria for the gold medal. Benjamin earned the silver medal and France's Mathieu Bozzetto defeated Stanislav Detkov of Russia for the bronze medal. American Tyler Jewell finished 13th in the final rankings.

American Michelle Gorgone, nicknamed "Pirelli" after the racing tires, finished 14th in the giant parallel slalom in her second Olympic Games. A member of the U.S. Snowboarding since 2003, Gorgone also loves to sing and has tried out twice for the TV show "American Idol." (PHOTO BY ADRIAN DENNIS/AFP/GETTY IMAGES)

American Faye Gulini (#12), Helene Olafsen of Norway and Olivia Nobs of Switzerland (#4) compete in the quarterfinals of snowboardcross. Gulini finished 12th overall. Nobs ultimately claimed the bronze medal. (Photo by Alex Livesey/Getty Images)

American Lindsey Jacobellis (#2) and Deborah Anthonioz of France compete in ladies' snowboardcross. Jacobellis finished fifth overall. Anthonioz went on to claim the silver medal. (Photo by Streeter Lecka/Getty Images)

Speedskating

Around the Oval

Story Contributors: Linda Jager and Amy Donaldson

peedskating has produced some of the most iconic athletes in U.S. Olympic history from Eric Heiden to Dan Jansen and Bonnie Blair. Arriving in Vancouver was a talented line-up of speedskaters including Shani Davis, dominating the World Cup circuit and defending gold medalist in the 1000m, and a changed Chad Hedrick, a family man fired up to compete and enjoy his final Olympic appearance.

The first event for Team USA, the men's 5000m, was held on the opening day of competition, Feb. 13, 2010 at the Richmond Olympic Oval. At 20, Trevor Marsicano was considered a medal contender going into the event based on his bronze medal performance at the World Championships last season, but over the last few years, the event has been dominated by Holland's Sven Kramer. Kramer won by over two full seconds while Hedrick finished 11th, Davis 12th, and Marsicano in 14th.

Kramer was on track to win a second gold medal in the 10,000m race, but a miscommunication with his coach caused him to miss a lane change and he was disqualified.

A thrilled Mark Tuitert (center) of the Netherlands denied a double gold bid by American Shani Davis, the reigning world champion in the 1500m. Davis shakes hands with bronze medalist Havard Bokko of Norway. (PHOTO BY JASPER JUINEN/GETTY IMAGES)

American Shani Davis celebrates the silver
medal in the men's 1500m speedskating final.
(PHOTO BY MARTIN BUREAU/ AFP/GETTY IMAGES)

It was a heartbreaking turn of events for Kramer as he owns the world record and was in the lead when the mistake occurred.

Olympic rookie Jonathan Kuck finished 8th and Ryan Bedford finished 12th in the 10,000m.

The men's sprint competition was plagued by mechanical problems with the ice resurfacing machines, and competitors dealt with a two-and-a-half hour race delay.

Tucker Fredricks, the overall World Cup champion, made some mistakes in his run and he finished 12th. Davis pulled out of the race to avoid potential injury. That left newcomers Nick Pearson and Mitch Whitmore, both of Wisconsin, to represent the United States. Pearson finished 26th and Whitmore was 37th,

The 500m sprint was won by Tae-Bum Mo of South Korea, who, along with Fredricks, was favored to win the event. Japan's Keiichiro Nagashima, finished second, and his teammate Joji Kato earned the bronze medal.

The Americans offered a very competitive group for the men's 1000m race, including Davis, Hedrick, Pearson and Marsicano, who'd been skating well at that distance.

Going into the 1000m Davis was the overall World Cup leader, world record-holder, and returning Olympic gold medalist. True to form, Davis skated an incredible race winning the gold medal posting a track record time. This marked the first time that anyone has ever repeated Olympic gold medals in the 1000m. Hedrick skated the best 1000m of his career to win the bronze medal. Pearson finished 7th and Marsicano skated to a 10th-place finish. Four Americans in the top 10 was a huge accomplishment for Team USA and a display of dominance in the event.

South Korea's Mo earned his second medal of the 2010 Games with a silver in the event.

If there was a heartbreak in the speedskating competition for the U.S., it came in the 1500m race.

Davis was heavily favored and the only man who'd beaten him at that distance—Hedrick—said it was his goal to win that race. In the end, it was Mark Tuitert of Netherlands who skated away with the gold in what most athletes consider the sport's marquee event.

Americans (from left to right) Trevor Marsicano, Jonathan Kuck, Chad Hedrick and Brian Hansen bask in their silver medal victory in the team pursuit event. (Photo by Jasper Juinen/Getty Images)

Americans Nancy Swider-Peltz Jr. (left), Jilleanne Rookard (#3) and Jennifer Rodriguez rejoice after pulling off a major upset and eliminating the world-record holders of Canada (above) by five hundredths of a second in the quarterfinals of the team pursuit event. (PHOTOS BY VINCENZO PINTO/AFP/GETTY IMAGES)

Germany's speedskater Stephanie Beckert strikes a pose with her three medals against the backdrop of Vancouver. Beckert won the gold in the team pursuit event and silver medals in the 3000m and in the 5000m races. (PHOTO BY DAVID HECKER/ AFP/GETTY IMAGES)

Davis finished second for the silver, while Hedrick was sixth. Marsicano finished 15th, and Hansen skated a great race to finish 18th.

The final men's speedskating event of the Games was the men's team pursuit races, which saw some of the most exciting upsets. In the men's race, Hedrick bounced back from the 1500m disappointment to lead a young squad— Brian Hansen, Jonathan Kuck and Trevor Marsicano—from quarterfinals to a podium finish. In a major upset, the Americans beat the Dutch in the semifinals and went on to win the silver. The Canadians again thrilled the hometown crowd with a win in the team pursuit.

WOMEN

The women debuted with the 3000m event. The lithe, 5-foot-7, 119-pound Czech Martina Sablikova won the event by 2.09 seconds over Germany's Stephanie Beckert.

The U.S. women have not won a medal in this event since Beth Heiden won bronze in 1980. Nancy Swider-Peltz, Jr. had a career-best race, finishing in ninth. Jilleanne Rookard was 12th and Catherine Raney-Norman was 17th.

For the women's 500 competition, the ice was race ready. Heather Richardson, finishing sixth, posted the best U.S. result. South Korea's Sang-Hwa Lee upset Germany's Jenny Wolf to earn the gold medal. Wolf finished second and China's Beixing Wang earned bronze.

Also skating for Team USA were Elli Ochowicz, who finished 17th, four-time Olympian Jennifer Rodriguez was 21st and Lauren Cholewinski 30th.

In the middle distances, Dutch speedskater Irene Wust, who struggled to keep up with Sablikova in the 3000m, found her moxie and won the 1500m with Canada's Kristina Groves in second and Sablikova in third. Canada struck gold in the 1000m with Christine Nesbitt edging Annette Gerritsen of the Netherlands by 0.02 seconds.

In spite of challenges, Team USA held out medal hopes in Rodriguez and Richardson in the women's 1000m. Coming off two successful World Cup seasons, Rodriguez saw inconsistencies in her skating and struggles in her life off the ice. During the summer of 2009, Rodriguez lost her mother to a long bout with cancer. Her mother was her number one supporter and the loss of her life really took its toll on Rodriguez. She went on to skate a great race but ended up missing a medal by only three tenths of a second. It was a performance her mother would have been proud to watch.

Richardson skated a great race, finishing in ninth, Ochowicz finished 26th and Olympic newcomer Rebekah Bradford was 29th.

In the 1500m, Richardson and Rodriguez both had an inconsistent day and ended up in 16th and 18th, respectively. The other Americans in the event were Rookard finishing 24th and Raney-Norman 31st.

The 5000m race saw a rematch of Sablikova and

In the 3000m event, American Catherine Raney-Norman (right) raced against the great Cindy Klassen, who won five medals in Torino. The Canadian, still not recovered from double knee surgery, finished 14th and Raney-Norman finished 17th. (PHOTO BY TOSHIFUMI KITAMURA/AFP/GETTY IMAGES)

Beckert. The 22-year-old Czech, the 5000m world record-holder and three-time reigning world champion, skated to her second gold and third medal of the Games. Beckert, 0.48 seconds behind, settled for her second silver. Canada's Clara Hughes won the bronze.

The 5000m is Rookard's specialty event, but like Rodriguez, she has also faced personal tragedy outside of the sport. Rookard, who had lost her father years ago, suffered the loss of her mother two months before the Games. The 27-year-old fought hard and skated races that her parents would have been proud of. Her 5000m was an absolutely incredible race to watch, skating consistent laps and battling hard through the last few laps to earn an eighth-place finish.

Maria Lamb also skated the 5000m, but unfortunately had to compete with subpar preparation due to an injury that she suffered shortly before the Games. Despite her injury she still managed to pull off a 15th-place finish.

In the women's final event, the team pursuit, the American squad of Swider-Peltz Jr., Rookard and Rodriguez upset the World Champion Canadian team to advance to the semifinals, denying the powerful Canadian team of a medal. With the Canadians out, Germany won the gold, Japan claimed the silver and Poland edged the American team of Raney-Norman, Rookard and Rodriguez to take the bronze medal.

Heather Richardson, who originally targeted 2014 for her Olympic debut, found herself on the U.S. Olympic Team after some stellar performances in the World Cup races. She finished sixth in the 500m race and also had a strong skate in the 1000m, finishing ninth overall. (PHOTO BY JAMIE SQUIRE/GETTY IMAGES)

American Tucker Fredricks, the overall World Cup champion in the 500m and one of the favorites to win this race, finished 12th. Some speculated whether the two-and-one-half hour delay to repair the ice played havoc with these elite athletes' performances. (PHOTO BY ALEX LIVESEY/GETTY IMAGES)

Downtime

Tucker Fredricks and Shani Davis share a laugh before the start of the speedskating training session at the Richmond Oval. (PHOTO BY SAEED KHAN/AFP/ GETTY IMAGES)

Closing Ceremony

The 2010 U.S. Olympic Team wrapped up the Vancouver Games with its best-ever performance of 37 medals. The result was a testament to the success of infusing non-traditional American winter sports, such as biathlon and nordic combined, with renewed commitment and resources.

Not since the 1932 Olympic Winter Games in Lake Placid has the United States topped the medal charts. The U.S. Olympic Team brought home nine gold, 15 silver and 13 bronze medals.

Nordic combined athlete Billy Demong, nominated to carry the flag by his teammates, was just one of the athletes contributing to the historic medal haul, adding a gold and a silver earned in the large hill event and team event, respectively.
(Photo by Clive Rose/Getty Images)

Competitions finished, the 2010 U.S. Olympic Team relaxes and soaks in the fanfare of Vancouver's Closing Ceremony. (PHOTO BY CLIVE ROSE/GETTY IMAGES)

(Photo by Robyn Beck/AFP/Getty Images)

(Photo by Clive Rose/Getty Images)

After the fanfare, the Olympic cauldron (below) was extinguished, marking the end of the Vancouver Games.   (Photo by Dimitar Dilkoff/AFP/Getty Images)

(Photo by Martin Bureau/AFP/Getty Images)

X Paralympic Winter Games
One Inspires Many

The view from the gondola at Whistler Creekside, where the Paralympic alpine skiing events were held. (Photo by Fabrice Coffrini /AFP/ Getty Images)

Dream Catchers

By Amy Donaldson

Some of them lost their sight to little-known diseases. Others lost their legs fighting for freedom. And then there are those who were born with physical disabilities that might have slowed them down but did not deter them from achieving their dreams.

Despite injuries, illnesses or accidents, these athletes' love of sport triumphed with determination, creativity and hard work.

The Paralympic Games aren't just an opportunity for the world's best athletes to compete at the highest level. They are enlightening the world about the ability of all athletes. The Paralympic Movement is growing globally and more than 500 athletes from 44 countries competed at the 2010 Paralympic Winter Games.

From the United States 58 athletes, representing their country and 20 different states, competed in the five sports—alpine skiing, biathlon, cross-country skiing, sled hockey and wheelchair curling. There were 64 medal events and the United States earned 13 Paralympic medals—four of those gold.

A record number of tickets were sold to all five sports at the 2010 Paralympic Winter Games. The support was impressive; the achievements outstanding. As Paralympians continue to redefine ability, athletes are hoping that additional sports, such as snowboarding and ski cross, will be added to future Paralympic Games.

Flagbearer Heath Calhoun, alpine skier and Army Veteran, proudly led the U.S. Paralympic Team into the stadium during the Opening Ceremony of the X Paralympic Winter Games held from March 12 - 22, 2010 in Vancouver. (PHOTO BY MARTIN ROSE/BONGARTS/GETTY IMAGES)

Like the Olympic Games, the Paralympic Games displayed impressive athletic accomplishment and competitive will.

One of the big surprises of the Paralympic Games was Japan's ice sled hockey team upset of the defending gold medalists and host country, Canada, to earn a spot in the gold-medal game against the United States. The Americans won that game, 2-0, and had a record-setting performance of five shutouts en route to the gold.

Life dealt the Paralympic champions physical challenges. They responded with physical, emotional and mental triumph.

ABOVE / *Fifteen-year-old Zach Beaumont lights the flame to officially open the X Paralympic Winter Games on March 12, 2010 in Vancouver, Canada. Beaumont, who had his right leg amputated as a baby, dreams of competing in snowboarding at the Paralympic Games one day.* (PHOTO BY MARTIN ROSE BONGARTS/ GETTY IMAGES)

OPPOSITE (TOP) / *Sumi, an animal spirit who name means "guardian spirit," is one of the three mascots of the 2010 Olympic Winter Games (Quatchi and Miga are the other two). Transformation, representing the connection and kinship between the human, animal and spirit world, is a common theme in Canada's West Coast First Nations. Revered animals are depicted in transformation through masks, totems and other forms of art and legend. The orca is the traveler and guardian of the sea. The bear often represents strength and friendship. And the thunderbird—which creates thunder by flapping its wings—is one of the most powerful of the supernatural creatures.* (PHOTO BY KEVIN C. COX/GETTY IMAGES)

(BOTTOM) / *Based on the theme 'One Inspires Many', the Opening Ceremony was a colorful event attended by a sell-out crowd of 60,000.* (PHOTO BY KEVIN C. COX/GETTY IMAGES)

Focusing on ability, not disability

"Many of you will go home
as champions,
you all go home as winners.

You have been
remarkable ambassadors
of the human spirit."

—John Furlong, CEO, VANOC

"What others perceive as challenges, to me they're just the way things are; I may have to adapt and modify accordingly, that's all. Being disabled, you just have to use what you got that works, and make it as strong as possible."

Those words come from world-class mono-skier Laurie Stephens, born with spina bifida, whose best finish in Vancouver was fourth in the sitting super-G event.

"It's important to realize that we're just like any other athlete: we train hard and we race to ski our best, and win. I just love skiing," added the 26-year-old American who competed in all five alpine disciplines.

(PHOTO BY EZRA SHAW/GETTY IMAGES)

Alpine Skiing

Eleven Medals

Story Contributors: Caroline Williams and Keely Ames

The 2010 U.S. Paralympic Alpine Skiing Team had a successful showing in Whistler Creekside, winning a total of 11 medals, including three gold, five silver and three bronze medals. That medal haul bettered the team's output of eight medals won in 2006. Additionally, the U.S. athletes, who thrive on the speed events and claim to be not as strong in the technical races, captured no less than one medal in each of the five disciplines: slalom, giant slalom, super-G, downhill and the super combined, which was held for the first time in Paralympic competition.

"Definitely the women sitting just did an extraordinary job," said U.S. Adaptive Alpine Ski Team head coach Ray Watkins upon the conclusion of the alpine races.

"The Umsteads—Danelle and Rob of Taos, N.M.—did an incredible job. For Mark Bathum of Seattle, Wash., to pop in there, that was just great. There were some really strong efforts by everybody. That's what our Paralympic team is about. Everyday we're working hard, fighting and representing our country the best we can."

The five-event competition, in which sitting skiers, standing skiers and visually impaired skiers make up the three classes of athletes, was originally slated to be spread out over nine days. However, the schedule was condensed into seven days due to fog and snow on the first day of racing, and a fast-moving storm front set to hit on the final day of competition.

Still, the U.S. team battled through rain, snow and fog over the first half of the competition, but managed to stay positive and on the winning track. The women's sitting skiers led the U.S. with a combined eight medals, while visually impaired men and women took in the remaining three. Additionally, the United States finished just one spot off the podium five times, three of which were within less than a half second away from a medal. The closest was four-time Paralympian Chris Devlin-Young, who was a heartbreaking sliver of a second (0.02) away from bronze in the super-G. Also in the super-G the 2009 U.S. Olympic Committee Paralympic Sportswoman of the Year Stephani Victor of Park City, Utah, was 0.13 of a second off the women's mono-ski podium. Finally, Bathum and guide Slater Storey of Sun Valley, Idaho, finished 0.30 of a second behind the bronze medalist. Excluding the 11 medal finishes, the USA Team placed among the top 10 competitors a total of 29 times.

As a young racer, Elitsa Storey saw racers taking off their legs. She saw wheelchair athletes. She saw how comfortable they were. "Seeing all the other athletes doing what they can...It just made me more determined. They all have a disability but face it in their own way. It was neat to see." Storey, 22, competed in her second Paralympic Winter Games. (Photo by Quinn Rooney/Getty Images)

Alana Nichols

Two years after breaking her back in a snowboarding accident in 2002, Alana Nichols took up mono-skiing.

Six years later, in her first Paralympic Winter Games, the Farmington, N.M., native became the first U.S. woman to win a gold medal in both the Paralympic Summer and Winter Games. She earned a gold medal in wheelchair basketball in Beijing, China, and then won gold in Vancouver in the giant slalom, women's sitting category.

She finished with four medals—two gold, one silver and one bronze—and plans to continue competing for the U.S. in both summer and winter sports.

ABOVE / *At age 16, an athletic Ralph Green fell victim to a random shooting in Brooklyn, NY, and lost his leg. The 32-year-old Green competed in his second Paralympic Winter Games finishing 22nd in the standing slalom and 29th in the giant slalom events.* (PHOTO BY HANNAH JOHNSTON/GETTY IMAGES)

The week also featured retiring athletes and emerging stars. Included among the retirees was five-time Paralympian and standing skier Monte Meier of Park City, Utah. The four-time Paralympic medalist bid adieu to his 19-year career on the national team in style by carrying the U.S. flag into the Closing Ceremony.

Women's sitting skier Alana Nichols, who only began skiing competitively two years ago, had a huge coming out party with a full set of medals, plus an extra gold. And the visually impaired team of Danelle Umstead and husband Rob picked up a pair of bronze medals in their first Paralympic Games.

Despite the loss of Meier and several of his longtime teammates, with athletes like Nichols and the Umsteads picking up the torch, the future certainly seems bright for the U.S. Adaptive Alpine Team.

ABOVE / *A few days shy of her 27th birthday, Alana Nichols earned her first gold medal in Vancouver in the sitting giant slalom event. Two days later she added another gold, this time in the downhill, and added two more medals, silver in the super-G and bronze in the super combined, for a total of four medals. She competed in all five disciplines, finishing fifth in the sitting slalom event.* (PHOTO BY EZRA SHAW/GETTY IMAGES)

ALPINE SKIING | SITTING

Stephani VICTOR

Victory for Victor

The defending Paralympic gold medalist in slalom, Stephani Victor would wait until her final event in the 2010 Paralympic Winter Games before earning the second Paralympic gold medal of her 11-year ski career.

The 40-year-old earned the silver medal in slalom and giant slalom, but finished fourth in downhill and fifth in the super-G. She was looking for nothing but gold in her final event March 20, 2010. To earn her third Olympic medal at Whistler, Victor had to deal with that wacky west coast weather.

"This week proved to me I can ski any course, any ski length, any terrain, any weather, any time," she said. "We've been tested to the ultimate this week. I knew I had to own all of that and embrace it."

Victor grew up in Sewickley, Pennsylvania with the same dream a lot of little girls have—to be a movie star. Victor, however, was on her way to making that dream a reality as she graduated, with honors, from the University of Southern California's film school.

On Dec. 19, 1995, Stephani was hit by an out-of-control car as she stood in a driveway. Just 26 years old at the time, she was crushed between that car and a parked vehicle, and in order to save her life, doctors had to amputate both of her legs above the knee.

Almost instantly, she saw her tragedy as a new opportunity. She filmed her first documentary, "The Lengths I Will Go," which chronicled her lengthy recovery.

In 1999, when she was attending the Sundance Film Festival in Park City, Utah, she tried adaptive skiing for the first time. The coaches immediately recognized the former soccer player's athletic ability and competitive spirit.

Now the owner of five Paralympic medals, Victor spends her time motivating others to live life to the fullest, regardless of their situations. She doesn't like the term amputee and she sees life in terms of opportunities rather than obstacles.

Stephani Victor gives a victory roar as she celebrates the silver medal in the sitting giant slalom event. The American also won the gold in the super combined in Vancouver. The 40-year-old skier is a motivational speaker who often connects with people who struggle to be seen for who they are, rather than what others see when they look at them. (PHOTO BY KEVIN C. COX/GETTY IMAGES)

(PHOTO BY HANNAH JOHNSTON/GETTY IMAGES)

Visually impaired skier Danelle Umstead competed in all five disciplines: slalom, giant slalom, downhill, super-G and finally super combined. The 38-year-old-skier, along with her husband and guide, Rob, won two bronze medals in the downhill and super combined. (PHOTO BY HANNAH JOHNSTON/GETTY IMAGES)

(PHOTO BY QUINN ROONEY/GETTY IMAGES)

The Umsteads

In her first Paralympic Games appearance, Danelle Umstead earned two bronze medals in alpine skiing with the help of her husband and guide, Rob.

A native of New Mexico, Danelle was diagnosed with Retinitis Pigmentosa, a genetic disease that slowly steals your sight. Her guide is her husband, Rob Umstead, whom she met at Taos Ski Valley, where he coached and she went to learn to ski.

Rob is a ski racer and coach, but put his career on hold to guide his wife down the mountain and through the gates of alpine courses around the world. They call themselves Team Vision4Gold, and in addition to winning races, they hope to raise awareness about Retinitis Pigmentosa.

Monte Meier

When Meier started competing internationally in 1994, there wasn't even an official World Cup circuit for Paralympic athletes.

"You just had to find races," said the 39-year-old Park City, Utah, resident. "We'd race FIS events with regular skiers, which brought out my competitive spirit. But I knew all eyes were on me. I knew everyone was looking at the one-legger. And I wanted to put on a good show. That made me push ever harder."

Meier lost his leg in 1979 in a garden-tilling accident, but his parents' philosophy was to encourage their outdoor-loving son in any and all endeavors. He took up skiing with his mom and found his passion when someone suggested racing.

"It is a huge honor being elected flag bearer for closing. Not only representing the whole U.S. Paralympic Team, all the sports, but also my country. I couldn't think of a better way to go out, carrying the flag at the closing."

—Monte Meier

Heath Calhoun

S taff Sgt. Heath Calhoun represented his country in a unique way when the Iraq war veteran carried the U.S. flag for the Opening Ceremony of the 2010 Paralympic Games.

The son and grandson of veterans, Calhoun's decision to become an Army Ranger was a surprise to no one. He had envisioned a career in the military when, on Nov. 7, 2003, his Humvee was hit by a rocket-propelled grenade. He was badly wounded and ended up losing both legs above the knee. Nine months of rehab led him to Aspen Colorado's Winter Sports Clinic where he instantly became hooked on skiing. He trained hard and made the 2010 Paralympic Team where he competed in super-G (eighth), super combined (10th) and slalom (DNF).

Tennessee native Heath Calhoun moved to Colorado to train in 2008. At the 2009 U.S. Adaptive Alpine National Championships, Calhoun took second place in the men's sitting ski slalom and won gold in the super-G. In Vancouver, the 30-year-old American finished in eighth place in the sitting super-G and 10th place in the super combined event. (PHOTO BY QUINN ROONEY/GETTY IMAGES)

Biathlon

Soule's Medal

Story Contributor: Allison Frederick

Skiing in both biathlon and cross-country events, Andrew Soule (Pearland, Texas) made his 2010 Paralympic Winter Games debut a memorable one. Soule made history at Whistler Paralympic Park, winning the first-ever medal for the United States.

A retired U.S. Army veteran of Afghanistan's Operation Enduring Freedom, Soule entered the biathlon competition at the Games ranked fourth overall in International Paralympic Committee World Cup points. He brought the crowd to its feet with an exciting come-from-behind finish in the final race of the men's sitting 2.4km biathlon pursuit to win the bronze medal with a final time of 10:53.

In the men's sitting 12.5km event, Soule shot four perfect rounds of five shots each, but the U.S. athlete could not catch the competition in the final lap and finished 1:15 outside of third place. Russia dominated the field of 21 competitors, taking the top three podium spots.

On the women's side, Kelly Underkofler (St. Paul, Minn.) also represented Team USA in both biathlon and cross-country events. A seasoned athlete, Underkofler competed in the 2002 and 2006 Paralympic Winter Games. In Torino, she placed fourth in the long distance biathlon and posted five other top-ten finishes.

Battling an injured leg muscle at the 2010 Paralympic Winter Games, Underkofler finished ninth in the women's standing 3km biathlon pursuit with a time of 14:39. In the women's standing 12.5km biathlon event, she posted another ninth-place finish with a time of 51:44.

Kelly Underkofler finished in ninth place in the 12.5km standing biathlon event. Born without the lower part of her left arm, the 25-year-old Minnesotan is a three-time Paralympian. (PHOTO BY KEVIN C. COX/GETTY IMAGES)

(PHOTOS BY HANNAH JOHNSTON/GETTY IMAGES)

Andy Soule

The tragedy of 9/11 moved Andy Soule from sadness to action. He joined the military and was sent to Afghanistan. He was severely injured when an explosive device detonated next to his Humvee. He lost both his legs in that accident.

The 30-year-old native of Pearland, Texas, was looking for ways to stay active after several years of rehabilitation when he happened upon a cross-country ski camp in Sun Valley, Idaho.

He was hooked.

He moved from Texas to Idaho in 2006 so he could train full time. His hard work and dedication paid off when he won the bronze medal in the 2.4 km biathlon in Vancouver.

Gaining Ground

Story Contributor: Allison Frederick

The U.S. posted several top ten finishes over the five days of cross-country competition but fell short of reaching the podium at the 2010 Paralympic Winter Games. The men's cross-country events were dominated by the Russians capturing 14 of the 30 medals. And of the 30 medals handed out in the women's events, Ukraine won nine, Russia eight and Belarus six.

Two-time cross-country Paralympian Chris Klebl led the U.S. in the long distance events at Whistler Paralympic Park. Klebl, who posted an 11th-place finish in Torino, was inside the top ten on several occasions during the World Cup circuit leading up to Vancouver. He was the top U.S. finisher in the men's sitting 15km with a time of 43:13.7 for eighth place.

Klebl also led the U.S. with the fastest time in the men's 1km sprint, crossing the finish line in ninth place with a time of 2:18.39, just 0.42 seconds outside the qualifying spot. In the men's sitting 10km, Klebl finished with a time of 29:39.7 for 16th place overall.

In what was one of the most exciting cross-country races of the Games, the men's sitting 10km, U.S. Air Force veteran Sean Halsted was in medal contention throughout much of the course. In the final laps, the top ten skiers were all within about nine seconds of each other in the extremely competitive field of 34 athletes. With Norway's Trygve Toskedal breathing down his neck, Halsted held his ground and charged the line, but fell short of a podium finish, clocking 28:35.8 for seventh place overall.

Halsted also finished ninth in the men's sitting 15km with a time of 43:25.6 and tenth in the men's sitting 1km sprint with a time of 2:18.72.

Biathlon bronze in tow, Andy Soule continued his quest for medals in cross-country competition. He finished just inside the top ten in the men's sitting 15km with a time of 43:32.8. Then in the men's sitting 10km, Soule battled Russian powerhouse Irek Zaripov for position on the course. A tumble on the downhill portion of the first lap cost Soule several precious seconds. He crossed the

Born in Germany and raised in Austria, Chris Klebl was paralyzed from the waist down in a snowboarding accident in 1995 — the result of a bad landing in a cliff jump. Klebl's best finish for the U.S. was eighth place in the men's 15km sitting event. (PHOTO BY QUINN ROONEY/GETTY IMAGES)

finish line in 29:18.7 for 12th place overall. Soule capped off his 2010 Paralympic Winter Games with an 11th-place finish in the men's sitting 1km sprint event.

Competing in his second Paralympic Winter Games, Greg Mallory had his best finish on the final day of the Games, placing 18th in the men's sitting 1km sprint with a time of 2:21.89. Mallory also finished 24th in the men's sitting 10 km and 26th in the men's sitting 15km event.

On the women's side, Kelly Underkofler showed her strength in the long distance events, posting a time of 58:19.6 in the women's standing 15km free event for an eighth-place finish. Underkofler went on to finish 10th in the women's standing 5km classic event with a final time of 18:37.2. In her final event, the women's standing 1km sprint, Underkofler fell outside of qualifying position, finishing in 13th place.

After finishing just out of medal contention in Torino, Monica Bascio (Evergreen, Colo.) returned to the world's stage this year with her young son, Henry, watching from the grandstands. In her first of three events, Bascio posted a ninth-place finish in the women's sitting 10km at Whistler Paralympic Park. After a near collision in the first lap of the race when Korea's Vo-Ra-Mi Seo crossed into her tracks, Bascio was able to quickly regain composure and cross the finish line with a time of 34:33.9.

In the women's sitting 5km event, Bascio posted a tenth-place finish with a time of 16:32.4. Liudmila Vauchok of Belarus dominated the field for the gold medal. Bascio's best performance came in the women's sitting 1km sprint event. With eight competitors to advance from the qualification round, Bascio clocked a time of 2:43.7 to secure the last spot in the semifinals. She went on to finish fourth in the first of two semifinals, falling outside the cut-off with a time of 2:56.9.

ABOVE / *Monica Bascio took up cross-country skiing when she moved from California to Colorado as a way to stay in shape during the winter. Bascio, who broke her back in a skiing accident, embraces the motto "going forward" in everything she does.* (PHOTO BY JAMIE MCDONALD/GETTY IMAGES)

OPPOSITE (TOP) / *American Gregory Mallory's best finish was in the men's sitting 1km sprint, placing 18th. When he's not skiing, Mallory practices law.* (PHOTO BY EZRA SHAW/GETTY IMAGES)

(BOTTOM) / *American Sean Halsted (#78) finished seventh in the men's sitting 10km cross-country event.* (PHOTO BY QUINN ROONEY/GETTY IMAGES)

Sled Hockey

Gold Tending

Story Contributor: Alex Clark

Sled hockey is one of the most popular sports at the Paralympic Winter Games. It was introduced in 1994 in Lillehammer, Norway. While internationally, it is known as sledge hockey, in the U.S., it is more commonly referred to as sled hockey.

The U.S. won its first gold in sled hockey in 2002, and followed that with bronze in Torino. In Vancouver, the U.S. team dominated, proving they really were the best sled hockey team in the world.

The U.S. Paralympic Sled Hockey Team became the first-ever sled hockey team to win its second Paralympic gold medal, winning all five of its games without surrendering a single goal. Entering the tournament as the top seed, Team USA swept through its preliminary-round opponents South Korea, the Czech Republic, and Japan, by a combined score of 14-0. By earning Group A's No. 1 slot, Team USA set up a semifinal match-up with Norway.

The U.S. and Norway had previously met in the semifinals of the 2006 Paralympic Winter Games in Torino, Italy, with Norway topping Team USA, 4-2, and forcing the Americans to settle for bronze. Team USA avenged its loss and blanked Norway, 3-0, to punch its ticket to the gold-medal game.

The U.S. faced an unlikely foe in its final game, as Japan upset host Canada in its semifinal tilt. Despite falling to Team USA, 6-0, in the preliminary round, Japan proved a tough challenge in the team's second encounter. But the U.S. defense and goaltending stood strong, helping the team emerge with a 2-0 win and the tournament's top prize. Team USA's Taylor Chace was named the tournament's top defenseman, while Steve Cash was named the tournament's top goaltender.

TOP PHOTO / *Alexi Salamone (#21), America's leading scorer during the tournament, squares off against Japanese captain Takayuki Endo (#10) in the gold-medal game. Salamone scored the first goal in the first period.* (PHOTO BY KEVIN C. COX/GETTY IMAGES)

OPPOSITE (BOTTOM) / *Team USA sings the National Anthem as they celebrate their 2-0 win over Japan in the gold-medal game.* (PHOTO BY KEVIN C. COX/GETTY IMAGES)

Alexi Salamone

The nuclear reactor meltdown at Chernobyl happened about 14 months before Alexi Salamone was born in nearby Briansk, Ukraine. He was born with a birth defect that caused his legs to be amputated when he was just four years old.

Two years later, he was adopted by the Salamone family and moved to New York.

He was introduced to skating first, and then hockey. It wasn't long before someone saw the talent in the young athlete. His hard work and determination have made him one of the world's best sled hockey players.

Steve Cash

U.S. goalie Steve Cash was key in the U.S. team's ability to win gold in Vancouver. He did not allow a single goal as the team earned a 5-0 record culminating with a 2-0 win over Japan for the gold on March 20, 2010. Japan stunned fans when it defeated Canada in the semifinals, 3-1. The Japanese squad only managed five shots on goal in the gold-medal game, and one of those was a penalty shot.

Cash had 33 saves in the 2010 tournament and was named the top goalie. His efforts helped Team USA to become the first sled hockey team in history to shut out all of their opponents.

Cash lost part of his right leg when he was an infant. Doctors were trying to rid his body of cancer, which had invaded his knee area. Blessed with parents who taught him everyone has the opportunity to turn a perceived weakness into strength, he grew up playing hockey.

Despite a determined Japanese team, American goaltender Steve Cash registered his fifth shutout of the tournament as the U.S. beat Japan, 2-0, in the gold-medal game. (PHOTO BY MARTIN ROSE/BONGARTS/GETTY IMAGES)

TOP / *Taylor Chace (#19) of the United States battles for control of the puck against Noritaka Ito (#59) of Japan during the gold-medal game.* (PHOTO BY KEVIN C. COX/GETTY IMAGES)

Taylor Chace

T aylor Chace grew up on ice. His goal was always to reach the highest level he could playing a game that he loved. He was playing hockey when, at 16, he suffered a spinal cord injury that resulted in permanent paralysis in parts of his legs.

He was selected to the U.S. Sled Hockey National Team in 2005 and has been one of the team's most important leaders since then. Chace loves the competitive drive and spirit that not only permeates the sport of sled hockey but all of the Paralympic Games.

RIGHT / *Captain of the U.S. team, Andy Yohe (#9) takes a victory lap after a 2-0 victory over Japan.* (PHOTO BY MARTIN ROSE/BONGARTS/GETTY IMAGES)

Twenty-year-old Nikko Landeros (#15) of the United States passes the puck against Daisuke Uehara (#32) of Japan during the gold-medal game.

▲ (Photo by Jamie McDonald/Getty Images)

(Photo by Kevin C. Cox/Getty Images)

TOP / *The sweet taste of victory as Team USA celebrates its 2-0 gold-medal win over Japan and later assembles for a team photo (opposite, bottom).*

BOTTOM / *Twenty-year-old Greg Shaw (#8) sets up a pass against Naohiko Ishida (#23) of Japan during the gold-medal game.*

Wheelchair Curling

Semifinal Play

Story Contributor: Terry Kolesar

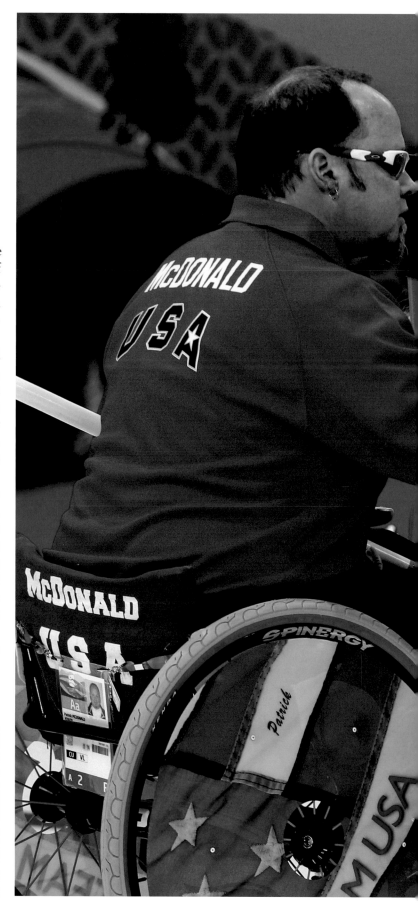

Augusto Perez and Team USA came into the 2010 Paralympic Winter Games fresh off two seasons of improved play that saw the team earn the bronze in 2008 and finish fourth in 2009 at the world wheelchair curling championship.

Skip Perez and teammates Patrick McDonald (Orangevale, Calif.), James Pierce (North Syracuse, N.Y.), Jacqui Kapinowski (Point Pleasant, N.J.) and James Joseph (New Hartford, N.Y.) were keen to surpass the USA's 2-5 performance four years ago in Torino when wheelchair curling debuted as a medal sport at the Paralympic Games.

New to the sport four years ago, they came to Vancouver ranked third and a sure medal contender.

The U.S. made it through the round robin with just two losses for a 7-2 record and earned the No. 2 playoff seed, marking the first-ever Paralympic semifinal game for the U.S. wheelchair curling program. They lost a tough battle with Korea, 7-5, in the semifinal to drop down to the bronze medal game. After a rough start, the Americans battled back but couldn't score enough to outlast Sweden, 7-5, to get on the podium. They finished a respectable fourth place with a 7-4 record.

Canada would go on to repeat as Paralympic champion edging Korea, 8-7.

ROUND ROBIN GAMES
USA 9, Korea 6
Canada 10, USA 5
USA 6, Germany 5
USA 8, Italy 2
USA 8, Great Britain 7 (EXTRA END)
Sweden 6, USA 4
USA 9, Norway 8
USA 8, Japan 3
USA 8, Switzerland 2

Score Box

SEMIFINAL
Korea 7, USA 5

BRONZE MEDAL GAME
Sweden 7, USA 5

Patrick McDonald (left), Jacqui Kapinowski, Jim Pierce and Augusto Perez huddle during the round robin game against Korea. Team USA won 9-6. (PHOTO BY MARTIN ROSE/BONGARTS/GETTY IMAGES)

Augusto Perez

Strategy

Born in Madrid, Spain, it was high school that lured Augusto Perez to the United States. He came for his senior year and ended up staying when Paul Smith's College offered him a scholarship.

Three bouts with cancer finally resulted in the amputation of his left leg. Nicknamed "Goose," he tried curling in 2005 and fell in love with the sport. He made the U.S. Paralympic Team just a couple of months later.

Vancouver was his second trip to the Paralympic Games, and this time he was the skip of the U.S. Curling Team. The team finished fourth in the 2010 competition, a huge improvement from their 2-5 performance in Torino.

When it comes to throwing a stone with the right weight, direction and rotation, it's all about technique. With wheelchair curlers, technique depends on their individual available muscle sets. Technique can be taught, practiced and improved but good technique happens when a curler works with—and doesn't fight—his or her body or wheelchair.

Having mastered weight, direction and rotation, then the subtleties of strategy and tactics, like ice-reading and shot calling, come into play.

ABOVE / *Augusto Perez (left) and Jacqui Kapinowski (right) consider their next throw against Sweden during the bronze medal game. Sweden won, 7-5, leaving the U.S. team with the consolation prize.* (PHOTO BY MARTIN ROSE/BONGARTS/GETTY IMAGES)

OPPOSITE / *Jim Pierce (left), Augusto Perez (right) and Patrick McDonald assess their next move against Canada, who won 10-5. The Canadians went on to defend their championship.* (PHOTO BY MARTIN ROSE/BONGARTS/GETTY IMAGES)

XXI Olympic Winter Games

February 12-28, 2010

Participating Nations | 82

ALB	Albania		JPN	Japan
ALG	Algeria		KAZ	Kazakhstan
AND	Andorra		KGZ	Kyrgyzstan
ARG	Argentina		LAT	Latvia
ARM	Armenia		LIB	Lebanon
AUS	Australia		LIE	Liechtenstein
AUT	Austria		LTU	Lithuania
AZE	Azerbaijan		MKD	Macedonia
BLR	Belarus		MEX	Mexico
BEL	Belgium		MDA	Moldova
BER	Bermuda		MON	Monaco
BIH	Bosnia & Herzegovina		MGL	Mongolia
BRA	Brazil		MNE	Montenegro
BUL	Bulgaria		MAR	Morocco
CAN	Canada		NEP	Nepal
CAY	Cayman Islands		NED	Netherlands
CHI	Chile		NZL	New Zealand
CHN	China		PRK	North Korea
COL	Colombia		NOR	Norway
CRO	Croatia		PAK	Pakistan
CYP	Cyprus		PER	Peru
CZE	Czech Republic		POL	Poland
DEN	Denmark		POR	Portugal
EST	Estonia		ROU	Romania
ETH	Ethiopia		RUS	Russia Federation
FIN	Finland		SMR	San Marino
FRA	France		SEN	Senegal
GEO	Georgia		SRB	Serbia
GER	Germany		SVK	Slovakia
GHA	Ghana		SLO	Slovenia
GBR	Great Britain		RSA	South Africa
GRE	Greece		KOR	South Korea
HKG	Hong Kong		ESP	Spain
HUN	Hungary		SWE	Sweden
ISL	Iceland		SUI	Switzerland
IND	India		TPE	Chinese Taipei
IRI	Iran		TJK	Tajikistan
IRL	Ireland		TUR	Turkey
ISR	Israel		UKR	Ukraine
ITA	Italy		USA	United States
JAM	Jamaica		UZB	Uzbekistan

Medal Count | 258

NATION		GOLD	SILVER	BRONZE	TOTAL
USA	United States	9	15	13	37
GER	Germany	10	13	7	30
CAN	Canada	14	7	5	26
NOR	Norway	9	8	6	23
AUT	Austria	4	6	6	16
RUS	Russian Fed.	3	5	7	15
KOR	South Korea	6	6	2	14
CHN	China	5	2	4	11
SWE	Sweden	5	2	4	11
FRA	France	2	3	6	11
SUI	Switzerland	6	0	3	9
NED	Netherlands	4	1	3	8
CZE	Czech Republic	2	0	4	6
POL	Poland	1	3	2	6
ITA	Italy	1	1	3	5
JPN	Japan	0	3	2	5
FIN	Finland	0	1	4	5
AUS	Australia	2	1	0	3
BLR	Belarus	1	1	1	3
SVK	Slovakia	1	1	1	3
CRO	Croatia	0	2	1	3
SLO	Slovenia	0	2	1	3
LAT	Latvia	0	2	0	2
GBR	Great Britain	1	0	0	1
EST	Estonia	0	1	0	1
KAZ	Kazakhstan	0	1	0	1

- Seven nations—the Cayman Islands, Colombia, Ghana, Montenegro, Pakistan, Peru and Serbia—made their Olympic Winter Games debut.
- Slovakia and Belarus won their first Olympic Winter gold medal.
- Canada broke the record for the most gold medals won at a single Olympic Winter Games , which was 13, set by the former Soviet Union in 1976 and tied by Norway in 2002.
- It was the second time the United States won the most medals at a Winter Games. The last time was in 1932.

OPPOSITE / *Following the free skate, Mirai Nagasu of the United States found herself in fourth place.* (PHOTO BY MATTHEW STOCKMAN/GETTY IMAGES)

Allison Jones competed in all five disciplines of alpine skiing (standing), finishing fifth in the super combined and the slalom, sixth in the downhill and ninth in the super-G (pictured) and giant slalom. Born without a femur, the 25-year-old American began skiing at age 5. Vancouver marked her fifth Paralympic Games. Jones, also a cyclist, won the silver medal in the individual time trial event at the Beijing Paralympic Games and competed in Athens in 2004. She won the gold medal in the slalom in Torino and silver medals in the super-G and giant slalom in Salt Lake City. (PHOTO BY JAMIE MCDONALD/GETTY IMAGES)

X Paralympic Winter Games

March 12-21, 2010

Participating Nations | 44

AND	Andorra	IRI	Iran
ARG	Argentina	ITA	Italy
ARM	Armenia	JPN	Japan
AUS	Australia	KAZ	Kazakhstan
AUT	Austria	MEX	Mexico
BLR	Belarus	MGL	Mongolia
BEL	Belgium	NED	Netherlands
BIH	Bosnia & Herzegovina	NZL	New Zealand
BUL	Bulgaria	NOR	Norway
CAN	Canada	POL	Poland
CHI	Chile	ROU	Romania
CHN	China	RUS	Russia Federation
CRO	Croatia	SRB	Serbia
CZE	Czech Republic	SVK	Slovakia
DEN	Denmark	SLO	Slovenia
FIN	Finland	RSA	South Africa
FRA	France	KOR	South Korea
GER	Germany	ESP	Spain
GBR	Great Britain	SWE	Sweden
GRE	Greece	SUI	Switzerland
HUN	Hungary	UKR	Ukraine
ISL	Iceland	USA	United States

- Argentina, Bosnia and Herzegovina and Romania participated in their first Paralympic Winter Games.
- Serbia, which split with Montenegro, also made its debut in Vancouver's Paralympic Games.

Medal Count | 192

NATION		GOLD	SILVER	BRONZE	TOTAL
RUS	Russian Fed.	12	16	10	38
GER	Germany	13	5	6	24
CAN	Canada	10	5	4	19
UKR	Ukraine	5	8	6	19
USA	United States	4	5	4	13
SVK	Slovakia	6	2	3	11
AUT	Austria	3	4	4	11
JPN	Japan	3	3	5	11
BLR	Belarus	2	0	7	9
ITA	Italy	1	3	3	7
FRA	France	1	4	1	6
NOR	Norway	1	3	2	6
AUS	Australia	0	1	3	4
ESP	Spain	1	2	0	3
SUI	Switzerland	1	2	0	3
FIN	Finland	0	1	1	2
SWE	Sweden	0	0	2	2
NZL	New Zealand	1	0	0	1
KOR	South Korea	0	1	0	1
CZE	Czech Republic	0	0	1	1
POL	Poland	0	0	1	1

Sport Classifications

Sport	Amputee | Dwarfism | Other	Blind | Visually Impaired	Spinal Cord Injury | Paralyzed | Wheelchair User	Traumatic Brain Injury | Cerebral Palsy |Stroke
Alpine Skiing	●	●	●	●
Biathlon	●	●	●	●
Cross-Country Skiing	●	●	●	●
Sled Hockey	●		●	●
Wheelchair Curling	●		●	●

Olympic Winter Games Results

ALPINE SKIING

Men's Downhill
Feb 15 | Final | 64 Athletes: 4 DNF;1 DSQ

#	CTRY	ATHLETE	TIME	DIFFERENCE
1	SUI	DEFAGO Didier	1:54.31	0.00
2	NOR	SVINDAL Aksel Lund	1:54.38	+0.07
3	USA	MILLER Bode	1:54.40	+0.09
4	AUT	SCHEIBER Mario	1:54.52	+0.21
5	CAN	GUAY Erik	1:54.64	+0.33
6	SUI	CUCHE Didier	1:54.67	+0.36
7	FRA	POISSON David	1:54.82	+0.51
8	LIE	BUECHEL Marco	1:54.84	+0.53
9	AUT	KROELL Klaus	1:54.87	+0.56
10	AUT	WALCHHOFER Michael	1:54.88	+0.57
20	USA	NYMAN Steven	1:55.71	+1.40
21	USA	WEIBRECHT Andrew	1:55.74	+1.43
—	USA	SULLIVAN Marco	DSQ	

Men's Super-G
Feb 19 | Final | 64 Athletes: 1 DNS; 15 DNF;3 DSQ

#	CTRY	ATHLETE	TIME	DIFFERENCE
1	NOR	SVINDAL Aksel Lund	1:30.34	0.00
2	USA	MILLER Bode	1:30.62	+0.28
3	USA	WEIBRECHT Andrew	1:30.65	+0.31
4	ITA	HEEL Werner	1:30.67	+0.33
5	CAN	GUAY Erik	1:30.68	+0.34
6	ITA	INNERHOFER Christof	1:30.73	+0.39
7	ITA	STAUDACHER Patrick	1:30.74	+0.40
8	SUI	JANKA Carlo	1:30.83	+0.49
9	SUI	GRUENENFELDER Tobias	1:30.90	+0.56
10	SUI	CUCHE Didier	1:31.06	+0.72
19	USA	LIGETY Ted	1:31.70	+1.36
23	USA	SULLIVAN Marco	1:32.09	+1.75

Men's Super Combined
Feb 21 | Downhill | 52 Athletes: 6 DNF
Feb 21 | Slalom | 46 Athletes: 1 DNS; 11 DNF

#	CTRY	ATHLETE	DOWN.	SLALOM	TOTAL
1	USA	MILLER Bode	1:53.91	51.01	2:44.92
2	CRO	KOSTELIC Ivica	1:54.20	51.05	2:45.25
3	SUI	ZURBRIGGEN Silvan	1:53.88	51.44	2:45.32
4	SUI	JANKA Carlo	1:53.65	51.89	2:45.54
5	USA	LIGETY Ted	1:55.06	50.76	2:45.82
6	AUT	RAICH Benjamin	1:54.70	51.43	2:46.13
7	CZE	BANK Ondrej	1:55.17	51.02	2:46.19
8	ITA	INNERHOFER Christof	1:54.55	51.90	2:46.45
9	NOR	JANSRUD Kjetil	1:55.44	51.06	2:46.50
10	USA	BRANDENBURG Will	1:56.28	50.78	2:47.06
11	USA	WEIBRECHT Andrew	1:55.23	52.35	2:47.58

Men's Giant Slalom
Feb 23 | 1st Run | 103 Athletes: 2 DNS; 9 DNF; 3 DSQ
Feb 23 | 2nd Run | 89 Athletes: 1 DNS; 7 DNF

#	CTRY	ATHLETE	RUN 1	RUN 2	TOTAL
1	SUI	JANKA Carlo	1:17.27	1:20.56	2:37.83
2	NOR	JANSRUD Kjetil	1:18.07	1:20.15	2:38.22
3	NOR	SVINDAL Aksel Lund	1:17.43	1:21.01	2:38.44
4	AUT	HIRSCHER Marcel	1:17.48	1:21.04	2:38.52
5	AUT	BAUMANN Romed	1:17.29	1:21.51	2:38.80
6	AUT	RAICH Benjamin	1:17.66	1:21.17	2:38.83
7	CRO	KOSTELIC Ivica	1:18.05	1:20.83	2:38.88
8	GER	NEUREUTHER Felix	1:18.24	1:20.82	2:39.06
9	USA	LIGETY Ted	1:17.87	1:21.24	2:39.11
10	SLO	GORZA Ales	1:17.95	1:21.26	2:39.21
26	USA	FORD Tommy	1:19.10	1:22.05	2:41.15
31	USA	ZAMANSKY Jake	1:19.85	1:22:50	2:42:35
—	USA	MILLER Bode	DNF		

ALPINE SKIING (cont'd)

Men's Slalom
Feb 27 | 1st Run | 102 Athletes: 1 DNS; 43 DNF; 4 DSQ
Feb 27 | 2nd Run | 54 Athletes: 3 DNF; 3 DSQ

#	CTRY	ATHLETE	RUN 1	RUN 2	TOTAL
1	ITA	RAZZOLI Giuliano	47.79	51.53	1:39.32
2	CRO	KOSTELIC Ivica	48.37	51.11	1:39.48
3	SWE	MYHRER Andre	49.03	50.73	1:39.76
4	AUT	RAICH Benjamin	48.33	51.48	1:39.81
5	AUT	HIRSCHER Marcel	48.92	51.28	1:40.20
6	SLO	VALENCIC Mitja	48.22	52.13	1:40.35
7	ITA	MOELGG Manfred	48.64	51.81	1:40.45
8	CAN	COUSINEAU Julien	49.59	51.07	1:40.66
9	FRA	LIZEROUX Julien	48.82	51.90	1:40.72
10	AUT	HERBST Reinfried	49.23	51.55	1:40.78
24	USA	KASPER Nolan	50.66	52.51	1:43.17
—	USA	COCHRAN Jimmy	54.94	DNF	
—	USA	LIGETY Ted	DNF		
—	USA	MILLER Bode	DNF		

Ladies' Downhill
Feb 17 | 45 Athletes: 1 DNS; 6 DNF;1 DSQ

#	CTRY	ATHLETE	TIME	DIFFERENCE
1	USA	VONN Lindsey	1:44.19	0.00
2	USA	MANCUSO Julia	1:44.75	+0.56
3	AUT	GOERGL Elisabeth	1:45.65	+1.46
4	AUT	FISCHBACHER Andrea	1:45.68	+1.49
5	SUI	SUTER Fabienne	1:46.17	+1.98
6	CAN	JANYK Britt	1:46.21	+2.02
7	FRA	MARCHAND-ARVIER Marie	1:46.22	+2.03
8	GER	RIESCH Maria	1:46.26	+2.07
9	ITA	RECCHIA Lucia	1:46.50	+2.31
10	GER	STECHERT Gina	1:46.93	+2.74
11	USA	COOK Stacey	1:46.98	+2.79
—	USA	MCKENNIS Alice	DSQ	

Ladies' Super G
Feb 20 | 53 Athletes: 15 DNF

#	CTRY	ATHLETE	TIME	DIFFERENCE
1	AUT	FISCHBACHER Andrea	1:20.14	0.00
2	SLO	MAZE Tina	1:20.63	+0.49
3	USA	VONN Lindsey	1:20.88	+0.74
4	ITA	SCHNARF Johanna	1:20.99	+0.85
5	AUT	GOERGL Elisabeth	1:21.14	+1.00
6	SUI	STYGER Nadia	1:21.25	+1.11
7	ITA	RECCHIA Lucia	1:21.43	+1.29
8	GER	RIESCH Maria	1:21.46	+1.32
9	USA	MANCUSO Julia	1:21.50	+1.36
10	FRA	JACQUEMOD Ingrid	1:21.77	+1.63
18	USA	SMITH Leanne	1:23.05	+2.91
—	USA	MARSHALL Chelsea	DNF	

Ladies' Super Combined
Feb 18 | Downhill | 35 Athletes: 1 DNS; 3 DNF
Feb 18 | Slalom | 31 Athletes: 3 DNF

#	CTRY	ATHLETE	DOWN.	SLALOM	TOTAL
1	GER	RIESCH Maria	1:24.49	44.65	2:09.14
2	USA	MANCUSO Julia	1:24.96	45.12	2:10.08
3	SWE	PAERSON Anja	1:25.57	44.62	2:10.19
4	AUT	ZETTEL Kathrin	1:26.01	44.49	2:10.50
5	SLO	MAZE Tina	1:25.97	44.56	2:10.53
6	SUI	SUTER Fabienne	1:25.29	45.56	2:10.85
7	CZE	ZAHROBSKA Sarka	1:27.33	43.69	2:11.02
8	ITA	SCHNARF Johanna	1:25.72	45.57	2:11.29
9	AUT	KIRCHGASSER Michaela	1:27.09	44.26	2:11.35
10	FRA	MARCHAND-ARVIER Marie	1:25.41	46.41	2:11.82
17	USA	RICHARDSON Kaylin	1:27.64	45.76	2:13.40
21	USA	SMITH Leanne	1:27.27	46.70	2:13.97
—	USA	VONN Lindsey	1:24.16	DNF	

Ladies' Giant Slalom
Feb 24 | 1st Run | 86 Athletes: 17 DNF; 1 DSQ
Feb 25 | 2nd Run | 68 Athletes: 4 DNS; 4 DNF

#	CTRY	ATHLETE	RUN 1	RUN 2	TOTAL
1	GER	REBENSBURG Viktoria	1:15.47	1:11.64	2:27.11
2	SLO	MAZE Tina	1:15.39	1:11.76	2:27.15
3	AUT	GOERGL Elisabeth	1:15.12	1:12.13	2:27.25
4	SUI	SUTER Fabienne	1:15.97	1:11.55	2:27.52
5	AUT	ZETTEL Kathrin	1:15.28	1:12.25	2:27.53
6	GER	HOELZL Kathrin	1:15.81	1:11.77	2:27.58
7	AUT	BREM Eva-Maria	1:15.38	1:12.24	2:27.62
8	USA	MANCUSO Julia	1:16.42	1:11.24	2:27.66
9	FRA	BARIOZ Taina	1:15.14	1:15.14	2:27.79
10	GER	RIESCH Maria	1:15.60	1:12.37	2:27.97
14	USA	SCHLEPER Sarah	1:16.19	1:12.17	2:28.36
32	USA	MCJAMES Megan	1:18.30	1:14.68	2:32.98
—	USA	VONN Lindsey	DNF		

ALPINE SKIING (cont'd)

Ladies' Slalom
Feb 27 | 1st Run | 87 Athletes: 15 DNF; 2 DSQ
Feb 27 | 2nd Run | 70 Athletes: 1 DNS; 14 DNF

#	CTRY	ATHLETE	RUN 1	RUN 2	TOTAL
1	GER	RIESCH Maria	50.75	52.14	1:42.89
2	AUT	SCHILD Marlies	51.40	51.92	1:43.32
3	CZE	ZAHROBSKA Sarka	51.15	52.75	1:43.90
4	SWE	PIETILAE-HOLMNER Maria	51.64	52.58	1:44.22
5	FRA	AUBERT Sandrine	51.68	52.78	1:44.46
6	FIN	POUTIAINEN Tanja	51.67	53.26	1:44.93
7	AUT	GOERGL Elisabeth	53.01	51.96	1:44.97
8	ITA	GIUS Nicole	51.71	53.30	1:45.01
9	SLO	MAZE Tina	52.28	52.81	1:45.09
10	SVK	ZUZULOVA Veronika	52.11	53.03	1:45.14
16	USA	SCHLEPER Sarah	51.83	51.83	1:45.88
30	USA	DUKE Hailey	54.02	54.02	1:48.69
—	USA	MCJAMES Megan	54.41	DNF	
—	USA	VONN Lindsey	DNF		

BIATHLON

Men's 10km Sprint
Feb 14 | Final | 88 Athletes: 1 DNF

#	CTRY	ATHLETE	TIME	PENALTIES
1	FRA	JAY Vincent	24:07.8	0
2	NOR	SVENDSEN Emil Hegle	24:20.0	1
3	CRO	FAK Jakov	24:21.8	0
4	SLO	BAUER Klemen	24:25.2	1
5	UKR	DERYZEMLYA Andriy	24:48.5	2
6	CAN	LEGUELLEC Jean Philippe	24:57.6	1
7	SLO	HURAJT Pavol	25:15.0	1
8	SWE	FERRY Bjorn	25:20.2	0
9	USA	TEELA Jeremy	25:21.7	2
10	RUS	TCHEREZOV Ivan	25:25.9	2
36	USA	BAILEY Lowell	26:26.6	0
47	USA	BURKE Tim	26:54.8	3
54	USA	HAKKINEN Jay	27:17.4	0

Men's 12.5km Pursuit
Feb 16 | Final | 60 Athletes

#	CTRY	ATHLETE	TIME	PENALTIES
1	SWE	FERRY Bjorn	33:38.4	1
2	AUT	SUMANN Christoph	+16.5	2
3	FRA	JAY Vincent	+28.2	2
4	AUT	EDER Simon	+31.0	3
5	GER	GREIS Michael	+51.2	1
6	RUS	TCHEREZOV Ivan	+51.2	2
7	NOR	BJOERNDALEN Ole Einar	+51.4	2
8	NOR	SVENDSEN Emil Hegle	+52.0	4
9	SLO	BAUER Klemen	+55.4	5
10	UKR	SEDNEV Serguei	+1:11.6	0
24	USA	TEELA Jeremy	+2:07.0	4
36	USA	BAILEY Lowell	+2:55.6	3
46	USA	BURKE Tim	+3:48.4	5
57	USA	HAKKINEN, Jay	+6:54.8	6

Men's 20km Individual
Feb 18 | Final | 88 Athletes

#	CTRY	ATHLETE	TIME	PENALTIES
1	NOR	SVENDSEN Emil Hegle	48:22.5	1
2	NOR	BJOERNDALEN Ole Einar	48:32.0	2
2	BEL	NOVIKOV Sergey	48:32.0	0
4	RUS	USTYUGOV Evgeny	49:11.8	1
5	SLO	HURAJT Pavol	49:39.0	1
6	AUT	EDER Simon	49:41.7	2
7	POL	SIKORA Tomasz	49:43.8	2
8	AUT	SUMANN Christoph	50:04.9	3
9	AUT	MESOTITSCH Daniel	50:32.0	2
10	GER	GREIS Michael	50:37.6	2
45	USA	BURKE Tim	53:22.6	5
57	USA	BAILEY Lowell	54:23.1	4
76	USA	HAKKINEN, Jay	57:01.8	7
88	USA	ROBERTS Wynn	58:49.2	8

Men's 15km Mass Start
Feb 21 | Final | 30 Athletes

#	CTRY	ATHLETE	TIME	PENALTIES
1	RUS	USTYUGOV Evgeny	35:35.7	0
2	FRA	FOURCADE Martin	+10.5	3
3	SLO	HURAJT Pavol	+16.6	0
4	AUT	SUMANN Christoph	+25.9	1
5	AUT	MESOTITSCH Daniel	+30.2	3
6	RUS	TCHEREZOV Iva	+33.5	3
7	AUT	LANDERTINGER Dominik	+34.0	4
8	FRA	JAY Vincent	+34.6	1
9	CRO	FAK Jakov	+34.8	3
10	GER	GREIS Michael	+35.0 8	3
18	USA	BURKE, Tim	+1:09.0	4
29	USA	TEELA Jeremy	+3:00.4	4

Legend

DNF	- Did not finish	OR	- Olympic Record
DNS	- Did not start	OT	- Overtime
DSQ	- Disqualified	WD	- Withdrew

BIATHLON (cont'd)

Men's 4x7.5-km Relay
Feb 26 | Final | 19 Teams

#	CTRY	ATHLETES	TIME	PENALTIES
1	NOR	HANEVOLD Halvard	1:21:38.1	0+7
		BOE Tarjei		
		SVENDSEN Emil Hegle		
		BJOERNDALEN Ole Einar		
2	AUT	EDER Simon	1:22:16.7	1+8
		MESOTITSCH Daniel		
		LANDERTINGER Dominik		
		SUMANN Christophs		
3	RUS	TCHEREZOV Ivan	1:22:16.9	0+4
		SHIPULIN Anton		
		TCHOUDOV Maxim		
		USTYUGOV Evgeny		
4	SWE	LINDSTROM Fredrik	1:23:02.0	1+10
		BERGMAN Carl Johan		
		NILSSON Mattias		
		FERRY Bjorn Total Penalties		
5	GER1	SCHEMPP Simon	1:23:16.0	2+7
		BIRNBACHER Andreas		
		PEIFFER Arnd		
		GREIS Michael		
6	FRA	JAY Vincent	1:23:16.2	1+9
		DEFRASNE Vincent		
		FOURCADE Simon		
		FOURCADE Martin		
7	CZE	SOUKUP Jaroslav	1:23:55.2	0+9
		VITEK Zdenek		
		DOSTAL Roman		
		SLESINGR Michal		
8	UKR	BILANENKO Olexander	1:24:25.1	0+4
		DERYZEMLYA Andriy		
		DERKACH Vyacheslav		
		SEDNEV Serguei		
9	SUI	FREI Thomas	1:24:36.8	0+9
		SIMMEN Matthias		
		WEGER Benjamin		
		HALLENBARTER Simon		
10	CAN	CLEGG Robin	1:24:50.7	0+7
		BEDARD Marc-Andre		
		GREEN Brendan		
		LEGUELLEC Jean Philippe		
13	USA	BAILEY Lowell	1:27:58.3	4+12
		HAKKINEN Jay		
		BURKE Tim		
		TEELA Jeremy		

Women's 7.5km Sprint
Feb 13 | Final | 89 Athletes: 1 DNS

#	CTRY	ATHLETE	TIME	PENALTIES
1	SVK	KUZMINA Anastazia	19:55.6	1
2	GER	NEUNER Magdalena	19:57.1	1
3	FRA	DORIN Marie	20:06.5	0
4	RUS	BOULYGINA Anna	20:07.7	0
5	KAZ	KHRUSTALEVA Elena	20:20.4	0
6	FRA	BRUNET Marie Laure	20:23.3	0
7	RUS	ZAITSEVA Olga	20:23.4	0
8	BEL	DOMRACHEVA Darya	20:27.4	0
9	SLO	GREGORIN Teja	20:29.2	0
10	NOR	FLATLAND	20:29.7	1
		Ann Kristin Aafedt		
45	USA	STUDEBAKER Sara	22:05.3	1
77	USA	SPECTOR Laura	23:18.1	2
78	USA	BARNES Lanny	23:26.0	1
80	USA	JOHNSON Haley	23:35.4	4

Women's 10km Pursuit
Feb 16 | Final | 60 Athletes

#	CTRY	ATHLETE	TIME	PENALTIES
1	GER	NEUNER Magdalena	30:16.0	2
2	SVK	KUZMINA Anastazia	+12.3	2
3	FRA	BRUNET Marie Laure	+28.3	0
4	SWE	OLOFSSON-ZIDEK	+39.4	1
		Anna Carin		
5	NOR	BERGER Tora	+51.2	0
6	RUS	BOULYGINA Anna	+52.1	1
7	RUS	ZAITSEVA Olga	+1:04.3	2
8	NOR	FLATLAND	+1:17.3	1
		Ann Kristin Aafedt		
9	SLO	GREGORIN Teja	+1:22.6	2
10	GER	HENKEL Andrea	+1:24.5	3
46	USA	STUDEBAKER Sara	+4:44.1	2

BIATHLON (cont'd)

Women's 15km Individual
Feb 18 | Final | 87 Athletes: 1 DNF

#	CTRY	ATHLETE	TIME	PENALTIES
1	NOR	BERGER Tora	40:52.8	1
2	KAZ	KHRUSTALEVA Elena	41:13.5	0
3	BLR	DOMRACHEVA Darya	41:21.0	1
4	GER	WILHELM Kati	41:57.3	1
5	POL	NOVAKOWSKA Weronika	41:57.5	1
6	GER	HENKEL Andrea	42:32.4	2
7	POL	CYL Agnieszka	42:32.5	1
8	UKR	KHVOSTENKO Oksana	42:38.6	0
9	BLR	KALINCHIK Liudmila	42:39.1	1
10	GER	NEUNER Magdalena	42:42.1	3
23	USA	BARNES Lanny	43:31.8	0
34	USA	STUDEBAKER Sara	44:27.3	1
65	USA	SPECTOR Laura	47:19.3	2
66	USA	JOHNSON Haley	47:19.4	4

Women's 12.5km Mass Start
Feb 21 | Final | 30 Athletes

#	CTRY	ATHLETE	TIME	PENALTIES
1	GER	NEUNER Magdalena	35:19.6	2
2	RUS	ZAITSEVA Olga	+5.5	1
3	GER	HAUSWALD Simone	+7.3	2
4	RUS	MEDVEDTSEVA Olga	+21.2	0
5	SLO	GREGORIN Teja	+29.4	1
6	BLR	DOMRACHEVA Darya	+33.6	1
7	FRA	BAILLY Sandrine	+42.4	2
8	SVK	KUZMINA Anastazia	+43.3	3
9	GER	HENKEL Andrea	+53.9	1
10	SWE	JONSSON Helena	+56.3	2

NOTE: No USA athlete competed

Women's 4x6-km Relay
Feb 23 | Final | 19 Teams

#	CTRY	ATHLETES	TIME	PENALTIES
1	RUS	SLEPTSOVA Svetlana	1:09:36.3	0+5
		BOGALIY-TITOVETS Anna		
		MEDVEDTSEVA Olga		
		ZAITSEVA Olga		
2	FRA	BRUNET Marie Laure	1:10:09.1	2+8
		BECAERT Sylvie		
		DORIN Marie		
		BAILLY Sandrine		
3	GER	WILHELM Kati	1:10:13.4	0+5
		HAUSWALD Simone		
		BECK Martina		
		HENKEL Andrea		
4	NOR	EIKELAND Liv Kjersti	1:10:34.1	0+3
		FLATLAND Ann Kristin Aafedt		
		ROGSTAD Solveig		
		BERGER Tora		
5	SWE	HOGBERG Elisabeth	1:10:47.2	0+3
		OLOFSSON-ZIDEK Anna Carin		
		NILSSON Anna Maria		
		ONSSON Helena		
6	UKR	PIDHRUSHNA Olena	1:11:08.2	0+8
		SEMERENKO Valj		
		KHVOSTENKO Oksana		
		SEMERENKO Vita		
7	BLR	KALINCHIK Liudmila	1:11:34.0	0+3
		DOMRACHEVA Darya		
		KUDRASHOVA Olga		
		SKARDINO Nadezhda		
8	SLO	RAVNIKAR Dijana	1:12:02.4	0+6
		MALI Andreja		
		BRANKOVIC-LIKOZAR Tadeja		
		GREGORIN Teja		
9	CHN	WANG Chunli	1:12:16.9	0+8
		LIU Xianying		
		KONG Yingchao		
		SONG Chaoqing		
10	ROM	PLOTOGEA Dana	1:12:32.9	0+7
		TOFALVI Eva		
		PURDEA Mihaela		
		FERENCZ Reka		
17	USA	STUDEBAKER Sara	1:15:47.5	1+12
		BARNES Lanny		
		JOHNSON Haley		
		SPECTOR Laura		

BOBSLED

Two Man
Feb 20 | Heat 1 | 27 Teams: 1 DNF; 2 DSQ
Feb 20 | Heat 2 | 23 Teams: 1 DNS; 1 DNF; 2 DSQ
Feb 21 | Heat 3 | 22 Teams: 1 DNF
Feb 21 | Heat 4 | 22 Teams: 2 DNS

#	CTRY	ATHLETES	HEAT 1 2 3 4 TOTAL		
1	GER1	LANGE Andre	51.59	51.72	51.57
		KUSKE Kevin	51.77	3:26.65	
2	GER2	FLORSCHUETZ Thomas	51.57	51.85	51.62
		ADJEI Richard	51.83	3:26.87	
3	RUS1	ZUBKOV Alexsandr	51.79	52.02	51.80
		VOEVODA Alexey	51.90	3:27.51	
4	SUI1	RUEEGG Ivo	51.76	52.18	51.92
		GRAND Cedric	51.99	3:27.85	
5	CAN2	LUEDERS Pierre	51.94	52.12	51.87
		LUMSDEN Jesse	51.94	3:27.87	
6	USA4	HOLCOMB Steven	51.89	52.04	51.98
		TOMASEVICZ Curtis	52.03	3:27.94	
7	RUS2	ABRAMOVICH Dmitry	52.03	52.40	52.11
		PRUDNIKOV Sergey	51.92	3:28.46	
8	LAT1	MASKALANS Edgars	52.16	52.32	52.17
		DREISKENS Daumants	52.43	3:29.083	
9	GER3	ANGERER Kar	52.23	52.43	52.19
		BERMBACH Gregor	52.44	3:29.29	
10	USA2	NAPIER John	52.28	52.45	52.31
		LANGTON Steven	52.36	3:29.40	
12	USA3	KOHN Mike	52.47	52.71	52.25
		CUNNINGHAM Nick	52.35	3:29.78	

Four Man
Feb 26 | Heat 1 | 25 Teams
Feb 26 | Heat 2 | 25 Teams: 3 DNS
Feb 27 | Heat 3 | 22 Teams: 1 DNS
Feb 27 | Heat 4 | 21 Teams: 1 DNS

#	CTRY	ATHLETES	HEAT 1 2 3 4 TOTAL		
1	USA1	HOLCOMB Steven	50.89	50.86	51.19
		MESLER Steve	51.52	3:24.46	
		TOMASEVICZ Curtis			
		OLSEN Justin			
2	GER1	LANGE Andre	51.14	51.05	51.29
		KUSKE Kevin	51.36	3:24.84	
		ROEDIGER Alexander			
		PUTZE Martin			
3	CAN1	RUSH Lyndon	51.12	51.03	51.24
		BISSETT David	51.46	3:24.85	
		BROWN Lascelles			
		Le BIHAN Chris			
4	GER2	FLORSCHUETZ Thomas	51.14	51.36	51.45
		LISTNER Ronny	51.63	3:25.58	
		BARUCHA Andreas			
		ADJEI Richard			
5	CAN2	LUEDERS Pierre	51.27	51.29	51.50
		KRIPPS Justin	51.54	3:25.60	
		WRIGHT Neville			
		LUMSDEN Jesse			
6	SUI1	RUEEGG Ivo	51.31	51.13	51.70
		LAMPARTER Thomas	51.57	3:25.71	
		GRAND Cedric			
		HEFTI Beat			
7	GER3	ANGERER Karl	51.18	51.41	51.70
		BREDAU Andreas	51.77	3:26.06	
		MANN Alex			
		BERMBACH Gregor			
8	RUS3	POPOV Evgeny	51.49	51.16	51.67
		KIREEV Alexey	51.81	3:26.13	
		MOISEYCHENKOV Denis			
		YURKOV Andrey			
9	ITA1	BERTAZZO Simone	51.57	51.38	51.62
		SANTARSIERO Danilo	51.68	3:26.25	
		ROMANINI Samuele			
		TURRI Mirko			
9	RUS1	ABRAMOVICH Dmitry	51.32	51.40	51.78
		ORESHNIKOV Roman	51.75	3:26.25	
		PRUDNIKOV Sergey			
		STEPUSHKIN Dmitry			
13	USA3	KOHN Mike	51.69	51.42	52.10
		CUNNINGHAM Nick	52.11	3:27.32	
		MORIARTY Jamie			
		SCHUFFENHAUER Bill			
—	USA2	NAPIER John	51.30	53.41	DNS
		FOGT Christopher			
		LANGTON Steven			
		BERKELEY Charles			

BOBSLED (cont'd)

Women's

Feb 23 | Heat 1 | 21 Teams
Feb 23 | Heat 2 | 21 Teams
Feb 24 | Heat 3 | 21 Teams
Feb 24 | Heat 4 | 21 Teams: 2 DNS; 1 DSQ

#	CTRY	ATHLETES	HEAT 1 2 3 4 TOTAL		
1	CAN1	HUMPHRIES Kaillie	53.19	53.01	52.85
		MOYSE Heather	53.23	3:32.28	
2	CAN2	UPPERTON Helen	53.50	53.12	53.34
		BROWN Shelley-Ann	53.17	3:33.13	
3	USA2	PAC Erin	53.28	53.05	53.29
		MEYERS Elana	53.78	3:33.40	
4	GER1	KIRIASIS Sandra	53.41	53.23	53.58
		SENKEL Christin	53.59	3:33.81	
5	USA3	SCHAAF Bree	53.76	53.33	53.56
		AZEVEDO Emily	53.40	3:34.05	
6	USA1	ROHBOCK Shauna	53.73	53.36	53.53
		RZEPKA Michelle	53.44	3:34.06	
7	GER3	SCHRAMM Claudia	53.65	53.81	53.57
		TISCHER Janine	53.65	3:34.68	
8	NED1	KAMPHUIS Esme	53.81	53.59	54.09
		VEENSTRA Tine	53.65	3:35.14	
9	RUS1	SKULKINA Anastasia	54.38	53.64	54.08
		DORONINA Elena	53.83	3:35.93	
10	SUI2	MEYER Fabienne	54.04	54.27	54.00
		SCHENK Hanne	53.82	3:36.13	

CROSS-COUNTRY SKIING

Men's 15km Free

Feb 15 | Final | 96 Athletes: 1 DNS

#	CTRY	ATHLETE	TIME	DIFFERENCE
1	SUI	COLOGNA Dario	33:36.3	0.0
2	ITA	PILLER COTTRER Pietro	34:00.9	+24.6
3	CZE	BAUER Lukas	34:12.0	+35.7
4	SWE	HELLNER Marcus	34:13.5	+37.2
5	FRA	VITTOZ Vincent	34:16.2	+39.9
6	FRA	MANIFICAT Maurice	34:27.4	+51.1
7	GER	ANGERER Tobias	34:28.5	+52.2
8	CAN	BABIKOV Ivan	34:30.0	+53.7
9	RUS	VYLEGZHANIN Maxim	34:31.6	+55.3
48	USA	SOUTHAM James	35:58.2	+2:21.9
58	USA	KUZZY Garrott	36:41.5	+3:05.2
59	USA	FREEMAN Kris	36:41.6	+3:05.3
64	USA	HAMILTON Simi	37:30.5	+3:54.2

Men's Individual Sprint Classic

Feb 15 | Qualifications | 62 Athletes
Feb 15 | Final | 6 Athletes

#	CTRY	ATHLETE	TIME	DIFFERENCE
1	RUS	KRIUKOV Nikita	3:36.3	
2	RUS	PANZHINSKIY Alexander		+0.0
3	NOR	NORTHUG Petter		+9.2
4	NOR	HATTESTAD Ola Vigen		+13.7
5	KAZ	POLTARANIN Alexey		+18.1
6	NOR	PETTERSEN Oeystein		+1:19.9
7	SWE	JOENSSON Emil		
8	RUS	DEVJATIAROV Mickail Jun.		
9	NOR	KJOELSTAD Johan		
10	FIN	LASSILA Kalle		
29	USA	HAMILTON Simi		
36	USA	KOOS Torin		
45	USA	NEWELL Andy		
47	USA	KUZZY Garrott		

Men's 30km Pursuit (15 Classic + 15 Free)

Feb 15 | Final | 64 Athletes: 8 DNF

#	CTRY	ATHLETE	TIME	DIFFERENCE
1	SWE	HELLNER Marcus	1:15:11.4	0.0
2	GER	ANGERER Tobias	1:15:13.5	+2.1
3	SWE	OLSSON Johan	1:15:14.2	+2.8
4	RUS	LEGKOV Alexander	1:15:15.4	+4.0
5	CAN	BABIKOV Ivan	1:15:20.5	+9.1
6	GER	FILBRICH Jens	1:15:25.0	+13.6
7	CZE	BAUER Lukas	1:15:25.2	+13.8
8	CAN	GREY George	1:15:32.0	+20.6
9	CAN	HARVEY Alex	1:15:43.0	+31.6
10	SWE	SOEDERGREN Anders	1:15:47.0	+35.6
34	USA	SOUTHAM James	1:20:46.2	+5:34.8
45	USA	FREEMAN Kris	1:23:02.6	+7:51.2

CROSS-COUNTRY SKIING (cont'd)

Men's 50km Mass Start Classic

Feb 28 | Final | 55 Athletes: 2 DNS; 5 DNF

#	CTRY	ATHLETE	TIME	DIFFERENCE
1	NOR	NORTHUG Petter	2:05:35.5	0.0
2	GER	TEICHMANN Axel	2:05:35.8	+0.3
3	SWE	OLSSON Johan	2:05:36.5	+1.0
4	GER	ANGERER Tobias	2:05:37.0	+1.5
5	CAN	KERSHAW Devon	2:05:37.1	+1.6
6	EST	VEERPALU Andrus	2:05:41.6	+6.1
7	SWE	RICHARDSSON Daniel	2:05:45.2	+9.7
8	RUS	VYLEGZHANIN Maxim	2:05:46.4	+10.9
9	SWE	SOEDERGREN Anders	2:05:47.1	+11.6
10	SUI	COLOGNA Dario	2:05:47.5	+12.0
28	USA	SOUTHAM James	2:10:08.3	+4:32.8
—	USA	FREEMAN Kris	DNF	

Men's Team Sprint Free

Feb 22 | Semifinals | 22 Teams
Feb 22 | Final | 10 Teams

#	CTRY	ATHLETES	TIME	DIFFERENCE
1	NOR	PETTERSEN Oeystein	19:01.0	0.0
		NORTHUG Petter		
2	GER	TSCHARNKE Tim	19:02.3	+1.3
		TEICHMANN Axel		
3	RUS	MORILOV Nikolay	19:02.5	+1.5
		PETUKHOV Alexey		
4	CAN	KERSHAW Devon	19:07.3	+6.3
		HARVEY Alex		
5	KAZ	CHEBOTKO Nikolay	19:07.5	+6.5
		POLTARANIN Alexey		
6	CZE	KOZISEK Dusan	19:13.8	+12.8
		KOUKAL Martin		
7	FRA	VITTOZ Vincent	19:18.7	+17.7
		MIRANDA Cyril		
8	ITA	ZORZI Cristian	19:21.1	+20.1
		PASINI Renato		
9	USA	KOOS Torin	19:21.6	+20.6
		NEWELL Andy		
10	FIN	PAAKKONEN Lasse	19:50.8	+49.8
		NOUSIAINEN Ville		

Men's 4x10km Relay

Feb 24 | Final | 14 Teams
1: Classic; 2: Classic; 3: Freestyle; 4: Freestyle

#	CTRY	ATHLETES	TIME	DIFFERENCE
1	SWE	RICHARDSSON Daniel	1:45:05.4	0.0
		OLSSON Johan		
		SOEDERGREN Anders		
		HELLNER Marcus		
2	NOR	JOHNSRUD SUNDBY Martin	1:45:21.3	+15.9
		HJELMESET Odd-Bjoern		
		BERGER Lars		
		NORTHUG Petter		
3	CZE	JAKS Martin	1:45:21.9	+16.5
		BAUER Lukas		
		MAGAL Jiri		
		KOUKAL Martin		
4	FRA	GAILLARD Jean Marc	1:45:26.3	+20.9
		VITTOZ Vincent		
		MANIFICAT Maurice		
		JONNIER Emmanuel		
5	FIN	JAUHOJAERVI Sami	1:45:30.3	+24.9
		HEIKKINEN Matti		
		KATTILAKOSKI Teemu		
		NOUSIAINEN Ville		
6	GER	FILBRICH Jens	1:45:49.4	+44.0
		TEICHMANN Axel		
		SOMMERFELDT Rene		
		ANGERER Tobias		
7	CAN	KERSHAW Devon	1:47:03.2	+1:57.8
		HARVEY Alex		
		BABIKOV Ivan		
		GREY George		
8	RUS	PANKRATOV Nikolay	1:47:04.7	+1:59.3
		SEDOV Petr		
		LEGKOV Alexander		
		VYLEGZHANIN Maxim		
9	ITA	CHECCHI Valerio	1:47:16.6	+2:11.2
		DI CENTA Giorgio		
		PILLER COTTRER Pietro		
		ZORZI Cristian		
10	SUI	LIVERS Toni	1:47:57.2	`+2:51.8
		PERL Curdin		
		FISCHER Remo		
		COLOGNA Dario		
13	USA	NEWELL Andy	1:51:27.7	+6:22.3
		KOOS Torin		
		KUZZY Garrott		
		HAMILTON Simi		

CROSS-COUNTRY SKIING (cont'd)

Ladies' 10km Free

Feb 15 | Final | 78 Athletes: 1 DSQ

#	CTRY	ATHLETE	TIME	DIFFERENCE
1	SWE	KALLA Charlotte	24:58.4	0.0
2	EST	SMIGUN-VAEHI Kristina	25:05.0	+6.6
3	NOR	BJOERGEN Marit	25:14.3	+15.9
4	SWE	HAAG Anna	25:19.3	+20.9
5	POL	KOWALCZYK Justyna	25:20.1	+21.7
6	FIN	ROPONEN Riitta-Liisa	25:24.3	+25.9
7	RUS	MEDVEDEVA Evgenia	25:26.5	+28.1
8	NOR	STEIRA Kristin Stoermer	25:50.5	+52.1
9	UKR	SHEVCHENKO Valentina	25:51.1	+52.7
10	KAZ	MALAHOVA-SHISHKINA Svetlana	25:53.9	+55.5
30	USA	COMPTON Caitlin	26:49.1	+1:50.7
34	USA	ARRITOLA Morgan	27:04.4	+2:06.0
41	USA	BROOKS Holly	27:17.6	+2:19.2
49	USA	STEPHEN Elizabeth	27:41.1	+2:42.7

Ladies' Individual Sprint Classic

Feb 17 | Qualifications | 54 Athletes
Feb 17 | Final | 6 Athletes

#	CTRY	ATHLETE	TIME	DIFFERENCE
1	NOR	BJOERGEN Marit	3:39.2	
2	POL	KOWALCZYK Justyna		+1.1
3	SLO	MAJDIC Petra		+1.8
4	SWE	OLSSON Anna		+2.5
5	ITA	GENUIN Magda		+9.9
6	NOR	BRUN-LIE Celine		+12.3
7	NOR	JACOBSEN Astrid Uhrenholdt		
8	USA	RANDALL Kikkan		
9	FIN	KUITUNEN Virpi		
10	SWE	PAJALA Magdalena		
38	USA	BROOKS Holly		

Ladies' 15km Pursuit (7.5 Classic + 7.5 Free)

Feb 15 | Final | 66 Athletes: 2 DNS; 4 DNF; 1 DSQ

#	CTRY	ATHLETE	TIME	DIFFERENCE
1	NOR	BJOERGEN Marit	39:58.1	0.0
2	SWE	HAAG Anna	40:07.0	+8.9
3	POL	KOWALCZYK Justyna	40:07.4	+9.3
4	NOR	STEIRA Kristin Stoermer	40:07.5	+9.4
5	FIN	SAARINEN Aino-Kaisa	40:40.6	+42.5
6	NOR	JOHAUG Therese	40:50.0	+51.9
7	ITA	LONGA Marianna	41:02.2	+1:04.1
8	SWE	KALLA Charlotte	41:18.5	+1:20.4
9	ITA	FOLLIS Arianna	41:21.6	+1:23.5
10	CAN	RENNER Sara	41:37.9	+1:39.8
37	USA	ARRITOLA Morgan	43:25.9	+3:27.8
42	USA	COMPTON Caitlin	44:23.3	+4:25.2
55	USA	BROOKS Holly	45:38.8	+5:40.7
57	USA	STEPHEN Elizabeth	45:53.8	+5:55.7

Ladies' 30km Mass Start Classic

Feb 27 | Final | 55 Athletes: 2 DNS; 5 DNF; 1 DSQ

#	CTRY	ATHLETE	TIME	DIFFERENCE
1	POL	KOWALCZYK Justyna	1:30:33.7	0.0
2	NOR	BJOERGEN Marit	1:30:34.0	+0.3
3	FIN	SAARINEN Aino-Kaisa	1:31:38.7	+1:05.0
4	GER	SACHENBACHER-STEHLE Evi	1:31:52.9	+1:19.2
5	JPN	ISHIDA Masako	1:31:56.5	+1:22.8
6	SWE	KALLA Charlotte	1:31:57.6	+1:23.9
7	NOR	JOHAUG Therese	1:32:01.3	+1:27.6
8	NOR	STEIRA Kristin Stoermer	1:32:04.4	+1:30.7
9	SWE	OLSSON Anna	1:33:00.3	+2:26.6
10	FRA	LAURENT PHILIPPOT Karine	1:33:11.4	+2:37.7
23	USA	RANDALL Kikkan	1:34:59.0	+4:25.3
35	USA	BROOKS Holly	1:38:14.5	+7:40.8
—	USA	ARRITOLA Morgan	DNF	

CROSS-COUNTRY SKIING (cont'd)

Ladies' Team Sprint Free
Feb 22 | Semifinals | 18 Teams: 1 DSQ (Poland)
Feb 22 | Final | 10 Teams

#	CTRY	ATHLETES	TIME	DIFFERENCE
1	GER	SACHENBACHER-STEHLE Evi NYSTAD Claudia	18:03.7	0.0
2	SWE	KALLA Charlotte HAAG Anna	18:04.3	+0.6
3	RUS	KHAZOVA Irina KOROSTELEVA Natalia	18:07.7	+4.0
4	ITA	GENUIN Magda FOLLIS Arianna	18:14.2	+10.5
5	NOR	JACOBSEN Astrid Uhrenholdt BRUN-LIE Celine	18:32.8	+29.1
6	USA	COMPTON Caitlin RANDALL Kikkan	18:51.6	+47.9
7	CAN	GAIAZOVA Daria RENNER Sara	18:51.8	+48.1
8	FIN	ROPONEN Riitta-Liisa SARASOJA Riikka	18:56.6	+52.9
9	FRA	LAURENT PHILIPPOT Karine BARTHELEMY Laure	19:04.2	+1:00.5
10	SLO	VISNAR Katja FABJAN Vesna		

Ladies' 4x5km Relay
Feb 25 | Final |16 Teams: 1 DSQ (Poland)
1: Classic; 2: Classic; 3: Freestyle; 4: Freestyle

#	CTRY	ATHLETES	TIME	DIFFERENCE
1	NOR	SKOFTERUD Vibeke JOHAUG Therese STEIRA Kristin Stoermer BJOERGEN Marit	55:19.5	0.0
2	GER	ZELLER Katrin SACHENBACHER-STEHLE Evi GOSSNER Miriam NYSTAD Claudia	55:44.1	+24.6
3	FIN	MURANEN Pirjo KUITUNEN Virpi ROPONEN Riitta-Liisa SAARINEN Aino-Kaisa	55:49.9	+30.4
4	ITA	FOLLIS Arianna LONGA Marianna RUPIL Silvia VALBUSA Sabina	56:04.9	+45.4
5	SWE	OLSSON Anna PAJALA Magdalena KALLA Charlotte INGEMARSDOTTER Ida	56:18.9	+59.4
6	FRA	CUINET Aurore LAURENT PHILIPPOT Karine BOURGEOIS Celia STORTI Cecile	56:30.6	+1:11.1
7	RUS	SAVIALOVA Olga KHAZOVA Irina MEDVEDEVA Evgenia KOROSTELEVA Natalia	57:00.9	+1:41.4
8	JPN	NATSUMI Madoka ISHIDA Masako FUKUDA Nobuko KASHIWABARA Michiko	57:40.4	+2:20.9
9	KAZ	KOLOMINA Elena JATSKAJA Oxana ROSHINA Tatjana MALAHOVA-SHISHKINA Svetlana	58:23.3	+3:03.8
10	BLR	SANNIKOVA Alena VASILJONOK Olga RUDAKOVA Ekaterina DUBAREZAVA Nastassia	58:28.4	+3:08.9
11	USA	RANDALL Kikkan BROOKS Holly ARRITOLA Morgan COMPTON Caitlin	58:57.5	+3:38.0

CURLING

Men's
Feb 16-27 | Round Robin | 10 Teams

#	CTRY	RECORD	FINAL	USA SCORES		
1	CAN	9 - 0	1st: 6-3	GER - USA	7-5	
2	NOR	7 - 2		NOR - USA	6-5	Extra End
3	SUI	6 - 3	3rd: 5-4	SUI - USA	7-6	Extra End
4	GBR	5 - 4		DEN - USA	7-6	Extra End
5	SWE	5 - 4		USA - FRA	4-3	
6	GER	4 - 5		USA - SWE	8-7	Extra End
7	FRA	3 - 6		GBR - USA	4-2	
8	CHN	2 - 7		CAN - USA	7-2	
9	DEN	2 - 7		CHN - USA	11-5	
10	USA	2 - 7				

USA TEAM: SHUSTER John (Skip) | SMITH Jason (Vice-Skip) | ISAACSON Jeff (Second) | BENTON John (Lead) | PLYS Chris (Alternate)

Women's
Feb 16-26 | Round Robin | 10 Teams

#	CTRY	RECORD	FINAL	USA SCORES		
1	SWE	7 - 2	1st: 7-6	JPN - USA	9-7	
2	CAN	8 - 1		GER - USA	6-5	
3	CHN	6 - 3	3rd: 12-6	DEN - USA	7-6	
4	SUI	6 - 3		USA - RUS	6-4	
5	DEN	4 - 5		USA - GBR	6-5	Extra End
6	GER	3 - 6		CAN - USA	9-2	
7	GBR	3 - 6		SWE - USA	9-3	
8	JPN	3 - 6		CHN - USA	6-5	
9	RUS	3 - 6		SUI - USA	10-3	
10	USA	2 - 7				

USA TEAM: McCORMICK Debbie (Skip) | POTTINGER Allison (Vice-Skip) | JORAANSTAD Nicole (Second) | NICHOLSON Natalie (Lead) | | SACHTJEN Tracy (Alternate)

FIGURE SKATING

Men's Singles
Feb 16 | Short Program | 30 Athletes
Feb 18 | Free Skating (Music shown) | 24 Athletes

#	CTRY	ATHLETE	SHORT	FREE	TOTAL
1	USA	LYSACEK Evan Music: *Scheherazade* by N. Rimsky-Korsakov	90.30	167.37	257.67
2	RUS	PLUSHENKO Evgeni Music: *Tango Amore* by E. Marton	90.85	165.51	256.36
3	JPN	TAKAHASHI Daisuke Music: *La Strada* by N. Rota	90.25	156.9	247.23
4	SUI	LAMBIEL Stephane Music: *La Traviata* by G. Verdi	84.63	162.09	246.72
5	CAN	CHAN Patrick Music: *Phantom of the Opera*	81.12	160.30	241.42
6	USA	WEIR Johnny Music: *Fallen Angels*	82.10	156.77	238.87
7	JPN	ODA Nobunari Music: *Charlie Chaplin Medley*	84.85	153.69	238.54
8	JPM	KOZUKA Takahiko Music: *Guitar Concerto* by M. Kamen	79.59	151.60	231.19
9	USA	ABBOTT Jeremy Music: *Symphony No. 3* by C. Saint-Seans	69.40	149.56	218.96
10	CZE	BREZINA Michal Music: *An American in Paris* by G. Gershwin	78.80	137.93	216.73

Ladies Singles
Feb 23 | Short Program | 30 Athletes
Feb 24 | Free Skating (Music shown) | 24 Athletes

#	CTRY	ATHLETE	SHORT	FREE	TOTAL
1	KOR	KIM Yu-Na Music: *Concerto in F* by G. Gershwin	78.50	150.06	228.56
2	JPN	ASADA Mao Music: *Bells of Moscow* by S. Rachmaninoff	73.78	131.72	205.50
3	CAN	ROCHETTE Joannie Music: *Samson and Delilah* by C. St. Saens	71.36	131.28	202.64
4	USA	NAGASU Mirai Music: *Carmen* Selection	63.76	126.39	190.15
5	JPN	ANDO Miki Music: *Cleopatra*	64.76	124.10	188.86
6	FIN	LEPISTO Laura Music: *Adios Nonino, Fuga y Misterio*	61.36	126.61	187.97
7	USA	FLATT Rachael Music: *Rhapsody on a Theme of Paganini* by S. Rachmaninov	64.64	117.85	182.49
8	JPN	SUZUKI Akiko Music: *West Side Story* by L. Bernstein	61.02	120.42	181.44
9	RUS	LEONOVA Alena Music: *Chicago* (soundtrack)	62.14	110.32	172.46
10	RUS	MAKAROVA Ksenia Music: *13th Warrior* by J. Goldsmith	59.22	112.69	171.91

FIGURE SKATING (cont'd)

Pairs
Feb 13 | Short Program | 20 Athletes
Feb 14 | Free Skating (Music shown) | 20 Athletes

#	CTRY	ATHLETES	SHORT	FREE	TOTAL
1	CHN	SHEN Xue ZHAO Hongbo Music: *Adagio in G Minor* by T. Albinoni	76.66	139.91	216.57
2	CHN	PANG Qing TONG Jian Music: *Impossible Dream* by J. Hisaishi	71.50	141.81	213.31
3	GER	SAVCHENKO Aliona SZOLKOWY Robin Music: *Out of Africa* by J. Barry	75.96	134.64	210.60
4	RUS	KAVAGUTI Yuko SMIRNOV Alexander Music: *Valse Sentimentale, On the Blue Danube*	74.16	120.61	194.77
5	CHN	ZHANG Dan ZHANG Hao Music: *Scheherazade* by N. Rimsky-Korsakov	71.28	123.06	194.34
6	CAN	DUBE Jessica DAVISON Bryce Music: *The Way We Were* by M. Hamlisch	65.36	121.75	187.11
7	RUS	MUKHORTOVA Maria TRANKOV Maxim Music: *Love Story* by F. Lai	63.44	122.35	185.79
8	UKR	VOLOSOZHAR Tatiana MOROZOV Stanislav Music: *Pearl Harbour* by H. Zimmer	62.14	119.64	181.78
9	CAN	LANGLOIS Anabelle HAY Cody Music: *Grand Canyon Suite*	64.20	115.77	179.97
10	USA	EVORA Amanda LADWIG Mark Music: *Piano Concerto No. 2* by S. Rachmaninoff	57.86	114.06	171.92
13	USA	DENNEY Caydee BARRETT Jeremy Music: *Scheherazade* by N. Rimsky-Korsakov	53.26	105.07	158.33

Ice Dance
Feb 19 | Compulsory Dance | 23 Teams
Feb 20 | Original Dance | 23 Teams
Feb 21 | Free Dance (Music shown) | 23 Teams

#	CTRY	ATHLETES	COMP+ORIG	FREE	TOTAL
1	CAN	VIRTUE Tessa MOIR Scott Music: *Symphony No 5* by G. Mahler	111.15	110.42	221.57
2	USA	DAVIS Meryl WHITE Charlie Music: *The Phantom of the Opera* by Andrew Lloyd Webber	108.55	107.19	215.74
3	RUS	DOMNINA Oksana SHABALIN Maxim Music: *The Double Life of Veronique*	106.60	101.04	207.64
4	USA	BELBIN Tanith AGOSTO Ben Music: *Ave Maria* by Giuilo Caccini, performed by Sumi Jo and *Amen* from Gioachino Rossini's *Stabat Mater*	103.33	99.74	203.07
5	ITA	FAIELLA Federica SCALI Massimo Music: *The Emigrants* by N. Rota	100.06	99.11	199.17
6	FRA	DELOBEL Isabelle SCHOENFELDER Olivier Music: *La Quete* by J. Brel	96.67	97.06	193.73
7	FRA	PECHALAT Nathalie BOURZAT Fabian Music: *Kika, Requiem for a Dream*	96.12	94.37	190.49
8	GBR	KERR Sinead KERR John Music: *Krwlng* by Linkin Park	93.78	92.23	186.01
9	RUS	KHOKHLOVA Jana NOVITSKI Sergei Music: *Firebird* by I. Stravinski	92.75	93.11	185.86
10	ISR	ZARETSKY Alexandra ZARETSKY Roman Music: *Schindler's List* by J. Williams	89.62	90.64	180.26
11	USA	SAMUELSON Emily BATES Evan Music: *Canto Della Terra* by Sarah Brightman and Andrea Bocelli	85.36	88.94	174.30

FREESTYLE SKIING

Men's Aerials

Feb 22 | Qualifications | 25 Athletes: 1 DNS
Feb 25 | Final | 12 Athletes

#	CTRY	ATHLETE	JUMP 1	JUMP 2	TOTAL
1	BLR	GRISHIN Alexei	120.58	127.83	248.41
2	USA	PETERSON Jeret	118.59	128.62	247.21
3	CHN	LIU Zhongqing	119.91	122.62	242.53
4	USA	ST. ONGE Ryan	115.27	124.66	239.93
5	CAN	NISSEN Kyle	126.92	112.39	239.31
6	CHN	JIA Zongyang	119.47	118.10	237.57
7	CHN	QI Guangpu	115.38	119.47	234.85
8	CAN	OMISCHL Steve	112.39	121.27	233.66
9	BLR	SLIVETS Timofei	115.84	109.74	225.58
10	CAN	SHOULDICE Warren	94.03	129.27	223.30
17	USA	DEPETERS Matthew	Elim. in qualifications		
23	USA	BAHRKE Scotty	Elim. in qualifications		

Men's Moguls

Feb 14 | Qualifications | 30 Athletes
Feb 14 | Final | 20 Athletes

#	CTRY	ATHLETE	TURNS	AIR	TIME	TOTAL
1	CAN	BILODEAU Alexandre	14.1	5.44	7.21	26.75
2	AUS	BEGG-SMITH Dale	14.2	5.43	6.95	26.58
3	USA	WILSON Bryon	13.8	5.46	6.82	26.08
4	CAN	MARQUIS Vincent	13.6	5.04	7.24	25.88
5	CAN	ROUSSEAU Pierre-Alexandre	13.9	5.05	6.88	25.83
6	FRA	COLAS Guilbaut	13.9	4.51	7.33	25.74
7	JPN	ENDO Sho	13.1	5.24	7.04	25.38
8	SWE	BJOERNLUND Jesper	13.5	4.95	6.67	25.12
9	JPN	NISHI Nobuyuki	13.4	4.85	6.86	25.11
10	RUS	SMYSHLYAEV Alexandr	13.2	4.24	6.94	24.38
15	USA	MORSE Michael	12.3	4.47	6.61	23.38
19	USA	DENEEN Patrick	Received no score in finals			
19	USA	ROBERTS Nathan	Received no score in finals			

Men's Ski Cross

Feb 14 | Qualifications | 33 Athletes: 1 DNF
Feb 14 | Final | 4 Athletes

#	CTRY	ATHLETE		
1	SUI	SCHMID Michael		
2	AUT	MATT Andreas		
3	NOR	GROENVOLD Audun		
4	CAN	DELBOSCO Christopher		
5	FRA	GAVAGGIO Enak		
6	CAN	BARR Davey		
7	AUS	KNELLER Scott		
8	SLO	FLISAR Filip		
9	JAM	KERR Errol		
10	CAN	HAYER Stanley		
23	USA	PUCKETT Casey	Elim. finals, 1st round	
28	USA	RAHLVES Daron	Elim. finals, 1st round	

Ladies' Aerials

Feb 20 | Qualifications | 23 Athletes
Feb 24 | Final | 12 Athletes

#	CTRY	ATHLETE	JUMP 1	JUMP 2	TOTAL
1	AUS	LASSILA Lydia	106.25	108.49	214.74
2	CHN	LI Nina	99.40	107.83	207.23
3	CHN	GUO Xinxin	98.82	106.40	205.22
4	BLR	SLIVETS Assoli	102.79	95.90	198.69
5	AUS	COOPER Jacqui	90.82	103.47	194.29
6	CHN	XU Mengtao	108.7	82.87	191.61
7	CHN	CHENG Shuang	94.64	93.23	187.87
8	BLR	TSUPER Alla	86.64	95.20	181.84
9	USA	SCHNOOR Lacy	89.88	83.01	172.89
10	USA	CALDWELL Ashley	86.53	84.57	171.10
11	USA	COOK Emily	65.03	83.89	148.92
17	USA	LINDSEY Jana	Elim. in qualifications		

FREESTYLE SKIING (cont'd)

Ladies' Moguls

Feb 13 | Qualifications | 27 Athletes
Feb 13 | Finals | 20 Athletes

#	CTRY	ATHLETE	TURNS	AIR	TIME	TOTAL
1	USA	KEARNEY Hannah	14.2	5.40	7.03	26.63
2	CAN	HEIL Jennifer	13.7	4.98	7.01	25.69
3	USA	BAHRKE Shannon	13.5	4.92	7.01	25.43
4	JPN	UEMURA Aiko	12.9	5.16	6.62	24.68
5	CAN	DUFOUR-LAPOINTE Chloe	12.7	4.93	6.24	23.87
6	AUT	MARBLER Margarita	13.0	4.32	6.37	23.69
7	RUS	STOLYAROVA Ekaterina	12.7	5.04	5.81	23.55
8	JPN	MURATA Arisa	12.5	4.56	6.16	23.22
9	RUS	RAKHIMOVA Regina	11.9	4.92	5.88	22.70
10	ITA	SCANZIO Deborah	11.8	4.32	6.07	22.19
17	USA	ROARK Michelle	5.9	4.71	5.29	15.90
18	USA	McPHIE Heather	4.8	3.90	5.82	14.52

Ladies' Ski Cross

Feb 23 | Finals | 4 Athletes
Feb 23 | Qualifications | 35 Athletes

#	CTRY	ATHLETE
1	CAN	McIVOR Ashleigh
2	NOR	BERNTSEN Hedda
3	FRA	JOSSERAND Marion
4	AUT	HUTTARY Karin
5	CAN	SERWA Kelsey
6	SWE	HOLMLUND Anna
7	SUI	SMITH Fanny
8	NOR	BRENDENGEN JENSEN Julie
9	FRA	DAVID Ophelie
10	SWE	ILJANS Magdalena

No USA athlete competed.

ICE HOCKEY

Men's

Feb 16-28 | 30 Games | 12 Teams

#	CTRY	WIN - OT WIN - OT LOSS - LOSS	SCORE
1	CAN	4 - 2 - 0 - 1	1st: 3-2 OT
2	USA	5 - 0 - 1 - 0	
3	FIN	4 - 0 - 0 - 2	3rd: 5-3
4	SVK	3 - 1 - 0 - 3	

USA Scores: Game 1 vs SUI: 3-1 | Game 2 vs NOR: 6-1 | Game 3 vs CAN: 5-3 | Game 4 vs SUI: 2-0 (Quarterfinals) | Game 5 vs FIN: 6-1 (Semifinals) | Game 6 vs CAN: 2-3 OT (Final)

Forwards: PARISE Zach (#9) | MALONE Ryan (#12) | LANGENBRUNNER Jamie (#15) | PAVELSKI Joe (#16) | KESLER Ryan (#17) | DRURY Chris (#23) | CALLAHAN Ryan (#24) | STASTNY Paul (#26) | BROWN Dustin (#32) | BACKES David (#42) | RYAN Bobby (#54) | KESSEL Phil (#81) | KANE Patrick (#88)

Defense: JOHNSON Jack (#3) | GLEASON Tim (#4) | JOHNSON Erik (#6) | WHITNEY Ryan (#19) | SUTER Ryan (#20) | RAFALSKI Brian (#28) | ORPIK Brooks (#44)

Goaltenders: QUICK Jonathan (#29) | THOMAS Tim (#30) | MILLER Ryan (#39)

Women's

Feb 13-25 | 20 Games | 8 Teams

#	CTRY	WIN - OT WIN - OT LOSS - LOSS	SCORE
1	CAN	5 - 0 - 0 - 0	1st: 2-0
2	USA	4 - 0 - 0 - 1	
3	FIN	2 - 1 - 0 - 2	3rd: 3-2 OT
4	SWE	2 - 0 - 1 - 2	

USA Scores: Game 1 vs CHN: 12-1 | Game 2 vs RUS: 13-0 Game 3 vs FIN: 6-0 | Game 4 vs SWE: 9-1 (Semifinals) Game 5 vs CAN: 0-2 (Final)

Forwards: LAWLER Erika (#2) | THATCHER Karen (#5) | LAMOUREUX Monique (#7) | DUGGAN Meghan (#10) | POTTER Jenny (#12) | CHU Julie (#13) | STACK Kelli (#16) | LAMOUREUX Jocelyne (#17) | MARVIN Gigi (#19) | DARWITZ Natalie (#20) | KNIGHT Hilary (#21) | ZAUGG-SIERGIEJ Jinelle (#27)

Defense: RUGGIERO Angela (#4) | CAHOW Caitlin (#8) | ENGSTROM Molly (#9) | CHESSON Lisa (#11) | BELLAMY Kacey (#22) | WEILAND Kerry (#23)

Goaltenders: SCHAUS Molly (#1) | McLAUGHLIN Brianne (#29) | VETTER Jessie (#31)

LUGE

Men's Singles

Feb 13 | Heat 1 | 39 Athletes: 1 DNS
Feb 13 | Heat 2 | 38 Athletes
Feb 14 | Heat 3 | 38 Athletes
Feb 14 | Heat 4 | 38 Athletes

#	CTRY	ATHLETE	HEAT 1 2 3 4 TOTAL		
1	GER	LOCH Felix	48.168	48.402	48.344
			48.171	3:13.085	
2	GER	MOELLER David	48.341	48.511	48.582
			48.330	3:13.764	
3	ITA	ZOEGGELER Armin	48.473	48.529	48.914
			48.459	3:14.375	
4	RUS	DEMTSCHENKO Albert	48.590	48.579	48.769
			48.467	3:14.405	
5	GER	LANGENHAN Andi	48.629	48.658	48.869
			48.473	3:14.629	
6	AUT	PFISTER Daniel	48.583	48.707	48.883
			48.553	3:14.726	
7	CAN	EDNEY Samuel	48.754	48.793	48.920
			48.373	3:14.840	
8	USA	BENSHOOF Tony	48.657	48.747	49.010
			48.714	3:15.128	
9	AUT	KINDL Wolfgang	48.707	48.755	49.080
			48.673	3:15.215	
10	AUT	PFISTER Manuel	48.677	48.835	49.064
			48.693	3:15.269	
13	USA	MAZDZER Chris	48.811	48.963	49.223
			48.816	3:15.813	
15	USA	WALDEN Bengt	49.002	48.865	49.323
			48.794	3:15.984	

Doubles

Feb 16 | Heat 1 | 20 Teams
Feb 17 | Heat 2 | 20 Teams

#	CTRY	ATHLETES	HEAT 1 2 TOTAL	
1	AUT1	LINGER Wolfgang LINGER Andreas	41.332 41.332	41.373 1:22.705
2	LAT1	SICS Andris SICS Juris	41.420	41.549 1:22.969
3	GER1	LEITNER Patric RESCH Alexander	41.566	41.474 1:23.040
4	ITA2	OBERSTOLZ Christian GRUBER Patrick	41.527	41.585 1:23.112
5	GER2	FLORSCHUETZ Andre WUSTLICH Torsten	41.545	41.645 1:23.190
6	USA1	JOYE Dan NICCUM Christian	41.602	41.689 1:23.291
7	CAN1	MOFFAT Chris MOFFAT Mike	41.675	41.723 1:23.398
8	AUT2	SCHIEGL Markus SCHIEGL Tobias	41.727	41.801 1:23.528
9	ITA1	HASELRIEDER Oswald PLANKENSTEINER Gerhard	41.789	41.860 1:23.649
10	RUS1	MACHNUTIN Vladimir JUZHAKOV Vladislav	41.798	41.948 1:23.746
13	USA2	GRIMMETTE Mark MARTIN Brian	41.821	42.184 1:24.005

Women's Singles

Feb 15 | Heat 1 | 29 Athletes: 1 DSQ
Feb 14 | Heat 2 | 28 Athletes: 1 DNF
Feb 16 | Heat 3 | 27 Athletes
Feb 16 | Heat 4 | 27 Athletes

#	CTRY	ATHLETE	HEAT 1 2 3 4 TOTAL		
1	GER	HUEFNER Tatjana	41.760	41.481	41.666
			41.617	2:46.524	
2	AUT	REITHMAYER Nina	41.728	41.563	41.884
			41.839	2:47.014	
3	GER	GEISENBERGER Natalie	41.743	41.657	41.800
			41.901	2:47.101	
4	RUS	IVANOVA Tatiana	41.816	41.601	41.914
			41.850	2:47.181	
5	GER	WISCHNEWSKI Anke	41.785	41.685	41.894
			41.889	2:47.253	
6	RUS	RODIONOVA Alexandra	41.828	41.731	41.984
			41.913	2:47.456	
7	SUI	KOCHER Martina	42.005	41.697	41.976
			41.897	2:47.575	
8	POL	STASZULONEK Ewelina	41.975	41.816	41.948
			41.882	2:47.621	
9	LAT	TIRUMA Maija	41.773	41.933	42.012
			41.936	2:47.654	
10	RUS	KHOREVA Natalia	41.932	41.785	42.175
			42.092	2:47.984	
16	USA	HAMLIN Erin	41.835	42.219	42.792
			42.262	2:49.108	
17	USA	CLUKEY Julia	42.059	42.075	42.472
			42.754	2:49.360	
22	USA	SWEENEY Megan	42.450	42.690	42.625
			42.450	2:50.215	

NORDIC COMBINED

Individual Normal Hill / 10km
Feb 14 | Final | 45 Athletes

#	CTRY	ATHLETE	JUMP	START(+)	FINISH	DIFF
1	FRA	LAMY CHAPPUIS Jason	124.0	0:46	25:47.1	0.0
2	USA	SPILLANE Johnny	124.5	0:44	25:03.5	+0.4
3	ITA	PITTIN Alessandro	123.5	0:48	24:59.9	+0.8
4	USA	LODWICK Todd	127.0	0:34	25:14.6	+1.5
5	AUT	STECHER Mario	122.5	0:52	25:08.7	+13.6
6	USA	DEMONG Billy	115.5	1:20	24:45.0	+17.9
7	JPN	KOBAYASHI Norihito	121.0	0:58	25:11.0	+21.9
8	FIN	KOIVURANTA Anssi	122.0	0:54	25:22.9	+29.8
9	NOR	MOAN Magnus	104.0	2:06	24:16.7	+35.6
10	GER	FRENZEL Eric	119.0	1:06	25:17.2	+36.1
36	USA	CAMEROTA Brett	121.5	0:56	27:00.6	+2:09.5

Individual Large Hill / 10km
Feb 25 | Final | 45 Athletes: 1 DNS

#	CTRY	ATHLETE	JUMP	START(+)	FINISH	DIFF
1	USA	DEMONG Billy	115.5	0:46	25:32.9	0.0
2	USA	SPILLANE Johnny	118.5	0:34	25:02.9	+4.0
3	AUT	GRUBER Bernhard	127.0	0:00	25:43.7	+10.8
4	FIN	MANNINEN Hannu	107.7	11:17	24:49.0	+33.1
5	CZE	CHURAVY Pavel	114.0	0:52	25:14.9	+34.0
6	NOR	TANDE Petter L.	109.8	1:09	25:02.2	+38.3
7	ITA	PITTIN Alessandro	108.7	1:13	25:00.6	+40.7
8	AUT	STECHER Mario	109.8	1:09	25:12.1	+48.2
9	JPN	WATABE Akito	112.5	0:58	25:23.7	+48.8
10	AUT	BIELER Christoph	116.8	0:41	25:40.7	+48.8
13	USA	LODWICK Todd	108.7	1:13	25:30.2	+1:10.3
45	USA	FLETCHER Taylor	38.0	5:56	26:17.5	+6:40.6

Team Large Hill / 4x5km
Feb 23 | Final | 10 Teams

#	CTRY	ATHLETES	JUMP	START(+)	FINAL TIME	DIFF
1	AUT	GRUBER Bernhard / KREINER David GOTTWALD Felix / STECHER Mario	479.9	0:36	49:31.6	0.0
2	USA	CAMEROTA Brett / LODWICK Todd SPILLANE Johnny / DEMONG Billy	505.8	0:02	49:36.8	+5.2
3	GER	RYDZEK Johannes / EDELMANN Tino FRENZEL Eric / KIRCHEISEN Bjoern	473.3	0:45	49:51.1	+19.5
4	FRA	LAHEURTE Maxime / BRAUD Francois LACROIX Sebastien / LAMY CHAPPUIS Jason	474.7	0:43	50:11.4	+39.8
5	NOR	SCHMID Jan / RIAN Espen TANDE Petter L / MOAN Magnus H.	468.4	0:51	50:25.9	+54.3
6	JPN	KATO Taihei / TAKAHASHI Daito WATABE Akito / KOBAYASHI Norihito	475.9	0:41	50:45.8	+1:14.2
7	FIN	RYYNAENEN Janne / TALLUS Jaakko KOIVURANTA Anssi / MANNINEN Hannu	507.0	0:00	51:53.1	+2:21.5
8	CZE	VODSEDALEK Ales / DVORAK Miroslav SLAVIK Tomas / CHURAVY Pavel	457.3	1:06	52:50.2	+3:18.6
9	SUI	HURSCHLER Seppi / HUG Tim SCHMID Tommy / HEER Ronny	436.6	1:34	53:49.8	+4:18.2
10	ITA	PITTIN Alessandro / MICHIELLI Giuseppe RUNGGALDIER Lukas / BAUER Armin	402.6	2:19	54:14.5	+4:42.9

SHORT TRACK SPEEDSKATING

Men's 500m
Feb 24 | 8 Heats | 32 Athletes
Feb 26 | Final | 4 Athletes

#	CTRY	ATHLETE	TIME
1	CAN	HAMELIN Charles	40.981
2	KOR	SUNG Si-Bak	41.340
3	CAN	TREMBLAY Francois-Louis	46.366
8	USA	OHNO Apolo Anton	DSQ in final
—	USA	CHO Simon	Elim.in1/4 finals
—	USA	MALONE Jordan	Elim. in Heat 3

Men's 1000m
Feb 17 | 8 Heats | 32 Athletes
Feb 20 | Final | 5 Athletes

#	CTRY	ATHLETE	TIME	
1	KOR	LEE Jung-Su	1:23.747	OR
2	KOR	LEE Ho-Suk	1:23.801	
3	USA	OHNO Apolo Anton	1:24.128	
4	CAN	HAMELIN Charles	1:24.329	
5	CAN	HAMELIN Francois	1:25.206	
—	USA	CELSKI J.R.	DSQ in semis	
—	USA	JAYNER Travis	Elim. in Heat 4	

Men's 1500m
Feb 13 | 6 Heats | 36 Athletes
Feb 13 | Final | 7 Athletes

#	CTRY	ATHLETE	TIME
1	KOR	LEE Jung-Su	2:17.611
2	USA	OHNO Apolo Anton	2:17.976
3	USA	CELSKI J.R.	2:18.053
4	CAN	JEAN Olivier	2:18.806
5	KOR	SUNG Si-Bak	2:45.010
6	CHN	LIANG Wenhao	2:48.192
7	KOR	LEE Ho-Suk	DSQ
—	USA	MALONE Jordan	DSQ in Heat 2

Men's 5000m Relay
Feb 13 | 2 Heats | 8 Teams
Feb 26 | Final | 5 Teams

#	CTRY	ATHLETES	TIME
1	CAN	HAMELIN Charles HAMELIN Francois JEAN Olivier TREMBLAY Francois-Louis	6:44.224
2	KOR	KWAK Yoon-Gy LEE Ho-Suk LEE Jung-Su SUNG Si-Bak	6:44.446
3	USA	CELSKI J.R. JAYNER Travis MALONE Jordan OHNO Apolo Anton CHO Simon (raced in semifinals)	6:44.498
4	CHN	HAN Jialiang LIU Xianwei MA Yunfeng SONG Weilong	6:44.630
5	FRA	CHATAIGNIER Maxime FAUCONNET Thibaut MASSON Jeremy MATTEI Jean Charles	6:51.566

SHORT TRACK SPEEDSKATING (cont'd)

Ladies' 500m
Feb 13 | 8 Heats | 32 Athletes
Feb 17 | Final | 4 Athletes

#	CTRY	ATHLETE	TIME
1	CHN	WANG Meng	43.048
2	CAN	ST-GELAIS Marianne	43.707
3	ITA	FONTANA Arianna	43.804
4	CAN	GREGG Jessica	44.204
—	USA	REUTTER Katherine	3rd in Final B
—	USA	DUDEK Alyson	Elim in 1/4 finals

Ladies' 1000m
Feb 24 | 8 Heats | 32 Athletes
Feb 20 | Final | 5 Athletes

#	CTRY	ATHLETE	TIME
1	CHN	WANG Meng	1:29.213
2	USA	REUTTER Katherine	1:29.324
3	KOR	PARK Seung-Hi	1:29.379
—	CHN	ZHOU Yang	DSQ
—	USA	BAVER Allison	DSQ in Heat 1
—	USA	DERRICK Kimberly	Elim. in Heat 7

Ladies' 1500m
Feb 13 | 6 Heats | 36 Athletes
Feb 20 | Final | 8 Athletes

#	CTRY	ATHLETE	TIME	
1	CHN	ZHOU Yang	2:16.993	OR
2	KOR	LEE Eun-Byul	2:17.849	
3	KOR	PARK Seung-Hi	2:17.927	
4	USA	REUTTER Katherine	2:18.396	
5	KOR	CHO Ha-Ri	2:18.831	
6	HUN	HUSZAR Erika	2:19.251	
7	BUL	RADANOVA Evgenia	2:19.411	
8	CAN	VICENT Tania	2:23.035	
—	USA	DERRICK Kimberly	Elim. in Heat 1	
—	USA	BAVER Allison	Elim. in Semis	

Ladies' 3000m Relay
Feb 13 | 2 Heats | 8 Teams
Feb 24 | Final | 5 Teams

#	CTRY	ATHLETES	TIME	
1	CHN	SUN Linlin WANG Meng ZHANG Hui ZHOU Yang	4:06.610	WR
2	CAN	GREGG Jessica ROBERGE Kalyna ST-GELAIS Marianne VICENT Tania	4:09.137	
3	USA	BAVER Allison DUDEK Alyson GEHRING Lana REUTTER Katherine DERRICK, Kimberly (raced in semifinals)	4:14.081	
—	KOR	CHO Ha-Ri KIM Min-Jung LEE Eun-Byul PARK Seung-Hi	DSQ	

SKELETON

Men's

Feb 18 | Heat 1 | 28 Athletes
Feb 18 | Heat 2 | 28 Athletes
Feb 19 | Heat 3 | 28 Athletes: 1 DNS; 1 DSQ
Feb 19 | Heat 4 | 26 Athletes

#	CTRY	ATHLETE	HEAT 1 2 3 4 TOTAL		
1	CAN	MONTGOMERY Jon	52.60	52.57	52.20
			52.36	3:29.73	
2	LAT	DUKURS Martins	52.32	52.59	52.28
			52.61	3:29.80	
3	RUS	TRETYAKOV Alexander	52.70	53.05	52.30
			52.70	3:30.75	
4	LAT	DUKURS Tomass	52.94	52.88	52.62
			52.69	3:31.13	
5	USA	LUND Zach	53.04	52.85	52.57
			52.81	3:31.27	
6	GBR	BROMLEY Kristan	52.91	52.89	52.70
			52.80	3:31.30	
7	GER	ROMMEL Frank	52.90	53.25	52.55
			52.70	3:31.40	
8	AUT	GUGGENBERGER Matthias	52.75	53.02	53.03
			53.01	3:31.81	
9	CAN	PAIN Jeff	53.03	53.18	53.00
			52.65	3:31.86	
10	GER	STIELICKE Sandro	53.18	53.24	52.64
			53.02	3:32.08	
14	USA	BERNOTAS Eric	53.23	53.55	53.33
			53.16	3:33.27	
17	USA	DALY John	54.08	53.65	53.23
			53.05	3:34.01	

Women's

Feb 18 | Heat 1 | 20 Athletes: 1 DSQ
Feb 18 | Heat 2 | 19 Athletes
Feb 19 | Heat 3 | 19 Athletes
Feb 19 | Heat 4 | 19 Athletes

#	CTRY	ATHLETE	HEAT 1 2 3 4 TOTAL		
1	GBR	WILLIAMS Amy	53.83	54.13	53.68
			54.00	3:35.64	
2	GER	SZYMKOWIAK Kerstin	54.15	54.11	53.91
			54.03	3:36.20	
3	GER	HUBER Anja	54.17	54.21	54.10
			53.88	3:36.36	
4	USA	PIKUS-PACE Noelle	54.30	54.21	53.88
			54.07	3:36.46	
5	CAN	HOLLINGSWORTH Mellisa	54.18	54.17	53.81
			54.44	3:36.60	
6	GBR	RUDMAN Shelley	54.66	54.26	53.95
			53.82	3:36.69	
7	CAN	GOUGH Amy	54.14	54.78	53.92
			54.17	3:37.01	
8	GER	TROTT Marion	54.53	54.53	53.88
			54.17	3:37.11	
9	SUI	PEDERSEN Maya	54.53	54.83	54.24
			53.91	3:37.51	
10	AUS	LINCOLN-SMITH Emma	54.28	54.41	54.54
			54.40	3:37.63	
11	USA	UHLAENDER Katie	54.51	54.53	54.54
			54.35	3:37.93	

SKI JUMPING

Normal Hill Individual

Feb 12 | Qualifications | 61 Athletes: 1 DSQ; 9 DNQ
Feb 13 | Round 1 | 51 Athletes: 1 DSQ; 20 DNQ
Feb 13 | Final | 30 Athletes: 1 DNS

#	CTRY	ATHLETE	ROUND 1	JUMP	POINTS	TOTAL
1	SUI	AMMANN Simon	135.5	108.0	141.0	276.5
2	POL	MALYSZ Adam	132.5	105.0	137.0	269.5
3	AUT	SCHLIERENZAUER Gregor	128.0	106.5	140.0	268.0
4	FIN	AHONEN Janne	129.5	104.0	133.5	263.0
5	GER	UHRMANN Michael	133.0	102.0	129.5	262.5
6	SLO	KRANJEC Robert	129.0	102.5	130.5	259.5
7	SLO	PREVC Peter	124.0	104.5	135.0	259.0
8	AUT	MORGENSTERN Thomas	130.0	101.5	128.5	258.5
9	NOR	JACOBSEN Anders	123.5	104.0	133.5	257.0
10	GER	SCHMITT Martin	123.0	103.5	133.0	256.0
41	USA	FRENETTE Peter	Elim. Round 1			
41	USA	ALEXANDER Nick	Elim. Round 1			
49	USA	JOHNSON Anders	Elim. Round 1			

Large Hill Individual

Feb 19 | Qualifications | 61 Athletes: 11 DNQ
Feb 20 | Round 1 | 50 Athletes: 1 DSQ; 18 DNQ
Feb 20 | Final | 31 Athletes: 1 DNS

#	CTRY	ATHLETE	ROUND 1	JUMP	POINTS	TOTAL
1	SUI	AMMANN Simon	144.7	138.0	138.9	283.6
2	POL	MALYSZ Adam	138.1	133.5	131.3	269.4
3	AUT	SCHLIERENZAUER Gregor	125.4	136.0	136.8	262.2
4	AUT	KOFLER Andreas	127.2	135.0	134.0	261.2
5	AUT	MORGENSTERN Thomas	123.6	129.5	123.1	246.7
6	GER	NEUMAYER Michael	122.5	130.0	123.0	245.5
7	CZE	HAJEK Antonin	119.4	129.0	121.2	240.6
8	JPN	KASAI Noriaki	105.7	135.0	133.5	239.2
9	SLO	KRANJEC Robert	99.3	135.5	134.4	233.7
10	AUT	LOITZL Wolfgang	124.1	121.5	106.2	230.3
32	USA	FRENETTE Peter	Elim. Round 1			
40	USA	ALEXANDER Nick	Elim. Round 1			
—	USA	JOHNSON Anders	Elim. qualifications			

Team

Feb 22 | Round 1 | 12 Teams
Feb 22 | Final | 8 Teams

#	CTRY	ATHLETES	ROUND 1	FINAL	TOTAL
1	AUT	LOITZL Wolfgang KOFLER Andreas MORGENSTERN Thomas SCHLIERENZAUER Gregor	547.3	560.6	1107.9
2	GER	NEUMAYER Michael WANK Andreas SCHMITT Martin UHRMANN Michael	509.3	526.5	1035.8
3	NOR	BARDAL Anders HILDE Tom EVENSEN Johan Remen JACOBSEN Anders	504.0	526.3	1030.3
4	FIN	HAUTAMAEKI Matti HAPPONEN Janne KEITURI Kalle OLLI Harri	490.2	524.4	1014.6
5	JPN	ITO Daiki TAKEUCHI Taku TOCHIMOTO Shohei KASAI Noriaki	484.7	523.0	1007.7
6	POL	HULA Stefan RUTKOWSKI Lukasz STOCH Kamil MALYSZ Adam	484.0	512.7	996.7
7	CZE	HAJEK Antonin KOUDELKA Roman HLAVA Lukas JANDA Jakub	477.4	504.4	981.8
8	SLO	PIKL Primoz MEZNAR Mitja PREVC Peter KRANJEC Robert	472.2	486.6	958.8
11	USA	JOHNSON Anders FRENETTE Peter FLETCHER Taylor ALEXANDER Nick	Elim. Round 1		

SNOWBOARDING

Men's Snowboardcross

Feb 15 | Qualifications | 35 Athletes
Feb 15 | Final | 4 Athletes

#	CTRY	ATHLETE
1	USA	WESCOTT Seth
2	CAN	ROBERTSON Mike
3	FRA	RAMOIN Tony
4	USA	HOLLAND Nate
5	CAN	FAGAN Robert
6	AUT	GRUENER Lukas
7	AUT	FUCHS Mario
8	GER	SPEISER David
9	FRA	VAULTIER Pierre
10	AUS	HAYLER Damon
18	USA	WATANABE Graham
20	USA	BAUMGARTNER Nick

Men's Halfpipe

Feb 17 | Qualifications | 40 Athletes: 1 DNS
Feb 17 | Final | 12 Athletes

#	CTRY	ATHLETE	SCORE
1	USA	WHITE Shaun	48.4
2	FIN	PIIROINEN Peetu	45.0
3	USA	LAGO Scotty	42.8
4	SUI	PODLADTCHIKOV Iouri	42.4
5	USA	VITO Louie	39.4
6	FIN	KOSKI Markku	36.4
7	CAN	LAMOUREUX Justin	35.9
8	JPN	KOKUBO Kazuhiro	35.7
9	JPN	AONO Ryo	32.9
10	FRA	CREPEL Mathieu	25.9
12	USA	BRETZ Greg	18.3

Men's Parallel Giant Slalom

Feb 27 | Qualifications | 30 Athletes: 1 DNF; 1 DSQ
Feb 27 | Big Final | 2 Athletes

#	CTRY	ATHLETE
1	CAN	ANDERSON Jasey Jay
2	AUT	KARL Benjamin
3	FRA	BOZZETTO Mathieu
4	RUS	DETKOV Stanislav
5	SUI	SCHOCH Simon
6	SLO	KOSIR Zan
7	USA	KLUG Chris
8	SLO	FLANDER Rok
9	AUT	PROMMEGGER Andreas
10	FRA	DUFOUR Sylvain
13	USA	JEWELL Tyler

Ladies' Snowboardcross

Feb 16 | Qualifications | 24 Athletes
Feb 16 | Final | 4 Athletes

#	CTRY	ATHLETE
1	CAN	RICKER Maelle
2	FRA	ANTHONIOZ Deborah
3	SUI	NOBS Olivia
4	NOR	OLAFSEN Helene
5	USA	JACOBELLIS Lindsey
6	FRA	MOENNE LOCCOZ Nelly
7	SUI	FRANCON Mellie
8	GBR	GILLINGS Zoe
9	SUI	MEILER Simona
10	AUT	KRINGS Doresia
11	SUI	FREI Sandra
12	USA	GULINI Faye
21	USA	CHYTHLOOK-SIFSOF Callan

Ladies' Halfpipe

Feb 18 | Qualifications | 30 Athletes
Feb 18 | Final | 12 Athletes

#	CTRY	ATHLETE	SCORE
1	AUS	BRIGHT Torah	45.0
2	USA	TETER Hannah	42.4
3	USA	CLARK Kelly	42.2
4	CHN	LIU Jiayu	39.3
5	FRA	RODRIGUEZ Sophie	34.4
6	CAN	NICOLL Mercedes	34.3
7	CHN	SUN Zhifeng	33.0
8	AUS	CRAWFORD Holly	30.3
9	SUI	HALLER Ursina	27.9
10	USA	HIGHT Elena	24.6
11	USA	BLEILER Gretchen	14.7

SNOWBOARDING (cont'd)

Ladies' Parallel Giant Slalom
Feb 26 | Qualifications | 30 Athletes: 1 DNF; 1 DNF
Feb 26 | Big Final | 2 Athletes

#	CTRY	ATHLETE
1	NED	SAUERBREIJ Nicolien
2	RUS	ILYUKHINA Ekaterina
3	AUT	KREINER Marion
4	GER	JOERG Selina
5	GER	KARSTENS Anke
6	AUT	MESCHIK Ina
7	AUT	RIEGLER Claudia
8	GER	KOBER Amelie
9	AUT	GUENTHER Doris
10	RUS	TUDEGESHEVA Ekaterina
11	FRA	DE FAUCOMPRET Camille
14	USA	GORGONE Michelle

SPEEDSKATING

Men's 500m
Feb 15 | Race 1 | 39 Athletes
Feb 15 | Race 2 | 39 Athletes: 1 WD

#	CTRY	ATHLETE	RACE 1	RACE 2	TOTAL	DIFF
1	KOR	MO Tae-Bum	34.923	34.906	69.82	0.00
2	JPN	NAGASHIMA Keiichiro	35.108	34.876	69.98	+0.16
3	JPN	KATO Joji	34.937	35.076	70.01	+0.19
4	KOR	LEE Kang-Seok	35.053	34.988	70.041	+0.22
5	FIN	POUTALA Mika	34.863	35.181	70.044	+0.22
6	NED	SMEEKENS Jan	35.160	35.051	70.21	+0.39
7	CHN	YU Fengtong	35.116	35.120	70.23	+0.41
8	CAN	GREGG Jamie	35.142	35.126	70.26	+0.44
9	CAN	WOTHERSPOON Jeremy	35.094	35.188	70.282	+0.46
10	CHN	ZHANG Zhongqi	35.175	35.113	70.288	+0.46
12	USA	FREDRICKS Tucker	35.218	35.138	70.35	+0.53
26	USA	PEARSON Nick	35.834	36.094	71.92	+2.10
37	USA	WHITMORE Mitch	36.734	36.314	73.04	+3.22
—	USA	DAVIS Shani	35.454		WD	

Men's 1000m
Feb 17 | Final | 38 Athletes

#	CTRY	ATHLETE	TIME	DIFF
1	USA	DAVIS Shani	1:08.94	0.00
2	KOR	MO Tae-Bum	1:09.12	+0.18
3	USA	HEDRICK Chad	1:09.32	+0.38
4	NED	GROOTHUIS Stefan	1:09.45	+0.51
5	NED	TUITERT Mark	1:09.48	+0.54
6	NED	KUIPERS Simon	1:09.65	+0.71
7	USA	PEARSON Nick	1:09.79	+0.85
8	FIN	POUTALA Mika	1:09.85	+0.91
9	KOR	LEE Kyou-Hyuk	1:09.92	+0.98
10	USA	MARSICANO Trevor	1:10.11	+1.17

Men's 1500m
Feb 17 | Final | 37 Athletes

#	CTRY	ATHLETE	TIME	DIFF
1	NED	TUITERT Mark	1:45.57	0.00
2	USA	DAVIS Shani	1:46.10	+0.53
3	NOR	BOKKO Havard	1:46.13	+0.56
4	RUS	SKOBREV Ivan	1:18.64	+2.16
5	KOR	MO Tae-Bum	1:46.47	+0.90
6	USA	HEDRICK Chad	1:46.69	+1.12
7	NED	KUIPERS Simon	1:46.76	+1.19
8	NOR	LARSEN Mikael Flygind	1:46.77	+1.20
9	CAN	MORRISON Denny	1:17.34	+0.86
10	ITA	FABRIS Enrico	1:47.02	+1.45
15	USA	MARSICANO Trevor	1:47.84	+2.27
18	USA	HANSEN Brian	1:48.45	+2.88

Men's 5000m
Feb 23 | Final | 28 Athletes: 1 DSQ

#	CTRY	ATHLETE	TIME	DIFF
1	NED	KRAMER Sven	6:14.60 OR	0.00
2	KOR	LEE Seung-Hoon	6:16.95	+2.35
3	RUS	SKOBREV Ivan	6:18.05	+3.45
4	NOR	BOKKO Havard	6:18.80	+4.20
5	NED	de JONG Bob	6:19.02	+4.42
6	FRA	CONTIN Alexis	6:19.58	+4.98
7	ITA	FABRIS Enrico	6:20.53	+5.93
8	NOR	CHRISTIANSEN Henrik	6:24.80	+10.20
9	NED	BLOKHUIJSEN Jan	6:26.30	+11.70
10	NOR	HAUGLI Sverre	6:27.05	+12.45
11	USA	HEDRICK Chad	6:27.07	+12.47
12	USA	DAVIS Shani	6:28.44	+13.84
14	USA	MARSICANO Trevor	6:30.93	+16.33

SPEEDSKATING (cont'd)

Men's 10,000m
Feb 23 | Final | 15 Athletes: 1 DSQ

#	CTRY	ATHLETE	TIME	DIFF
1	KOR	LEE Seung-Hoon	12:58.55 OR	0.0
2	RUS	SKOBREV Ivan	13:02.07	+3.52
3	NED	de JONG Bob	13:06.73	+8.18
4	FRA	CONTIN Alexis	13:12.11	+13.56
5	NOR	BOKKO Havard	13:14.92	+16.37
6	NOR	HAUGLI Sverre	13:18.74	+20.19
7	NOR	CHRISTIANSEN Henrik	13:25.65	+27.10
8	USA	KUCK Jonathan	13:31.78	+33.23
9	NED	van de KIEFT Arjen	13:33.37	+34.82
10	GER	WEBER Marco	13:35.73	+37.18
12	USA	BEDFORD Ryan	13:40.20	+41.65

Men's Team Pursuit
Feb 26 | Quarterfinals | 8 Teams
Feb 27 | Final | 2 Teams

#	CTRY	ATHLETES	TIME
1	CAN	GIROUX Mathieu MAKOWSKY Lucas MORRISON Denny | ROBERGE Francois-Olivier	3:41.37
2	USA	HANSEN Brian HEDRICK Chad KUCK Jonathan | MARSICANO Trevor*	3:41.58
3	NED	BLOKHUIJSEN Jan KRAMER Sven TUITERT Mark | KUIPERS Simon	3:39.95
4	NOR	BOKKO Havard CHRISTIANSEN Henrik LARSEN Mikael Flygind | van der HORST Fredrik	3:40.50
5	KOR	HA Hong-Sun LEE Jong-Woo LEE Seung-Hoon | MO Tae-Bum	
6	ITA	ANESI Matteo FABRIS Enrico IORIATTI Ermanno | STEFANI Luca	
7	SWE	ERIKSSON Joel FRIBERG Daniel ROJLER Johan	
8	JPN	DEJIMA Shigeyuki DOI Shingo HIRAKO Hiroki | SUGIMORI Teruhiro	

GREY TYPE: Athlete did not race in final.
* Participated in semifinal race.

Ladies' 500m
Feb 16 | Race 1 | 36 Athletes
Feb 16 | Race 2 | 36 Athletes: 1 DSQ

#	CTRY	ATHLETE	RACE 1	RACE 2	TOTAL	DIFF
1	KOR	LEE Sang-Hwa	38.249	37.850	76.09	0.00
2	GER	WOLF Jenny	38.307	37.838	76.14	+0.05
3	CHN	WANG Beixing	38.487	38.144	76.63	+0.54
4	NED	BOER Margot	38.511	38.365	76.87	+0.78
5	JPN	YOSHII Sayuri	38.566	38.432	76.99	+0.90
6	USA	RICHARDSON Heather	38.698	38.477	77.17	+1.08
7	CHN	ZHANG Shuang	38.530	38.807	77.33	+1.24
8	CHN	JIN Peiyu	38.686	38.771	77.45	+1.36
9	DPR	KO Hyon-Suk	38.893	38.577	77.47	+1.38
10	CAN	NESBITT Christine	38.881	38.694	77.57	+1.48
17	USA	OCHOWICZ Elli	39.002	39.048	78.05	+1.96
21	USA	RODRIGUEZ Jennifer	39.182	39.281	78.46	+2.37
30	USA	CHOLEWINSKI Lauren	39.514	39.587	79.10	+3.01

Ladies' 1000m
Feb 17 | Final | 36 Athletes: 1 DNF

#	CTRY	ATHLETE	TIME	DIFF
1	CAN	NESBITT Christine	1:16.56	0.00
2	NED	GERRITSEN Annette	1:16.58	+0.02
3	NED	van RIESSEN Laurine	1:16.72	+0.16
4	CAN	GROVES Kristina	1:16.78	+0.22
5	JPN	KODAIRA Nao	1:16.80	+0.24
6	NED	BOER Margot	1:16.94	+0.38
7	USA	RODRIGUEZ Jennifer	1:17.08	+0.52
8	NED	WUST Ireen	1:17.28	+0.72
9	USA	RICHARDSON Heather	1:17.37	+0.81
10	NOR	BOKKO Hege	1:17.43	+0.87
26	USA	OCHOWICZ Elli	1:18.33	+1.77
29	USA	BRADFORD Rebekah	1:18.788	+2.22

SPEEDSKATING (cont'd)

Ladies' 1500m
Feb 21 | Final | 36 Athletes

#	CTRY	ATHLETE	TIME	DIFF
1	NED	WUST Ireen	1:56.89	0.00
2	CAN	GROVES Kristina	1:57.14	+0.25
3	CZE	SABLIKOVA Martina	1:57.96	+1.07
4	NED	BOER Margot	1:58.10	+1.21
5	JPN	KODAIRA Nao	1:58.20	+1.31
6	CAN	NESBITT Christine	1:58.33	+1.44
7	NED	GERRITSEN Annette	1:58.46	+1.57
8	RUS	SHIKHOVA Yekaterina	1:58.54	+1.65
9	GER	FRIESINGER-POSTMA Anna	1:58.67	+1.78
10	GER	ANSCHUTZ THOMS Daniela	1:58.85	+1.96
16	USA	RICHARDSON Heather	1:59.56	+2.67
18	USA	RODRIGUEZ Jennifer	2:00.08	+3.19
24	USA	ROOKARD Jilleanne	2:01.95	+5.06
31	USA	RANEY-NORMAN Catherine	2:03.02	+6.13

Ladies' 3000m
Feb 14 | Final | 28 Athletes

#	CTRY	ATHLETE	TIME	DIFF
1	CZE	SABLIKOVA Martina	4:02.53	0.00
2	GER	BECKERT Stephanie	4:04.62	+2.09
3	CAN	GROVES Kristina	4:04.84	+2.31
4	GER	ANSCHUTZ THOMS Daniela	4:04.87	+2.34
5	CAN	HUGHES Clara	4:06.01	+3.48
6	JPN	HOZUMI Masako	4:07.36	+4.83
7	NED	WUST Ireen	4:08.09	+5.56
8	NOR	HAUGLI Maren Lane	4:10.01	+7.48
9	USA	SWIDER-PELTZ JR. Nancy	4:11.16	+8.63
10	NED	GROENEWOLD Renate	4:11.25	+8.72
11	NED	VALKENBURG Diane	4:11.71	+9.18
12	USA	ROOKARD Jilleanne	4:13.05	+10.52
17	USA	RANEY-NORMAN Catherine	4:16.59	+14.06

Ladies' 5000m
Feb 24 | Final | 16 Athletes: 1 DSQ

#	CTRY	ATHLETE	TIME	DIFF
1	CZE	SABLIKOVA Martina	6:50.91	0.00
2	GER	BECKERT Stephanie	6:51.39	+0.48
3	CAN	HUGHES Clara	6:55.73	+4.82
4	GER	ANSCHUTZ THOMS Daniela	6:58.64	+7.73
5	NOR	HAUGLI Maren	7:02.19	+11.28
6	CAN	GROVES Kristina	7:04.57	+13.66
7	JPN	HOZUMI Masako	7:04.96	+14.05
8	USA	ROOKARD Jilleanne	7:07.48	+16.57
9	JPN	ISHIZAWA Shiho	7:12.23	+21.32
10	NED	VOORHUIS Jorien	7:13.27	+22.36
15	USA	LAMB Maria	7:25.15	+34.24

Ladies' Team Pursuit
Feb 26 | Quarterfinals | 8 Teams
Feb 27 | Final | 2 Teams

#	CTRY	ATHLETES	TIME
1	GER	ANSCHUTZ THOMS Daniela BECKERT Stephanie MATTSCHERODT Katrin FRIESINGER-POSTMA Anna	3:02.82
2	JPN	HOZUMI Masako KODAIRA Nao TABATA Maki | TAKAGI Miho	3:02.84
3	POL	BACHLEDA-CURUS Katarzyna WOZNIAK Katarzyna ZLOTKOWSKA Luiza | CZERWONKA Natalia	3:03.73
4	USA	RANEY-NORMAN Catherine RODRIGUEZ Jennifer ROOKARD Jilleanne | SWIDER-PELTZ JR. Nancy*	3:05.30
5	CAN	GROVES Kristina NESBITT Christine SCHUSSLER Brittany | KLASSEN Cindy	
6	NED	VALKENBURG Diane VOORHUIS Jorien WUST Ireen | GROENEWOLD Renate	
7	RUS	LOBYSHEVA Yekaterina SHABANOVA Alla SHIKHOVA Yekaterina | LIKHACHOVA Galina	
8	KOR	LEE Ju-Youn NOH Seon-Yeong PARK Do-Yeong	

GREY TYPE: Athlete did not race in final
* Participated in semifinal race.

Paralympic Winter Games Results

ALPINE SKIING

Men's Downhill—Sitting
Mar 18 | Final | 28 Athletes: 1 DNS; 8 DNF;1 DSQ

#	CTRY	ATHLETE	TIME
1	SUI	KUNZ Christoph	1:18.19
2	JPN	MORII Taiki	1:18.63
3	JPN	KANO Akira	1:19.19
4	GER	NOLTE Thomas	1:19.60
5	CAN	DUECK Josh	1:19.88
6	FRA	TABERLET Yohann	1:19.92
7	GBR	ROSE Sean	1:20.41
8	SUI	PLEISCH Hans	1:21.36
9	SRB	BAMBUR Jasmin	1:21.41
10	AUT	SAMPL Reinhold	1:21.88
13	USA	DEVLIN-YOUNG Christopher	1:22.65
—	USA	WALKER Tyler	DNF
—	USA	TOMPKINS Joseph	DNF

Men's Downhill—Standing
Mar 18 | Final | 28 Athletes: 3 DNF

#	CTRY	ATHLETE	TIME
1	GER	SCHONFELDER Gerd	1:20.80
2	SUI	BRUGGER Michael	1:22.78
2	AUS	MAYBERRY Marty	1:22.78
4	AUS	RAHLES-RAHBULA Cameron	1:22.88
5	FRA	GAUTHIER-MANUEL Vincent	1:23.24
6	AUT	MEUSBURGER Robert	1:23.70
7	AUT	MANDL Hubert	1:23.85
8	SUI	PFYL Thomas	1:24.17
9	ITA	LANTHALER Christian	1:25.01
10	AUS	KANE Toby	1:25.26
14	USA	WASHBURN Bradley	1:26.40
21	USA	SANSONETIS George	1:28.47
22	USA	MEIER Monte	1:28.48

Men's Downhill—Visually Impaired
Mar 18 | Final | 12 Athletes: 3 DNF;1 DSQ

#	CTRY	ATHLETE	TIME
1	ESP	ANTACANA MAIZTEGUI Jon	1:18.23
2	USA	BATHUM Mark	1:18.63
3	GER	GRADWOHL Gerd	1:20.40
4	SVK	KRAKO Jakub	1:20.84
5	FRA	BEREJNY Nicolas	1:20.96
6	AUT	PRETTNER Christoph	1:21.83
7	SVK	DUDAS Radomir	1:21.88
8	RUS	FRANTSEV Ivan	1:31.89

Men's Super G—Sitting
Mar 19 | Final | 40 Athletes: 1 DNS; 7 DNF; 3 DSQ

#	CTRY	ATHLETE	TIME
1	JPN	KANO Akira	1:19.98
2	GER	BRAXENTHALER Martin	1:20.63
3	JPN	MORII Taiki	1:20.98
4	USA	DEVLIN-YOUNG Christopher	1:21.00
5	JPN	SUZUKI Takeshi	1:22.28
6	AUT	FROHLE Robert	1:24.00
7	AUT	SAMPL Reinhold	1:24.05
8	USA	CALHOUN Heath	1:24.77
9	FRA	TABERLET Yohann	1:24.79
10	AUT	DORN Dietmar	1:24.94
22	USA	WALKER Tyler	1:29.28
—	USA	BURNETT Carl	DNF
—	USA	CATANZARITE Nicholas	DNF

Men's Super G—Standing
Mar 19 | Final | 40 Athletes: 5 DNF; 2 DSQ

#	CTRY	ATHLETE	TIME
1	GER	SCHONFELDER Gerd	1:20.11
2	FRA	GAUTHIER-MANUEL Vincent	1:21.24
3	AUT	MANDL Hubert	1:21.97
4	FRA	BRUN Lionel	1:22.42
5	AUS	RAHLES-RAHBULA Cameron	1:22.65
6	SUI	BRUGGER Michael	1:23.00
7	NZL	HALL Adam	1:23.34
8	AUT	SALCHER Markus	1:23.68
9	JPN	KOIKE Gakuta	1:25.29
10	AUS	GOURLEY Mitchell	1:25.38
17	USA	WASHBURN Bradley	1:27.93
27	USA	MEIER Monte	1:31.91
28	USA	WHITNEY John	1:32.97
31	USA	SANSONETIS George	1:35.74
—	USA	GREEN Ralph	DSQ

ALPINE SKIING (cont'd)

Men's Super G—Visually Impaired
Mar 19 | Final | 15 Athletes

#	CTRY	ATHLETE	TIME
1	FRA	BEREJNY Nicolas	1:21.55
2	SVK	KRAKO Jakub	1:21.71
3	SVK	HARAUS Miroslav	1:22.75
4	USA	BATHUM Mark	1:23.05
5	ESP	SANTACANA MAIZTEGUI Jon	1:23.21
6	CAN	WILLIAMSON Chris	1:23.74
7	ITA	DAL MAISTRO Gianmaria	1:24.84
8	SVK	DUDAS Radomir	1:25.76
9	AUT	PRETTNER Christoph	1:26.58
10	SVK	HOLIK Norbert	1:28.27

Men's Super Combined—Sitting
Mar 20 | Super G | 21 Athletes: 6 DNF
Mar 20 | Slalom | 15 Athletes: 1 DNF; 2 DSQ

#	CTRY	ATHLETE	TIME
1	GER	BRAXENTHALER Martin	2:10.16
2	AUT	EGLE Jurgen	2:12.80
3	AUT	BONADIMANN Philipp	2:12.96
4	JPN	MORII Taiki	2:13.99
5	JPN	SUZUKI Takeshi	2:15.90
6	FRA	MORE Cyril	2:16.39
7	USA	DEVLIN-YOUNG Christopher	2:16.71
8	KOR	HAN Sang-Min	2:16.79
9	FRA	TABERLET Yohann	2:17.62
10	USA	CALHOUN Heath	2:18.99
12	USA	BURNETT Carl	2:31.05

Men's Super Combined—Standing
Mar 20 | Super G | 21 Athletes: 3 DNF
Mar 20 | Slalom | 18 Athletes

#	CTRY	ATHLETE	TIME
1	GER	SCHONFELDER Gerd	2:11.84
2	FRA	GAUTHIER-MANUEL Vincent	2:12.04
3	AUS	RAHLES-RAHBULA Cameron	2:13.85
4	AUT	MEUSBURGER Robert	2:14.00
5	FRA	BRUN Lionel	2:15.34
6	JPN	MISAWA Hiraku	2:15.78
7	AUT	MANDL Hubert	2:16.92
8	NZL	HALL Adam	2:17.02
9	AUT	SALCHER Markus	2:19.72
10	SUI	PFYL Thomas	2:20.25
14	USA	MEIER Monte	2:24.20

Men's Super Combined—Visually Impaired
Mar 20 | Super G | 12 Athletes: 1 DNF
Mar 20 | Slalom | 11 Athletes: 2 DNF

#	CTRY	ATHLETE	TIME
1	SVK	KRAKO Jakub	2:14.61
2	ITA	DAL MAISTRO Gianmaria	2:16.18
3	SVK	HARAUS Miroslav	2:16.31
4	CAN	WILLIAMSON Chris	2:18.42
4	FRA	BEREJNY Nicolas	2:18.42
6	SVK	HOLIK Norbert	2:22.05
7	RUS	FRANTSEV Ivan	2:22.67
8	ESP	GORCE YEPES Gabriel	2:24.04
9	ESP	BOIRA DIAZ Andres	2:34.31
—	USA	BATHUM Mark	DNF

Men's Giant Slalom—Sitting
Mar 16 | Run 1 | 51 Athletes: 11 DNF; 3 DSQ
Mar 16 | Run 2 | 37 Athletes: 1 DNS; 5 DNF; 4 DSQ

#	CTRY	ATHLETE	TIME
1	GER	BRAXENTHALER Martin	2:37.40
2	SUI	KUNZ Christoph	2:40.35
3	JPN	SUZUKI Takeshi	2:45.61
4	FRA	MORE Cyril	2:46.85
5	AUT	EGLE Jurgen	2:48.57
6	AUS	DALLAS Shannon	2:49.52
7	JPN	MORII Taiki	2:49.54
8	AUT	FROHLE Robert	2:49.83
9	FRA	TABERLET Yohann	2:50.65
10	AUT	BONADIMANN Philipp	2:50.82
14	USA	BURNETT Carl	2:56.45
16	USA	WALKER Tyler	3:02.56
23	USA	CATANZARITE Nicholas	3:37.68
—	USA	DEVLIN-YOUNG Christopher	DNF
—	USA	HAYDEN Gerald	DNF

ALPINE SKIING (cont'd)

Men's Giant Slalom—Standing
Mar 17 | Run 1 | 50 Athletes: 1 DNS; 9 DNF
Mar 17 | Run 2 | 40 Athletes

#	CTRY	ATHLETE	TIME
1	GER	SCHONFELDER Gerd	2:23.92
2	AUT	MEUSBURGER Robert	2:26.08
3	FRA	GAUTHIER-MANUEL Vincent	2:26.33
4	AUT	MANDL Hubert	2:27.22
5	FRA	BRUN Lionel	2:27.43
6	AUS	RAHLES-RAHBULA Cameron	2:29.07
7	SUI	PFYL Thomas	2:29.08
8	SUI	BRUGGER Michael	2:29.19
9	JPN	MISAWA Hiraku	2:30.65
10	AUS	KANE Toby	2:31.03
16	USA	WASHBURN Bradley	2:34.85
27	USA	SANSONETIS George	2:45.42
28	USA	WHITNEY John	2:47.17
29	USA	GREEN Ralph	2:48.96
32	USA	JANSING Ian	2:52.79

Men's Giant Slalom—Visually Impaired
Mar 17 | Run 1 | 19 Athletes: 1 DSQ
Mar 17 | Run 2 | 18 Athletes: 1 DNS; 4DNF

#	CTRY	ATHLETE	TIME
1	SVK	KRAKO Jakub	2:41.99
2	ESP	SANTACANA MAIZTEGUI Jon	2:42.20
3	ITA	DAL MAISTRO Gianmaria	2:44.25
4	CAN	WILLIAMSON Chris	2:44.65
5	SVK	HOLIK Norbert	2:50.82
6	SVK	DUDAS Radomir	2:51.28
7	RUS	FRANTSEV Ivan	2:51.73
8	SVK	HARAUS Miroslav	2:55.62
9	POL	KREZEL Maciej	2:57.66
10	ESP	GORCE YEPES Gabriel	3:01.69
—	USA	BATHUM Mark	DSQ

Men's Slalom—Sitting
Mar 16 | Run 1 | 47 Athletes: 7 DNF; 1 DSQ
Mar 16 | Run 2 | 42 Athletes: 6 DNF; 1 DSQ

#	CTRY	ATHLETE	TIME
1	GER	BRAXENTHALER Martin	1:41.63
2	CAN	DUECK Josh	1:46.29
3	AUT	BONADIMANN Philipp	1:46.34
4	AUT	KAPFINGER Andreas	1:48.46
5	AUT	SAMPL Reinhold	1:50.02
6	JPN	KANO Akira	1:52.31
7	JPN	MORII Taiki	1:52.55
8	GBR	ROSE Sean	1:52.74
9	USA	BURNETT Carl	1:53.27
10	USA	WALKER Tyler	1:53.34
—	USA	DEVLIN-YOUNG Christopher	DNF
—	USA	CALHOUN Heath	DNF

Men's Slalom—Standing
Mar 15 | Run 1 | 50 Athletes: 2 DNS; 3 DNF; 3 DSQ
Mar 15 | Run 2 | 42 Athletes: 2 DNF

#	CTRY	ATHLETE	TIME
1	NZL	HALL Adam	1:45.40
2	GER	SCHONFELDER Gerd	1:45.97
3	AUS	RAHLES-RAHBULA Cameron	1:47.69
4	AUT	MEUSBURGER Robert	1:47.75
5	FRA	GAUTHIER-MANUEL Vincent	1:47.79
6	FRA	BRUN Lionel	1:48.35
7	SUI	PFYL Thomas	1:48.38
8	USA	MEIER Monte	1:49.29
9	USA	WASHBURN Bradley	1:49.61
10	RUS	ALYABYEV Alexandr	1:50.72
22	USA	GREEN Ralph	1:56.78
23	USA	WHITNEY John	1:57.29
—	USA	SANSONETIS George	DSQ

Men's Slalom—Visually Impaired
Mar 14 | Run 1 | 19 Athletes: 3 DSQ
Mar 14 | Run 2 | 16 Athletes: 4 DNF; 1 DSQ

#	CTRY	ATHLETE	TIME
1	SVK	KRAKO Jakub	1:45.82
2	ESP	SANTACANA MAIZTEGUI Jon	1:46.91
3	ITA	DAL MAISTRO Gianmaria	1:48.32
4	SVK	HARAUS Miroslav	1:48.38
5	SVK	HOLIK Norbert	1:50.10
6	CAN	WILLIAMSON Chris	1:51.12
7	ESP	BOIRA DIAZ Andres	1:54.78
8	POL	KREZEL Maciej	1:56.81
9	GER	GRADWOHL Gerd	1:57.26
10	SVK	BELADIC Michal	1:59.65
11	USA	BATHUM Mark	2:10.45

Women's Downhill—Sitting
Mar 18 | Final | 6 Athletes: 2 DNF

#	CTRY	ATHLETE	TIME
1	USA	NICHOLS Alana	1:23.31
2	USA	STEPHENS Laurie	1:28.26
3	AUT	LOESCH Claudia	1:29.89
4	USA	VICTOR Stephani	1:36.99

Women's Downhill—Standing
Mar 18 | Final | 13 Athletes: 2 DNS

#	CTRY	ATHLETE	TIME
1	CAN	WOOLSTENCROFT Lauren	1:25.54
2	FRA	JAMBAQUE Solene	1:29.94
3	GER	ROTHFUSS Andrea	1:30.58
4	ITA	CORRADINI Melania	1:30.70
5	CAN	WISNIEWSKA Karolina	1:30.82
6	USA	JONES Allison	1:32.32
7	SVK	SMARZOVA Petra	1:35.23
8	FRA	BOCHET Marie	1:35.58
9	CAN	DZIEWIOR Andrea	1:37.53
10	SVK	CHLEBAKOVA Iveta	1:37.55
—	USA	STOREY Elitsa	DNS

Women's Downhill—Visually Impaired
Mar 18 | Final | 10 Athletes: 2 DNF

#	CTRY	ATHLETE	TIME
1	CAN	FOREST Viviane	1:27.51
2	SVK	FARKASOVA Henrieta	1:28.17
3	USA	UMSTEAD Danelle	1:30.18
4	AUT	GASTEIGER Sabine	1:32.00
5	AUS	PERRINE Melissa	1:33.30
6	RUS	FRANTSEVA Alexandra	1:38.71
7	ESP	COHI FORNELL Anna	1:45.94
8	BEL	de TROYER Natasha	1:48.85
—	USA	SARUBBI Caitlin	DNF

Women's Super G—Sitting
Mar 19 | Final | 8 Athletes: 1 DNS

#	CTRY	ATHLETE	TIME
1	AUT	LOESCH Claudia	1:33.89
2	USA	NICHOLS Alana	1:36.68
3	GER	SCHAFFELHUBER Anna	1:38.25
4	USA	STEPHENS Laurie	1:38.38
5	USA	VICTOR Stephani	1:40.36
6	JPN	AOKI Tatsuko	1:42.72
7	ITA	DAMENO Daila	1:51.91

Women's Super G—Standing
Mar 19 | Final | 16 Athletes: 2 DNS

#	CTRY	ATHLETE	TIME
1	CAN	WOOLSTENCROFT Lauren	1:26.46
2	ITA	CORRADINI Melania	1:31.92
3	GER	ROTHFUSS Andrea	1:32.47
4	FRA	JAMBAQUE Solene	1:32.82
5	SVK	CHLEBAKOVA Iveta	1:35.11
6	SVK	SMARZOVA Petra	1:36.09
7	CAN	WISNIEWSKA Karolina	1:36.22
8	FRA	BOCHET Marie	1:36.48
9	USA	JONES Allison	1:38.84
10	RUS	MEDVEDEVA Inga	1:38.97

Women's Super G—Visually Impaired
Mar 19 | Final | 10 Athletes: 2 DNS

#	CTRY	ATHLETE	TIME
1	SVK	FARKASOVA Henrieta	1:33.81
2	CAN	FOREST Viviane	1:37.54
3	CZE	KULISKOVA Anna	1:38.02
4	USA	UMSTEAD Danelle	1:40.62
5	BEL	de TROYER Natasha	1:44.03
6	ESP	COHI FORNELL Anna	1:46.12
7	AUS	PERRINE Melissa	1:46.35
8	USA	SARUBBI Caitlin	1:50.33

Women's Super Combined—Sitting
Mar 20 | Super G | 8 Athletes: 1 DNS; 1 DNF
Mar 20 | Slalom | 6 Athletes: 1 DSQ

#	CTRY	ATHLETE	TIME
1	USA	VICTOR Stephani	2:40.71
2	AUT	LOESCH Claudia	2:44.28
3	USA	NICHOLS Alana	2:47.54
4	GER	SCHAFFELHUBER Anna	2:52.84
5	USA	STEPHENS Laurie	2:53.01

Women's Super Combined—Standing
Mar 20 | Super G | 13 Athletes: 1 DNS; 1 DNF
Mar 20 | Slalom | 11 Athletes: 1 DSQ

#	CTRY	ATHLETE	TIME
1	CAN	WOOLSTENCROFT Lauren	2:22.67
2	FRA	JAMBAQUE Solene	2:34.82
3	CAN	WISNIEWSKA Karolina	2:35.47
4	FRA	BOCHET Marie	2:36.14
5	USA	JONES Allison	2:36.73
6	SVK	SMARZOVA Petra	2:37.37
7	ITA	CORRADINI Melania	2:38.01
8	RUS	MEDVEDEVA Inga	2:39.95
9	FIN	SAARINEN Katja	2:45.41
10	CAN	SCHWARTZ Melanie	2:54.51

Women's Super Combined—Visually Impaired
Mar 20 | Super G | 6 Athletes
Mar 20 | Slalom | 6 Athletes

#	CTRY	ATHLETE	TIME
1	SVK	FARKASOVA Henrieta	2:34.61
2	CAN	FOREST Viviane	2:35.94
3	USA	UMSTEAD Danelle	2:48.75
4	ESP	COHI FORNELL Anna	2:51.85
5	BEL	de TROYER Natasha	2:53.45
6	USA	SARUBBI Caitlin	3:02.02

Women's Giant Slalom—Sitting
Mar 16 | Run 1 | 15 Athletes: 1 DNS;1 DSQ
Mar 16 | Run 2 | 13 Athletes: 2 DNF; 1 DSQ

#	CTRY	ATHLETE	TIME
1	USA	NICHOLS Alana	2:57.57
2	USA	VICTOR Stephani	3:01.78
3	JPN	OBINATA Kuniko	3:08.71
4	JPN	AOKI Tatsuko	3:08.80
5	USA	STEPHENS Laurie	3:09.16
6	USA	KILGORE Ricci	3:17.44
7	GER	SCHAFFELHUBER Anna	3:20.29
8	AUT	LOESCH Claudia	3:23.13
9	USA	LOWERY Luba	3:26.30
10	SUI	FUHRER Anita	3:40.38

Women's Giant Slalom—Standing
Mar 15 | Run 1 | 21 Athletes: 2 DNF; 1 DSQ
Mar 15 | Run 2 | 18 Athletes: 1 DNS; 1 DSF

#	CTRY	ATHLETE	TIME
1	CAN	WOOLSTENCROFT Lauren	2:34.03
2	GER	ROTHFUSS Andrea	2:41.60
3	SVK	SMARZOVA Petra	2:41.63
4	CAN	WISNIEWSKA Karolina	2:44.03
5	SVK	CHLEBAKOVA Iveta	2:45.05
6	FRA	JAMBAQUE Solene	2:45.93
7	FRA	BOCHET Marie	2:46.77
8	ITA	CORRADINI Melania	2:48.28
9	USA	JONES Allison	2:52.26
10	AUT	PERTERER Marina	2:54.01
15	USA	PENNINGTON Hannah	3:18.40
—	USA	STORY Elitsa	DNF

Women's Giant Slalom—Visually Impaired
Mar 16 | Run 1 | 15 Athletes: 1 DNS; 1 DNF; 2 DSQ
Mar 16 | Run 2 | 11 Athletes: 1 DNF; 1 DSQ

#	CTRY	ATHLETE	TIME
1	SVK	FARKASOVA Henrieta	2:56.65
2	AUT	GASTEIGER Sabine	3:02.18
3	CAN	FOREST Viviane	3:11.17
4	GBR	GALLAGHER Kelly	3:14.53
5	ESP	COHI FORNELL Anna	3:15.66
6	USA	SARUBBI Caitlin	3:23.62
7	AUS	GALLAGHER Jessica	3:24.64
8	USA	UMSTEAD Danelle	3:41.64
9	AND	RAMIREZ CAPITAN Paquita	4:16.96

Women's Slalom—Sitting
Mar 14 | Run 1 | 17 Athletes: 1 DNS; 2 DSF
Mar 14 | Run 2 | 14 Athletes: 3 DNF; 2 DSQ

#	CTRY	ATHLETE	TIME
1	AUT	LOESCH Claudia	2:12.05
2	USA	VICTOR Stephani	2:12.63
3	JPN	OBINATA Kuniko	2:18.60
4	GER	SCHAFFELHUBER Anna	2:20.35
5	USA	STEPHENS Laurie	2:28.89
6	GBR	TURNEY Anna	2:40.83
7	USA	LOWERY Luba	2:43.49
8	USA	NICHOLS Alana	2:46.41
9	SWE	OTTOSSON EIDE Linnea	2:56.75

Women's Slalom—Standing
Mar 15 | Run 1 | 21 Athletes: 2 DNF; 1 DSQ
Mar 15 | Run 2 | 18 Athletes: 1 DNS; 1 DNF

#	CTRY	ATHLETE	TIME
1	CAN	WOOLSTENCROFT Lauren	1:51.97
2	GER	ROTHFUSS Andrea	1:58.35
3	CAN	WISNIEWSKA Karolina	1:58.84
4	FRA	BOCHET Marie	2:00.12
5	USA	JONES Allison	2:01.19
6	RUS	MEDVEDEVA Inga	2:03.07
7	AUT	PERTERER Marina	2:05.67
8	FRA	JAMBAQUE Solene	2:07.03
9	FRA	TYACK Nathalie	2:07.94
10	FIN	SAARINEN Katja	2:08.05
16	USA	PENNINGTON Hannah	2:24.24
—	USA	STOREY Elitsa	DNS

Women's Slalom—Visually Impaired
Mar 14 | Run 1 | 15 Athletes: 2 DNF
Mar 14 | Run 2 | 13 Athletes: 2 DNF

#	CTRY	ATHLETE	TIME
1	AUT	GASTEIGER Sabine	2:00.56
2	CAN	FOREST Viviane	2:01.45
3	AUS	GALLAGHER Jessica	2:04.35
4	SUI	BAUMGARTNER Nadja	2:06.99
5	SVK	FARKASOVA Henrieta	2:13.66
6	GBR	GALLAGHER Kelly	2:15.26
7	BEL	de TROYER Natasha	2:18.19
8	AUS	PERRINE Melissa	2:22.47
9	ESP	COHI FORNELL Anna	2:24.32
10	CZE	KULISKOVA Anna	2:33.57
11	AND	RAMIREZ CAPITAN Paquita	2:48.87
—	USA	SARUBBI Caitlin	DNF
—	USA	UMSTEAD Danelle	DNF

BIATHLON

Men's 12.5km—Sitting
Mar 17 | Final | 21 Athletes

#	CTRY	ATHLETE	TIME
1	RUS	ZARIPOV Irek	42:22.4
2	RUS	KISELEV Vladimir	42:29.9
3	RUS	PETUSHKOV Roman	43:11.0
4	USA	SOULE Andy	44:26.2
5	UKR	KOSTIUK Iurii	44:33.8
6	JPN	KUBO Kozo	44:39.6
7	NOR	LARSEN Trygve Toskedal	47:15.5
8	RUS	SHILOV Sergey	47:16.5
9	UKR	KHYZHNYAK Sergiy	47:29.4
10	BEL	DAVIDOVICH Aliaksandr	48:26.6

Men's 12.5km—Standing
Mar 17 | Final | 17 Athletes

#	CTRY	ATHLETE	TIME
1	NOR	ULSET Nils-Erik	38:29.4
2	UKR	VOVCHYNSKYI Grygorii	39:28.5
3	GER	GIESEN Josef	41:25.0
4	RUS	MIKHAYLOV Kirill	41:47.2
5	BLR	SILCHANKA Siarhei	41:51.8
6	UKR	LESHCHYSHYN Oleh	42:18.8
7	FRA	BOURSEAUX Yannick	42:34.7
8	UKR	SYTNYK Vitalii	43:19.8
9	AUT	KURZ Michael	44:35.8
10	GER	OELSNER Thomas	44:49.4

No USA athlete competed.

Men's 12.5km—Visually Impaired
Mar 17 | Final | 11 Athletes: 1 DNS

#	CTRY	ATHLETE	TIME
1	GER	BREM Wilhelm	38:28.6
2	RUS	POLUKHIN Nikolay	38:32.7
3	UKR	LUKYANENKO Vitaliy	38:55.5
4	BLR	SHAPTSIABOI Vasili	40:47.6
5	FRA	CLARION Thomas	41:44.9
6	UKR	MUNTS Oleg	45:58.3
7	RUS	MANNANOV Irek	46:18.0
8	UKR	SHULGA Dmytro	50:19.6
9	UKR	UTKIN Iurii	51:05.5
10	CAN	NOVIKOV Alexei	56:30.2

No USA athlete competed.

BIATHLON (cont'd)

Men's 2.4km Pursuit—Sitting
Mar 13 | Qualifications | 12 Athletes
Mar 13 | Final | 12 Athletes

#	CTRY	ATHLETE	TIME
1	RUS	ZARIPOV Irek	9:51.0
2	UKR	KOSTIUK Iurii	10:38.9
3	USA	SOULE Andy	10:53.1
4	UKR	KHYZHNYAK Sergiy	10:59.8
5	RUS	KISELEV Vladimir	11:00.9
6	RUS	SHILOV Sergey	11:04.6
7	SVK	GAJDICIAR Vladimir	11:13.1
8	BLR	DAVIDOVICH Aliaksandr	11:44.5
9	JPN	KUBO Kozo	12:25.0
10	SIU	HUBER Bruno	12:27.9

Men's 3km Pursuit—Standing
Mar 13 | Qualifications | 19 Athletes9
Mar 13 | Final | 12 Athletes

#	CTRY	ATHLETE	TIME
1	RUS	MIKHAYLOV Kirill	10:32.2
2	NOR	ULSET Nils-Erik	10:51.3
3	UKR	VOVCHYNSKYI Grygorii	10:58.9
4	GER	GIESEN Josef	10:59.6
5	RUS	LAYKOV Vyacheslav	11:06.3
6	RUS	DAROVSKIKH Valery	11:06.5
7	CAN	ARENDZ Mark	11:32.0
8	UKR	SYTNYK Vitalii	11:38.4
9	FRA	BOURSEAUX Yannick	11:45.9
10	JPN	NITTA Yoshihiro	11:48.7

No USA athlete competed.

Men's 3km Pursuit—Visually Impaired
Mar 13 | Qualifications | 16 Athletes: 2 DNS
Mar 13 | Final | 10 Athletes

#	CTRY	ATHLETE	TIME
1	UKR	LUKYANENKO Vitaliy	10:54.3
2	RUS	POLUKHIN Nikolay	11:09.2
3	BLR	SHAPTSIABOI Vasili	11:16.0
4	GER	BREM Wilhelm	11:48.3
5	RUS	MANNANOV Irek	12:01.7
6	CAN	McKEEVER Brian	12:02.7
7	UKR	SHULGA Dmytro	12:54.0
8	FRA	CLARION Thomas	13:09.3
9	UKR	UTKIN Iurii	13:44.5
10	KOR	IM Hak-Su	14:39.5

No USA athlete competed.

Women's 10km—Sitting
Mar 17 | Final | 9 Athletes

#	CTRY	ATHLETE	TIME
1	RUS	IOVLEVA Maria	38:46.6
2	UKR	IURKOVSKA Olena	39:07.8
3	GER	ESKAU Andrea	39:54.2
4	UKR	PAVLENKO Lyudmyla	41:10.6
5	RUS	POLYAKOVA Irina	41:56.5
6	UKR	STEFURAK Nadiia	43:52.1
7	UKR	TRYFONOVA Svitlana	45:04.2
8	UKR	TYMOSHCHENKO Tetyana	46:26.9
9	RUS	YAROSHEVICH Svetlana	55:32.1

No USA athlete competed.

Women's 12.5km—Standing
Mar 17 | Final | 12 Athletes

#	CTRY	ATHLETE	TIME
1	UKR	KONONOVA Oleksandra	46:01.4
2	RUS	BURMISTROVA Anna	48:04.0
3	UKR	BATENKOVA Iuliia	48:22.5
4	POL	ROGOWIEC Katarzyna	49:21.4
5	RUS	GORBUNOVA Alena	49:29.4
6	FIN	LOYTYNOJA Maija	50:44.6
7	CAN	BARBER Jody	51:06.5
8	JPN	DEKIJIMA Momoko	51:30.2
9	USA	UNDERKOFLER Kelly	51:44.1
10	ITA	NOVAGLIO Pamela	52:31.9

Women's 12.5km—Visually Impaired
Mar 17 | Final | 9 Athletes

#	CTRY	ATHLETE	TIME
1	GER	BENTELE Verena	43:57.3
2	RUS	VASILYEVA Liubov	46:59.4
3	RUS	LYSOVA Mikhalina	47:59.1
4	BLR	SKORABAHATAYA Yadviha	49:00.2
5	RUS	ILYUCHENKO Tatiana	50:05.1
6	UKR	SHYSHKOVA Oksana	51:42.7
7	DEN	BREDAHL Anne-Mette	53:23.4
8	FRA	MORIN Nathalie	56:15.1
9	CAN	WELDON Robbi	59:58.0

No USA athlete competed.

BIATHLON (cont'd)

Women's 2.4km Pursuit—Sitting
Mar 13 | Qualifications | 9 Athletes
Mar 13 | Final | 6 Athletes

#	CTRY	ATHLETE	TIME
1	UKR	IURKOVSKA Olena	9:55.5
2	RUS	IOVLEVA Maria	10:12.6
3	UKR	PAVLENKO Lyudmyla	10:20.7
4	RUS	POLYAKOVA Irina	11:59.3
5	UKR	TRYFONOVA Svitlana	13:01.1
6	GER	ESKAU Andrea	13:50.5

No USA athlete competed.

Women's 3km Pursuit—Standing
Mar 13 | Qualifications | 13 Athletes
Mar 13 | Final | 10 Athletes

#	CTRY	ATHLETE	TIME
1	RUS	BURMISTROVA Anna	11:24.1
2	FIN	LOYTYNOJA Maija	12:59.8
3	RUS	GORBUNOVA Alena	13:25.1
4	UKR	BATENKOVA Iuliia	13:34.5
5	POL	ROGOWIEC Katarzyna	13:36.3
6	UKR	KONONOVA Oleksandra	14:04.6
7	JPN	OTA Shoko	14:06.2
8	ITA	NOVAGLIO Pamela	14:37.6
9	USA	UNDERKOFLER Kelly	14:39.0
10	CAN	BARBER Jody	14:41.2

Women's 3km Pursuit—Visually Impaired
Mar 13 | Qualifications | 11 Athletes
Mar 13 | Final | 6 Athletes

#	CTRY	ATHLETE	TIME
1	GER	BENTELE Verena	12:51.8
2	RUS	VASILYEVA Liubov	13:23.4
3	RUS	LYSOVA Mikhalina	13:40.8
4	RUS	ILYUCHENKO Tatiana	15:05.6
5	UKR	SHYSHKOVA Oksana	16:43.6
6	CAN	WELDON Robbi	20:34.7

No USA athlete competed.

CROSS-COUNTRY SKIING

Men's 10km—Sitting
Mar 18 | Final | 34 Athletes: 1 DNF

#	CTRY	ATHLETE	TIME
1	RUS	ZARIPOV Irek	27:12.1
2	ITA	MASIELLO Enzo	28:21.1
3	BLR	LOBAN Dzmitry	28:25.1
4	UKR	KOSTIUK Iurii	28:25.6
5	RUS	PETUSHKOV Roman	28:27.6
6	RUS	KISELEV Vladimir	28:32.4
7	USA	HALSTED Sean	28:35.8
8	BLR	DAVIDOVICH Aliaksandr	28:38.0
9	NOR	LARSEN Trygve Toskedal	28:44.4
10	CHN	FU Chunshan	29:02.6
12	USA	SOULE Andy	29:18.7
24	USA	MALLORY Greg	30:35.3

Men's 10km Classic—Standing
Mar 18 | Final | 30 Athletes: 1 DNS; 2 DNF; 1 DSQ

#	CTRY	ATHLETE	TIME
1	JPN	NITTA Yoshihiro	26:29.5
2	RUS	MIKHAYLOV Kirill	27:01.7
3	UKR	VOVCHYNSKYI Grygorii	27:03.7
4	NOR	DAHLE Vegard	27:32.8
5	GER	UHLIG Tino	28:22.4
6	RUS	BALUKHTO Oleg	28:26.2
7	RUS	LAYKOV Vyacheslav	28:36.4
8	RUS	MINNEGULOV Rushan	28:42.2
9	FIN	TUOMISTO Ilkka	28:46.3
10	UKR	SYTNYK Vitalii	29:14.2

No USA athlete competed.

Men's 10km Classic—Visually Impaired
Mar 18 | Final | 30 Athletes: 1 DNS; 2 DNF; 1 DSQ

#	CTRY	ATHLETE	TIME
1	CAN	McKEEVER Brian	26:01.6
2	NOR	FLO Helge	27:27.3
3	RUS	POLUKHIN Nikolay	27:40.7
4	BLR	SHAPTSIABOI Vasili	27:46.4
5	UKR	MUNTS Oleg	28:55.6
6	KOR	IM Hak-Su	29:07.2
7	GER	HOFLE Frank	29:21.9
8	UKR	UTKIN Iurii	30:06.7
9	SWE	MODIN Zebastian	30:21.5
10	RUS	KUPCHINSKIY Valery	30:59.5

No USA athlete competed.

CROSS-COUNTRY SKIING (cont'd)

Men's 15km—Sitting
Mar 14 | Final | 31 Athletes: 1 DNS; 1 DNF

#	CTRY	ATHLETE	TIME
1	RUS	ZARIPOV Irek	41:01.1
2	RUS	PETUSHKOV Roman	41:11.1
3	ITA	MASIELLO Enzo	41:54.9
4	NOR	LARSEN Trygve Toskedal	42:17.3
5	UKR	KOSTIUK Iurii	42:17.7
6	BLR	DAVIDOVICH Aliaksandr	42:43.1
7	JPN	KUBO Kozo	42:55.5
8	USA	KLEBL Chris	43:13.7
9	USA	HALSTED Sean	43:25.6
10	USA	SOULE Andy	43:32.8
26	USA	MALLORY Greg	46:30.6

Men's 20km Free—Standing
Mar 15 | Final | 22 Athletes: 1 DNS; 2 DNF

#	CTRY	ATHLETE	TIME
1	RUS	MIKHAYLOV Kirill	52:07.7
2	NOR	ULSET Nils-Erik	53:34.1
3	RUS	KONONOV Vladimir	53:53.4
4	BLR	SILCHANKA Siarhei	54:51.6
5	RUS	MINNEGULOV Rushan	54:59.8
6	AUT	KURZ Michael	55:06.8
7	CHN	DU Haitao	55:29.9
8	NOR	DAHLE Vegard	55:42.9
9	FRA	BOURSEAUX Yannick	55:55.7
10	GER	OELSNER Thomas	58:02.6

No USA athlete competed.

Men's 20km Free—Standing
Mar 15 | Final | 14 Athletes: 1 DNF

#	CTRY	ATHLETE	TIME
1	CAN	McKEEVER Brian	51:14.7
2	RUS	POLUKHIN Nikolay	51:55.6
3	BLR	SHAPTSIABOI Vasili	52:22.5
4	GER	BREM Wilhelm	52:28.9
5	GER	HOFLE Frank	52:38.8
6	FRA	CLARION Thomas	52:39.8
7	UKR	MUNTS Oleg	53:03.8
8	NOR	FLO Helge	54:22.7
9	KOR	IM Hak-Su	55:53.6
10	RUS	KUPCHINSKIY Valery	57:03.8

No USA athlete competed.

Men's 1km Sprint—Sitting
Mar 21 | Qualifications| 35 Athletes
Mar 21 | Final | 4 Athletes

#	CTRY	ATHLETE	TIME
1	RUS	SHILOV Sergey	2:31.8
2	RUS	ZARIPOV Irek	2:31.9
3	RUS	KISELEV Vladimir	2:36.6
4	UKR	KOSTIUK Iurii	2:44.3
—	USA	KLEBL Chris	Elim. in qualifications
—	USA	HALSTED Sean	Elim. in qualifications
—	USA	SOULE Andy	Elim. in qualifications
—	USA	MALLORY Greg	Elim. in qualifications

Men's 1km Sprint Classic—Standing
Mar 21 | Qualifications| 33 Athletes: 2 DNS
Mar 21 | Final | 4 Athletes

#	CTRY	ATHLETE	TIME
1	JPN	NITTA Yoshihiro	3:30.7
2	RUS	MIKHAYLOV Kirill	3:32.3
3	FIN	TUOMISTO Ilkka	3:33.9
4	NOR	DAHLE Vegard	3:35.0

No USA athlete competed.

Men's 1km Sprint Classic—Visually Impaired
Mar 21 | Qualifications| 21 Athletes
Mar 21 | Final | 4 Athletes

#	CTRY	ATHLETE	TIME
1	CAN	McKEEVER Brian	3:42.9
2	RUS	POLUKHIN Nikolay	3:47.0
3	SWE	MODIN Zebastian	3:50.2
4	GER	HOFLE Frank	3:55.5

No USA athlete competed.

CROSS-COUNTRY SKIING (cont'd)

Men's Relay 1x4km + 2x5km
Mar 20 | Final | 8 Teams

#	CTRY	ATHLETE	TIME
1	RUS	POLUKHIN Nikolay	38:54.8
		SHILOV Sergey	
		MIKHAYLOV Kirill	
2	UKR	LUKYANENKO Vitaliy	39:16.8
		VOVCHYNSKYI Grygorii	
		KOSTIUK Iurii	
3	NOR	DAHLE Vegard	39:49.0
		LARSEN Trygve Toskedal	
		ULSET Nils-Erik	
4	BLR	SILCHANKA Siarhei	41:20.2
		PRONKA Barys	
		SHAPTSIABOI Vasili	
5	JPN	SATO Keiichi	41:48.8
		KUBO Kozo	
		NITTA Yoshihiro	
6	FRA	CLARION Thomas	42:10.9
		BOURSEAUX Yannick	
		BETTEGA Georges	
7	CAN	MOSHER Tyler	43:52.0
		FORTIER Sebastien	
		ARENDZ Mark	
8	CHN	CHENG Shishuai	44:06.6
		ZOU Dexin	
		FU Chunshan	

No USA athlete competed.

Women's 5km—Sitting
Mar 18 | Final | 16 Athletes: 1 DNS

#	CTRY	ATHLETE	TIME
1	BLR	VAUCHOK Liudmila	14:56.6
2	GER	ESKAU Andrea	15:11.4
3	CAN	BOURGONJE Colette	15:16.4
4	UKR	IURKOVSKA Olena	15:19.7
5	UKR	PAVLENKO Lyudmyla	15:23.9
6	ITA	PORCELLATO Francesca	15:25.3
7	RUS	IOVLEVA Maria	15:47.8
8	NOR	VESTBOSTAD Mariann	15:53.9
9	RUS	POLYAKOVA Irina	16:26.1
10	USA	BASCIO Monica	16:32.4

Women's 5km Classic—Standing
Mar 18 | Final | 18 Athletes: 1 DNF; 1 DSQ

#	CTRY	ATHLETE	TIME
1	UKR	KONONOVA Oleksandra	16:01.3
2	UKR	BATENKOVA Iuliia	16:03.7
3	BLR	VARONA Larysa	17:38.2
4	SWE	SELLIN Stina	17:54.7
5	CHN	PENG Yuanyuan	17:57.8
6	CAN	BARBER Jody	18:00.4
7	SUI	DEVITTORI-VALNEGRI Chiara	18:05.6
8	RUS	GORBUNOVA Alena	18:06.2
9	FIN	LOYTYNOJA Maija	18:28.7
10	USA	UNDERKOFLER Kelly	18:37.2

Women's 5km Classic—Visually Impaired
Mar 18 | Final | 13 Athletes

#	CTRY	ATHLETE	TIME
1	GER	BENTELE Verena	15:08.8
2	RUS	LYSOVA Mikhalina	16:00.3
3	RUS	ILYUCHENKO Tatiana	17:18.4
4	RUS	VASILYEVA Liubov	17:25.4
5	BLR	SKORABAHATAYA Yadviha	17:34.8
6	CAN	WELDON Robbi	17:40.9
7	UKR	SHYSHKOVA Oksana	17:44.9
8	JPN	KANUMA Yurie	18:32.9
9	FRA	MORIN Nathalie	19:16.0
10	RUS	NEVIDIMOVA Valentina	19:45.6

No USA athlete competed.

Women's 10km—Sitting
Mar 14 | Final | 12 Athletes: 1 DNF

#	CTRY	ATHLETE	TIME
1	BLR	VAUCHOK Liudmila	30:52.9
2	CAN	BOURGONJE Colette	31:49.8
3	UKR	IURKOVSKA Olena	32:43.5
4	UKR	TRYFONOVA Svitlana	32:50.0
5	NOR	VESTBOSTAD Mariann	33:27.8
6	RUS	IOVLEVA Maria	33:29.8
7	UKR	PAVLENKO Lyudmyla	33:30.1
8	GER	ESKAU Andrea	33:46.0
9	USA	BASCIO Monica	34:33.9
10	DEN	MAIBOLL Marianne	35:36.0

CROSS-COUNTRY SKIING (cont'd)

Women's 15km Free—Standing
Mar 15 | Final | 11 Athletes: 1 DNF

#	CTRY	ATHLETE	TIME
1	RUS	BURMISTROVA Anna	49:16.3
2	UKR	BATENKOVA Iuliia	49:23.5
3	POL	ROGOWIEC Katarzyna	51:04.1
4	UKR	KONONOVA Oleksandra	51:29.5
5	SUI	DEVITTORI-VALNEGRI Chiara	52:58.8
6	CAN	BARBER Jody	55:37.0
7	CHN	PENG Yuanyuan	55:43.3
8	USA	UNDERKOFLER Kelly	58:19.6
9	RUS	GORBUNOVA Alena	58:43.7
10	SWE	SELLIN Stina	59:01.8

Women's 15km Free—Visually Impaired
Mar 15 | Final | 9 Athletes: 1 DNS; 1 DNF

#	CTRY	ATHLETE	TIME
1	GER	BENTELE Verena	45:11.1
2	RUS	VASILYEVA Liubov	48:34.1
3	BLR	SKORABAHATAYA Yadviha	49:19.3
4	RUS	ILYUCHENKO Tatiana	50:50.9
5	CAN	WELDON Robbi	53:36.9
6	FRA	MORIN Nathalie	54:42.1
7	CAN	GORBOUNOVA Margarita	1:01:59.1

No USA athlete competed.

Women's 1km Sprint—Sitting
Mar 21 | Final | 15 Athletes
Mar 21 | Final | 4 Athletes

#	CTRY	ATHLETE	TIME
1	ITA	PORCELLATO Francesca	2:58.5
2	UKR	IURKOVSKA Olena	3:00.0
3	BLR	VAUCHOK Liudmila	3:01.9
4	UKR	PAVLENKO Lyudmyla	3:02.3
—	USA	BASCIO Monica	Elim. in semis

Women's 1km Sprint—Standing
Mar 21 | Final | 19 Athletes:`1 DNS
Mar 21 | Final | 4 Athletes

#	CTRY	ATHLETE	TIME
1	UKR	KONONOVA Oleksandra	4:21.4
2	JPN	OTA Shoko	4:26.8
3	RUS	BURMISTROVA Anna	4:31.3
4	BLR	VARONA Larysa	4:34.5
—	USA	UNDERKOFLER Kelly Elim. In qualifications	

Women's 1km Sprint—Visually Impaired
Mar 21 | Final | 12 Athletes:`1 DSQ
Mar 21 | Final | 4 Athletes

#	CTRY	ATHLETE	TIME
1	GER	BENTELE Verena	4:14.2
2	RUS	LYSOVA Mikhalina	4:44.2
3	RUS	VASILYEVA Liubov	4:54.4
4	RUS	ILYUCHENKO Tatiana	4:58.0

No USA athlete competed.

Women's Relay 3x2.5km
Mar 20 | Final | 8 Teams

#	CTRY	ATHLETE	TIME
1	RUS	LYSOVA Mikhalina	20:23.3
		VASILYEVA Liubov	
		IOVLEVA Maria	
2	UKR	IURKOVSKA Olena	20:42.8
		KONONOVA Oleksandra	
		BATENKOVA Iuliia	
3	BLR	VAUCHOK Liudmila	22:04.2
		SKORABAHATAYA Yadviha	
		VARONA Larysa	
4	CAN	WELDON Robbi	22:21.3
		BOURGONJE Colette	
		BARBER Jody	
5	JPN	DEKIJIMA Momoko	22:21.6
		KANUMA Yurie	
		OTA Shoko	
6	POL	ROGOWIEC Katarzyna	24:14.7
		DUDZIAK Arleta	
		MAYER Anna	

No USA athlete competed.

SLED HOCKEY

Men's
Mar 13-20 | 20 Games | 8 Teams

#	CTRY	RECORD	FINAL
1	USA	5 - 0	1st: 2-0
2	JPN	3 - 2	
3	NOR	3 - 1	3rd: 5-3
4	CAN	3 - 2	
5	CZE	3 - 2	5th: 2-1
6	KOR	1 - 4	
7	ITA	1 - 4	7th: 4-0
8	SWE	1 - 4	

USA Scores: Game 1 vs KOR: 5-0 | Game 2 vs CZE: 3-0 | Game 3 vs JPN: 6-0 | Game 4 vs NOR: 3-0 (Semifinals) | Game 5 vs JPN: 2-0 (Final)

USA TEAM: BLABAC Mike | CASH Steve | CHACE Taylor | CONNELLY Jimmy | EMMERSON Brad | HOWARD Joe | JONES Tim | LANDEROS Nikko | LIPSETT Taylor | PAGE Adam | PAULS Josh | SALAMONE Alexi | SHAW Greg | TORRES Bubba | YOHE Andy

WHEELCHAIR CURLING

Co-ed
Mar 13-20 | Round Robin | 10 Teams

#	CTRY	RECORD	FINAL
1	CAN	10 - 1	1st: 8-7
2	KOR	7 - 4	
3	SWE	7 - 5*	3rd: 7-5
4	USA	7 - 4	

* Tie-breaker Game: SWE vs ITA: 6-5

USA Scores: Game 1 vs KOR: 9-6 | Game 2 vs CAN: 5-10 | Game 3 vs GER: 6-5 | Game 4 vs ITA: 8-2 | Game 5 vs GBR: 8-7 | Game 6 vs SWE: 4-6 | Game 7 vs NOR: 9-8 | Game 8 vs JPN: 8-3 | Game 9 vs SUI: 8-2 | Game 10 vs KOR: 5-7 (Semifinals) | Game 11 vs SWE: 5-7 (3rd)

USA TEAM: PEREZ Augusto | McDONALD Patrick | PIERCE Jim | KAPINOWSKI Jacqui | JOSEPH Jimmy

Will Brandenburg
BIRTH DATE: 1.1.1987
Spokane, WA
EVENT: Super Combined

Jimmy Cochran
BIRTH DATE: 5.29.1981
Keene, NH
EVENT: Slalom

Stacey Cook
BIRTH DATE: 7.3.1984
Mammoth Lakes, CA
EVENT: Downhill

Hailey Duke
BIRTH DATE: 9.17.1985
Boise, ID
EVENT: Slalom

Erik Fisher
BIRTH DATE: 3.21.1985
Middleton, ID
EVENT: Downhill—Did not
compete

Tommy Ford
BIRTH DATE: 3.20.1989
Bend, OR
EVENT: Giant Slalom

Tim Jitloff
BIRTH DATE: 1.11.1985
Reno, NV
EVENT: Giant Slalom—Did
not compete

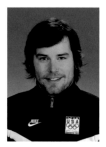

Nolan Kasper
BIRTH DATE: 3.27.1989
Warren, VT
EVENT: Slalom

Ted Ligety
BIRTH DATE: 8.31.1984
Park City, UT
EVENT: Super Combined,
Super-G, Giant Slalom,
Slalom

Julia Mancuso
BIRTH DATE: 3.9.1984
Olympic Valley, CA
EVENT: Downhill, Super-G,
Super Combined,
Giant Slalom

Chelsea Marshall
BIRTH DATE: 8.14.1986
Pittsfield, VT
EVENT: Super-G

Megan McJames
BIRTH DATE: 9.24.1987
Park City, UT
EVENT: Giant Slalom.
Slalom

Alice McKennis
BIRTH DATE: 8.18.1989
Glenwood Springs, CO
EVENT: Downhill

Bode Miller
BIRTH DATE: 10.12.1977
Franconia, NH
EVENT: Downhill, Super-G,
Super Combined, Giant
Slalom, Slalom

Steve Nyman
BIRTH DATE: 2.12.1982
Sundance, UT
EVENT: Downhill

Kaylin Richardson
BIRTH DATE: 9.28.1984
Edina, MN
EVENT: Super Combined

Sarah Schleper
BIRTH DATE: 2.19.1979
Vail, CO
EVENT: Giant Slalom,
Slalom

Leanne Smith
BIRTH DATE: 5.28.1987
Conway, NH
EVENT: Super Combined,
Super-G

Marco Sullivan
BIRTH DATE: 4.27.1980
Squaw Valley, CA
EVENT: Downhill, Super-G

Lindsey Vonn
BIRTH DATE: 10.18.1984
Vail, CO
EVENT: Downhill, Super-G,
Super Combined,
Giant Slalom, Slalom

Andrew Weibrecht
BIRTH DATE: 2.10.1986
Lake Placid, NY
EVENT: Downhill, Super-G,
Super Combined

Jake Zamansky
BIRTH DATE: 6.26.1981
Aspen, CO
EVENT: Giant Slalom

Biathlon

Lowell Bailey
BIRTH DATE: 7.15.1981
🏠 Lake Placid, NY
EVENT: 10km Sprint,
12.5km Pursuit, 20km
Indiv., Relay

Lanny Barnes
BIRTH DATE: 4.26.1982
🏠 Durango, CO
EVENT: 7.5km Sprint, 15km
Indiv., Relay

Tim Burke
BIRTH DATE: 2.3.1982
🏠 Paul Smiths, NY
EVENT: 10km Sprint,
12.5km Pursuit, 20km
Indiv., 15km Mass Start,
Relay

Jay Hakkinen
BIRTH DATE: 7.19.1977
🏠 Kasilof, AK
EVENT: 10km Sprint.
12.5km Pursuit, 20km
Indiv., Relay

Haley Johnson
BIRTH DATE: 12.8.1981
🏠 Lake Placid, NY
EVENT: 7.5km Sprint, 15km
Indiv., Relay

Wynn Roberts
BIRTH DATE: 3.1.1988
🏠 Battle Lake, MN
EVENT: 20km Indiv.

Laura Spector
BIRTH DATE: 10.30.1987
🏠 Lenox, MA
EVENT: 7.5km Sprint, 15km
Indiv., Relay

Sara Studebaker
BIRTH DATE: 10.7.1984
🏠 Boise, ID
EVENT: 7.5km Sprint, 10km
Pursuit, 15km Indiv., Relay

Jeremy Teela
BIRTH DATE: 11.28.1976
🏠 Heber City, UT
EVENT: 10km Sprint,
12.5km Pursuit, 15km
Mass Start, Relay

Twenty-two-year old Laura Spector balances studying at Dartmouth College and training for biathlon to pursue her Olympic dreams. Vancouver was her Olympic debut. (PHOTO BY JAVIER SORIANO/AFP/GETTY IMAGES)

Bobsled

Emily Azevedo
BIRTH DATE: 4.28.1983
🏛 Chico, CA
EVENT: Women's,
Brakeman (USA3)

Chuck Berkeley
BIRTH DATE: 8.21.1976
🏛 Pittsfield, MA
EVENT: 4-man, Brakeman
(USA2)

Nick Cunningham
BIRTH DATE: 5.8.1985
🏛 Monterey, CA
EVENT: 4-man, 2nd Pusher
(USA 3)

Chris Fogt
BIRTH DATE: 5.29.1983
🏛 Alpine, UT
EVENT: 4-man, 2nd Pusher
(USA2)

Steve Holcomb
BIRTH DATE: 4.14.1980
🏛 Park City, UT
EVENT: 2-man, 4-man, Pilot
(USA1)

Mike Kohn
BIRTH DATE: 5.26.1972
🏛 Fairfax, VA
EVENT: 2-man, 4-man, Pilot
(USA3)

Steve Langton
BIRTH DATE: 4.15.1983
🏛 Melrose, MA
EVENT: 2-man, Brakeman;
4-man, 3rd Pusher
(USA2)

Steve Mesler
BIRTH DATE: 8.27.1978
🏛 Buffalo, NY
EVENT: 4-man, 2nd Pusher
(USA1)

Elana Meyers
BIRTH DATE: 10.10.1984
🏛 Douglasville, GA
EVENT: Women's,
Brakeman (USA2)

Jamie Moriarty
BIRTH DATE: 3.26.1981
🏛 Glencoe, IL
EVENT: 4-man, 3rd Pusher
(USA3)

John Napier
BIRTH DATE: 12.12.1986
🏛 Lake Placid, NY
EVENT: 2-man, 4-man, Pilot
(USA2)

Justin Olsen
BIRTH DATE: 4.16.1987
🏛 San Antonio, TX
EVENT: 4-man, Brakeman
(USA1)

Erin Pac
BIRTH DATE: 5.30.1980
🏛 Farmington, CT
EVENT: Women's, Pilot
(USA2)

Shauna Rohbock
BIRTH DATE: 4.4.1977
🏛 Orem, UT
EVENT: Women's, Pilot
(USA1)

Michelle Rzepka
BIRTH DATE: 8.4.1983
🏛 Novi, MI
EVENT: Women's,
Brakeman (USA1)

Bree Schaaf
BIRTH DATE: 5.28.1980
🏛 Bremerton, WA
EVENT: Women's, Pilot
(USA3)

Bill Schuffenhauer
BIRTH DATE: 6.24.1973
🏛 Ogden, UT
EVENT: 4-man, Brakeman
(USA3)

Curt Tomasevicz
BIRTH DATE: 9.17.1980
🏛 Shelby, NE
EVENT: 2-man, Brakeman;
4-man, 3rd Pusher
(USA1)

OPPOSITE / *Holly Brooks, a nordic ski coach at Alaska Pacific University, made her Olympic debut at the age of 27. Backcountry skiing, peak bagging, kayaking, pack-rafting, and crust skiing are all a part of Brooks' repertoire in Alaska's playground.* (PHOTO BY LARS BARON/ BONGARTS/GETTY IMAGES)

Cross-Country Skiing

Morgan Arritola
BIRTH DATE: 5.13.1986
🏠 Ketchum, ID
EVENT: 10km Free, 15km
Pursuit, 30km Classic,
Relay

Holly Brooks
BIRTH DATE: 4.17.1982
🏠 Anchorage, AK
EVENT: 10km Free, Indiv.
Sprint Classic, 15km Pur-
suit, 30km Classic, Relay

Caitlin Compton
BIRTH DATE: 11.7.1980
🏠 Minneapolis, MN
EVENT: 10km Free, 15km
Pursuit, Team Sprint Free,
Relay

Kris Freeman
BIRTH DATE: 10.14.1980
🏠 Andover, NH
EVENT: 15km Free, 30km
Pursuit, 50km Classic

Simi Hamilton
BIRTH DATE: 5.14.1987
🏠 Aspen, CO
EVENT: 15km Free, Relay

Torin Koos
BIRTH DATE: 7.19.1980
🏠 Leavenworth, WA
EVENT: Team Sprint Free,
Relay

Garrott Kuzzy
BIRTH DATE: 11.26.1982
🏠 Minneapolis, MN
EVENT: 15km Free, Relay

Andy Newell
BIRTH DATE: 11.30.1983
🏠 Shaftsbury, VT
EVENT: Team Sprint Free,
Relay

Kikkan Randall
BIRTH DATE: 12.31.1982
🏠 Anchorage, AK
EVENT: Indiv. Sprint Classic,
30km Classic, Team Sprint
Free, Relay

James Southam
BIRTH DATE: 6.5.1978
🏠 Anchorage, AK
EVENT: 15km Free, 30km
Pursuit, 50km Classic

Liz Stephen
BIRTH DATE: 1.12.1987
🏠 East Montpelier, VT
EVENT: 10km Free, 15km
Pursuit

Curling

John Benton
BIRTH DATE: 6.23.1969
St. Michael, MN
POSITION: Lead

Jeff Isaacson
BIRTH DATE: 7.14.1983
Duluth, MN
POSITION: Second

Chris Plys
BIRTH DATE: 8.13.1987
Duluth, MN
POSITION: Alternate

John Shuster
BIRTH DATE: 11.3.1982
Chisholm, MN
POSITION: Skip

Jason Smith
BIRTH DATE: 9.18.1983
Chisholm, MN
POSITION: Vice-Skip

Nicole Joraanstad
BIRTH DATE: 11.10.1980
Seattle, WA
POSITION: Second

Debbie McCormick
BIRTH DATE: 1.8.1974
Madison, WI
POSITION: Skip

Natalie Nicholson
BIRTH DATE: 3.10.1976
Bemidji, MN
POSITION: Lead

Allison Pottinger
BIRTH DATE: 7.5.1973
Eden Prairie, MN
POSITION: Vice-Skip

Tracy Sachtjen
BIRTH DATE: 2.20.1969
Lodi, WI
POSITION: Alternate

USA coach Rodger Schmidt (left) considers a shot with team skip Debbie McCormick and team members Nicole Joraanstad, Allison Pottinger and Natalie Nicholson during their round robin match against Russia. The Americans won 6-4. (PHOTO BY ROBYNBECK/ AFP/GETTY IMAGES)

Figure Skating

Jeremy Abbott
BIRTH DATE: 6.5.1987
🏛 Aspen, CO
EVENT: Individual

Ben Agosto
BIRTH DATE: 1.15.1982
🏛 Chicago, IL
EVENT: Ice Dance
(Partner: Belbin)

Jeremy Barrett
BIRTH DATE: 4.10.1984
🏛 Venice, FL
EVENT: Pairs
(Partner: Denney)

Evan Bates
BIRTH DATE: 2.23.1989
🏛 Ann Arbor, MI
EVENT: Ice Dance
(Partner: Samuelson)

Tanith Belbin
BIRTH DATE: 7.11.1984
🏛 Kirkland, Canada
EVENT: Ice Dance
(Partner: Agosto)

Meryl Davis
BIRTH DATE: 1.1.1987
🏛 West Bloomfield, MI
EVENT: Ice Dance
(Partner: White)

Caydee Denney
BIRTH DATE: 6.22.1993
🏛 Wesley Chapel, FL
EVENT: Pairs
(Partner: Barrett)

Amanda Evora
BIRTH DATE: 11.17.1984
🏛 Sugar Land, TX
EVENT: Pairs
(Partner: Ladwig)

Rachael Flatt
BIRTH DATE: 7.21.1992
🏛 Del Mar, CA
EVENT: Individual

Mark Ladwig
BIRTH DATE: 5.6.1980
🏛 Fargo, ND/Mooreland, MN
EVENT: Pairs
(Partner: Evora)

Evan Lysacek
BIRTH DATE: 6.4.1985
🏛 Naperville, IIL
EVENT: Individual

Mirai Nagasu
BIRTH DATE: 4.16.1993
🏛 Arcadia, CA
EVENT: Individual

Emily Samuelson
BIRTH DATE: 5.14.1990
🏛 Novi, MI
EVENT: Ice Dance
(Partner: Bates)

Johnny Weir
BIRTH DATE: 7.2.1984
🏛 Quarryville, PA
EVENT: Individual

Charlie White
BIRTH DATE: 10.24.1987
🏛 Bloomfield Hills, MI
EVENT: Ice Dance
(Partner: Davis)

Freestyle Skiing

Scotty Bahrke
BIRTH DATE: 7.19.1985
⌂ Tahoe City, CA
EVENT: Aerials

Shannon Bahrke
BIRTH DATE: 11.7.1980
⌂ Tahoe City, CA
EVENT: Moguls

Ashley Caldwell
BIRTH DATE: 9.14.1993
⌂ Hamilton, VA
EVENT: Aerials

Emily Cook
BIRTH DATE: 7.1.1979
⌂ Belmont, MA
EVENT: Aerials

Patrick Deneen
BIRTH DATE: 12.25.1987
⌂ Cle Elum, WA
EVENT: Moguls

Matt DePeters
BIRTH DATE: 8.20.1987
⌂ Buffalo, NY
EVENT: Aerials

Hannah Kearney
BIRTH DATE: 2.26.1986
⌂ Norwich, VT
EVENT: Moguls

Jana Lindsey
BIRTH DATE: 9.18.1984
⌂ Black Hawk, SD
EVENT: Aerials

Heather McPhie
BIRTH DATE: 5.28.1984
⌂ Bozeman, MT
EVENT: Moguls

Michael Morse
BIRTH DATE: 4.2.1981
⌂ Duxbury, MA
EVENT: Moguls

Jeret Peterson
BIRTH DATE: 12.12.1981
⌂ Boise, ID
EVENT: Aerials

Casey Puckett
BIRTH DATE: 9.22.1972
⌂ Aspen, CO
EVENT: Ski Cross

Daron Rahlves
BIRTH DATE: 6.12.1973
⌂ Sugar Bowl, CA
EVENT: Ski Cross

Michelle Roark
BIRTH DATE: 11.16.1974
⌂ Denver, CO
EVENT: Moguls

Nate Roberts
BIRTH DATE: 3.24.1982
⌂ Park City, UT
EVENT: Moguls

Lacy Schnoor
BIRTH DATE: 6.12.1985
⌂ Draper, UT
EVENT: Aerials

Ryan St. Onge
BIRTH DATE: 2.7.1983
⌂ Winter Park, CO
EVENT: Aerials

Bryon Wilson
BIRTH DATE: 4.7.1988
⌂ Butte, MT
EVENT: Moguls

Ice Hockey — Men

David Backes
BIRTH DATE: 5.1.1984
🏛 Blaine, MN
POSITION: Forward
(St. Louis Blues)

Dustin Brown
BIRTH DATE: 11.4.1984
🏛 Ithaca, NY
POSITION: Forward
(Los Angeles Kings)

Ryan Callahan
BIRTH DATE: 3.21.1985
🏛 Rochester, NY
POSITION: Forward
(New York Rangers)

Chris Drury
BIRTH DATE: 8.20.1976
🏛 Trumbull, CT
POSITION: Forward
(New York Rangers)

Tim Gleason
BIRTH DATE: 1.29.1983
🏛 Clawson, MI
POSITION: Defenseman
(Carolina Hurricanes)

Jack Johnson
BIRTH DATE: 1.13.1987
🏛 Ann Arbor, MI
POSITION: Defenseman
(Los Angeles Kings)

Erik Johnson
BIRTH DATE: 3.21.1988
🏛 Bloomington, MN
POSITION: Defenseman
(St. Louis Blues)

Patrick Kane
BIRTH DATE: 11.19.1988
🏛 Buffalo, NY
POSITION: Forward
(Chicago Blackhawks)

Phil Kessel
BIRTH DATE: 10.2.1987
🏛 Madison, WI
POSITION: Forward
(Toronto Maple Leafs)

Ryan Kesler
BIRTH DATE: 8.31.1984
🏛 Livonia, MI
POSITION: Forward
(Vancouver Canucks)

Jamie Langenbrunner
BIRTH DATE: 7.24.1975
🏛 Cloquet, MN
POSITION: Forward
(New Jersey Devils)

Ryan Malone
BIRTH DATE: 12.1.1979
🏛 Pittsburgh, PA
POSITION: Forward
(Tampa Bay Lightning)

Ryan Miller
BIRTH DATE: 7.17.1980
🏛 East Lansing, MI
POSITION: Goaltender
(Buffalo Sabres)

Brooks Orpik
BIRTH DATE: 9.26.1980
🏛 San Francisco, CA
POSITION: Defenseman
(Pittsburgh Penguins)

Zach Parise
BIRTH DATE: 7.28.1984
🏛 Prior Lake, MN
POSITION: Forward
(New Jersey Devils)

Joe Pavelski
BIRTH DATE: 7.11.1984
🏛 Plover, WI
POSITION: Forward
(San Jose Sharks)

Jonathan Quick
BIRTH DATE: 1.21.1986
🏛 Hamden, CT
POSITION: Goaltender
(Los Angeles Kings)

Brian Rafalski
BIRTH DATE: 9.28.1973
🏛 Dearborn, MI
POSITION: Defenseman
(Detroit Red Wings)

Bobby Ryan
BIRTH DATE: 3.17.1987
🏛 Cherry Hill, NJ
POSITION: Forward
(Anaheim Ducks)

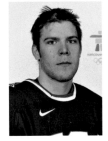

Paul Stastny
BIRTH DATE: 12.27.1985
🏛 St. Louis, MO
POSITION: Forward
(Colorado Avalanche)

Ryan Suter
BIRTH DATE: 1.21.1985
🏛 Madison, WI
POSITION: Defenseman
(Nashville Predators)

Tim Thomas
BIRTH DATE: 4.15.1974
🏛 Flint, MI
POSITION: Goaltender
(Boston Bruins)

Ryan Whitney
BIRTH DATE: 2.19.1983
🏛 Scituate, MA
POSITION: Defenseman
(Anaheim Ducks)

Ice Hockey — Women

Kacey Bellamy
BIRTH DATE: 4.22.1987
🏛 Westfield, MA
POSITION: Defenseman

Caitlin Cahow
BIRTH DATE: 5.20.1985
🏛 Branford, CT
POSITION: Defenseman

Lisa Chesson
BIRTH DATE: 8.18.1986
🏛 Plainfield, IL
POSITION: Defenseman

Julie Chu
BIRTH DATE: 3.13.1982
🏛 Fairfield, CT
POSITION: Forward

Natalie Darwitz
BIRTH DATE: 10.13.1983
🏛 Eagan, MN
POSITION: Forward

Megan Duggan
BIRTH DATE: 9.3.1987
🏛 Danvers, MA
POSITION: Forward

Molly Engstrom
BIRTH DATE: 3.1.1983
🏛 Siren, WI
POSITION: Defenseman

Hilary Knight
BIRTH DATE: 7.12.1989
🏛 Hanover, NH
POSITION: Forward

Jocelyne Lamoureux
BIRTH DATE: 7.3.1989
🏛 Grand Forks, ND
POSITION: Forward

Monique Lamoureux
BIRTH DATE: 7.3.1989
🏛 Grand Forks, ND
POSITION: Forward

Erika Lawler
BIRTH DATE: 2.5.1987
🏛 Fitchburg, MA
POSITION: Forward

Gigi Marvin
BIRTH DATE: 3.7.1987
🏛 Warroad, MN
POSITION: Forward

Brianne McLaughlin
BIRTH DATE: 6.20.1987
🏛 Sheffield Village, OH
POSITION: Goaltender

Jenny Potter
BIRTH DATE: 1.12.1979
🏛 Edina, MN
POSITION: Forward

Angela Ruggiero
BIRTH DATE: 1.3.1980
🏛 Simi Valley, CA
POSITION: Defenseman

Molly Schaus
BIRTH DATE: 7.29.1988
🏛 Natick, MA
POSITION: Goaltender

Kelli Stack
BIRTH DATE: 1.13.1988
🏛 Brooklyn Heights, OH
POSITION: Forward

Karen Thatcher
BIRTH DATE: 2.29.1984
🏛 Blaine, WA
POSITION: Forward

Jessie Vetter
BIRTH DATE: 12.19.1985
🏛 Cottage Grove, WI
POSITION: Goaltender

Kerry Weiland
BIRTH DATE: 10.18.1980
🏛 Palmer, AK
POSITION: Defenseman

Jinelle Zaugg-Siergiej
BIRTH DATE: 3.27.1986
🏛 Eagle River, WI
POSITION: Forward

Luge

Tony Benshoof
BIRTH DATE: 7.7.1975
🏠 White Bear Lake, MN
EVENT: Singles

Julia Clukey
BIRTH DATE: 4.29.1985
🏠 Augusta, ME
EVENT: Singles

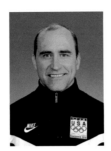

Mark Grimmette
BIRTH DATE: 1.23.1971
🏠 Muskegon, MI
EVENT: Doubles
(Partner: Martin)

Erin Hamlin
BIRTH DATE: 11.19.1986
🏠 Remsen, NY
EVENT: Singles

Dan Joye
BIRTH DATE: 2.19.1985
🏠 Carmel, NY
EVENT: Doubles
(Parnter: Niccum)

Brian Martin
BIRTH DATE: 1.19.1974
🏠 Palo Alto, CA
EVENT: Doubles
(Partner: Grimmette)

Chris Mazdzer
BIRTH DATE: 6.26.1988
🏠 Saranac Lake, NY
EVENT: Singles

Christian Niccum
BIRTH DATE: 1.27.1978
🏠 Woodinville, WA
EVENT: Doubles
(Parnter: Joye)

Megan Sweeney
BIRTH DATE: 2.17.1987
🏠 Suffield, CT
EVENT: Singles

Bengt Walden
BIRTH DATE: 4.16.1973
🏠 Nacka, Sweden
EVENT: Singles

Nordic Combined

Brett Camerota
BIRTH DATE: 1.9.1985
🏠 Park City, UT
EVENT: Indiv. Normal Hill,
Team Large Hill

Billy Demong
BIRTH DATE: 3.29.1980
🏠 Vermontville, NY
EVENT: Indiv. Normal Hill,
Indiv. Large Hill,
Team Large Hill

Taylor Fletcher
BIRTH DATE: 5.11.1990
🏠 Steamboat Springs, CO
EVENT: Indiv. Large Hill
(also competed in Ski
Jumping Team event)

Todd Lodwick
BIRTH DATE: 11.21.1976
🏠 Steamboat Springs, CO
EVENT: Indiv. Normal Hill,
Indiv. Large Hill,
Team Large Hill

Johnny Spillane
BIRTH DATE: 11.24.1980
🏠 Steamboat Springs, CO
EVENT: Indiv. Normal Hill,
Indiv. Large Hill,
Team Large Hill

Short Track Speedskating

Allison Baver
BIRTH DATE: 8.11.1980
🏛 Sinking Spring, PA
EVENT: 1000m, 1500m,
3000m Relay

J.R. Celski
BIRTH DATE: 7.17.1990
🏛 Federal Way, WA
EVENT: 1000m, 1500m,
5000m Relay

Simon Cho
BIRTH DATE: 10.7.1991
🏛 Laurel, MD
EVENT: 500m,
5000m Relay

Kimberly Derrick
BIRTH DATE: 4.28.1985
🏛 Memphis, TN
EVENT: 1000m, 1500m,
3000m Relay

Alyson Dudek
BIRTH DATE: 7.30.1990
🏛 Hales Corners, WI
EVENT: 500m,
3000m Relay

Lana Gehring
BIRTH DATE: 8.21.1990
🏛 Glenview, IL
EVENT: 3000m Relay

Travis Jayner
BIRTH DATE: 5.9.1982
🏛 Midland, MI
EVENT: 1000m,
5000m Relay

Jordan Malone
BIRTH DATE: 4.20.1984
🏛 Denton, TX
EVENT: 500m, 1500m,
5000m Relay

Apolo Anton Ohno
BIRTH DATE: 5.22.1982
🏛 Seattle, WA
EVENT: 500m, 1000m,
1500m, 5000m Relay

Katherine Reutter
BIRTH DATE: 7.30.1988
🏛 Champaign, IL
EVENT:500m, 1000m,
1500m, 3000m Relay

Skeleton

Eric Bernotas
BIRTH DATE: 8.5.1971
🏛 Avondale, PA
EVENT: Singles

John Daly
BIRTH DATE: 6.10.1985
🏛 Smithtown, NY
EVENT: Singles

Zach Lund
BIRTH DATE: 3.22.1979
🏛 Salt Lake City, UT
EVENT: Singles

Noelle Pikus-Pace
BIRTH DATE: 12.8.1982
🏛 Orem, UT
EVENT: Singles

Katie Uhlaender
BIRTH DATE: 7.17.1984
🏛 Breckenridge, CO
EVENT: Singles

Ski Jumping

Nick Alexander
BIRTH DATE: 8.24.1988
🏠 Lebanon, NH
EVENT: Normal Hill Indiv.,
Large Hill Indiv., Team

Peter Frenette
BIRTH DATE: 2.24.1992
🏠 Saranac Lake, NY
EVENT: Normal Hill Indiv.,
Large Hill Indiv., Team

Taylor Fletcher
BIRTH DATE: 5.11.1990
🏠 Steamboat Springs, CO
EVENT: Team (also
competed in Nordic
Combined)

Anders Johnson
BIRTH DATE: 4.23.1989
🏠 Park City, UT
EVENT: Normal Hill Indiv.,
Large Hill Indiv., Team

Two days after his final competition—the team ski jumping event—Peter Frenette turned 18. He was the youngest male competing on the U.S. Olympic Team in Vancouver. (PHOTO BY LARS BARON/BONGARTS/GETTY IMAGES)

Snowboarding

Nick Baumgartner
BIRTH DATE: 12.17.1981
🏠 Iron River, MI
EVENT: Snowboardcross

Gretchen Bleiler
BIRTH DATE: 4.10.1981
🏠 Aspen, CO
EVENT: Halfpipe

Greg Bretz
BIRTH DATE: 12.19.1990
🏠 Mammoth Lakes, CA
EVENT: Halfpipe

Callan Chythlook-Sifsof
BIRTH DATE: 2.14.1989
🏠 Girdwood, AK
EVENT: Snowboardcross

Kelly Clark
BIRTH DATE: 7.26.1983
🏠 Mt. Snow, VT
EVENT: Halfpipe

Michelle Gorgone
BIRTH DATE: 10.18.1983
🏠 Boston, MA
EVENT: Parallel Giant Slalom

Faye Gulini
BIRTH DATE: 3.24.1992
🏠 Salt Lake City, UT
EVENT: Snowboardcross

Elena Hight
BIRTH DATE: 8.17.1989
🏠 South Lake Tahoe, CA
EVENT: Halfpipe

Nate Holland
BIRTH DATE: 11.8.1978
🏠 Squaw Valley, CA
EVENT: Snowboardcross

Lindsey Jacobellis
BIRTH DATE: 8.19.1985
🏠 Stratton Mountain, VT
EVENT: Snowboardcross

Tyler Jewell
BIRTH DATE: 2.21.1977
🏠 Steamboat Springs, CO
EVENT: Parallel Giant Slalom

Chris Klug
BIRTH DATE: 11.18.1972
🏠 Aspen, CO
EVENT: Parallel Giant Slalom

Scotty Lago
BIRTH DATE: 11.12.1987
🏠 Seabrook, NH
EVENT: Halfpipe

Hannah Teter
BIRTH DATE: 1.27.1987
🏠 Belmont, VT
EVENT: Halfpipe

Louie Vito
BIRTH DATE: 3.20.1988
🏠 Sandy, UT
EVENT: Halfpipe

Graham Watanabe
BIRTH DATE: 3.19.1982
🏠 Sun Valley, ID
EVENT: Snowboardcross

Seth Wescott
BIRTH DATE: 6.28.1976
🏠 Sugarloaf, ME
EVENT: Snowboardcross

Shaun White
BIRTH DATE: 9.3.1986
🏠 Carlsbad, CA
EVENT: Halfpipe

Speedskating

Ryan Bedford
BIRTH DATE: 10.20.1986
⌂ Midland, MI
EVENT: 10,000m

Rebekah Bradford
BIRTH DATE: 4.30.1983
⌂ Apple Valley, MN
EVENT: 1000m

Lauren Cholewinski
BIRTH DATE: 11.15.1988
⌂ York, SC
EVENT: 500m

Shani Davis
BIRTH DATE: 8.13.1982
⌂ Chicago, IL
EVENT: 500m, 1000m,
1500m, 5000m

Tucker Fredricks
BIRTH DATE: 4.16.1984
⌂ Janesville, WI
EVENT: 500m

Brian Hansen
BIRTH DATE: 9.3.1990
⌂ Glenview, IL
EVENT: 1500m,
Team Pursuit

Chad Hedrick
BIRTH DATE: 4.17.1977
⌂ Spring, TX
EVENT: 1000m, 1500m,
5000m, Team Pursuit

Jonathan Kuck
BIRTH DATE: 3.14.1990
⌂ Champaign, IL
EVENT: 10,000m,
Team Pursuit

Maria Lamb
BIRTH DATE: 1.4.1986
⌂ River Falls, WI
EVENT: 5000m

Trevor Marsicano
BIRTH DATE: 4.5.1989
⌂ Ballston Spa, NY
EVENT: 1000m, 1500m,
5000m, Team Pursuit

Elli Ochowicz
BIRTH DATE: 12.15.1983
⌂ Hartland, WI
EVENT: 500m, 1000m

Nick Pearson
BIRTH DATE: 8.13.1979
⌂ West Allis, WI
EVENT: 500m, 1000m

**Catherine Raney-
Norman**
BIRTH DATE: 6.20.1980
⌂ Elm Grove, WI
EVENT: 1500m, 3000m,
Team Pursuit

Heather Richardson
BIRTH DATE: 3.20.1989
⌂ High Point, NC
EVENT: 500m, 1000m,
1500m

Jennifer Rodriguez
BIRTH DATE: 6.8.1976
⌂ Miami, FL
EVENT: 500m, 1000m,
1500m, Team Pursuit

Jilleanne Rookard
BIRTH DATE: 1.9.1983
⌂ Woodhaven, MI
EVENT: 1500m, 3000m,
5000m, Team Pursuit

Nancy Swider-Peltz, Jr.
BIRTH DATE: 1.10.1987
⌂ Wheaton, IL
EVENT: 3000m, Team
Pursuit

Mitch Whitmore
BIRTH DATE: 12.18.1989
⌂ Waukesha, WI
EVENT: 500m

Alpine Skiing

Mark Bathum
BIRTH DATE: 10.1.1958
🏠 Seattle, WA
EVENT: Visually Impaired—
Downhill, Super G, Super
Combined, Giant Slalom,
Slalom

Carl Burnett
BIRTH DATE: 6.14.1981
🏠 Cape Elizabeth, ME
EVENT: Sitting—Super G,
Super Combined, Giant
Slalom, Slalom

Heath Calhoun
BIRTH DATE: 6.29.1979
🏠 Grundy, VA
EVENT: Sitting—Super G,
Super Combined, Slalom

Nick Catanzarite
BIRTH DATE: 5.23.1977
🏠 Mishawaka, IN
EVENT: Sitting—Super G,
Giant Slalom

Chris Devlin-Young
BIRTH DATE: 12.26.1961
🏠 San Diego, CA
EVENT: Sitting—Downhill,
Super G, Super Combined,
Giant Slalom, Slalom

Ralph Green
BIRTH DATE: 6.1.1977
🏠 Brooklyn, NY
EVENT: Standing—Super G,
Giant Slalom, Slalom

Gerald Hayden
BIRTH DATE: 5.18.1980
🏠 Winter Park, CO
EVENT: Sitting—Giant
Slalom

Ian Jansing
BIRTH DATE: 12.26.1985
🏠 St. Louis, MO
EVENT: Standing—Giant
Slalom

Allison Jones
BIRTH DATE: 5.12.1984
🏠 Colorado Springs, CO
EVENT: Standing—
Downhill, Super G, Super
Combined, Giant Slalom,
Slalom

Ricci Kilgore
BIRTH DATE: 4.4.1980
🏠 Reno, NV
EVENT: Sitting—Giant
Slalom

Luba Lowery
BIRTH DATE: 3.17.1988
🏠 Cumberland Foreside, ME
EVENT: Sitting—Giant Slalom,
Slalom

Monte Meier
BIRTH DATE: 4.27.1971
🏠 Park City, UT
EVENT: Standing—
Downhill, Super G, Super
Combined, Slalom

Alana Nichols
BIRTH DATE: 3.21.1983
🏠 Farmington, NM
EVENT: Sitting—Downhill,
Super G, Super Combined,
Giant Slalom, Slalom

Hannah Pennington
BIRTH DATE: 5.8.1978
🏠 Winter Park, CO
EVENT: Standing—Slalom

George Sansonetis
BIRTH DATE: 10.20.1972
🏠 Fraser, CO
EVENT: Standing—
Downhill, Super G,
Giant Slalom, Slalom

Caitlin Sarubbi
BIRTH DATE: 2.22.1990
🏠 Brooklyn, NY
EVENT: Visually Impaired—
Downhill, Super G, Super
Combined, Giant Slalom,
Slalom

Laurie Stephens
BIRTH DATE: 3.5.1984
🏠 Wenham, MA
EVENT: Sitting—Downhill,
Super G, Super Combined,
Giant Slalom, Slalom

Elitsa Storey
BIRTH DATE: 12.26.1987
🏠 Sun Valley, ID
EVENT: Standing—Downhill,
Slalom

Slater Storey
BIRTH DATE: 1.9.1986
🏠 Sun Valley, ID
EVENT: Guide—Mark
Bathum

Joe Tompkins
BIRTH DATE: 8.20.1968
🏠 Juneau, AK
EVENT: Sitting—Downhill

Danelle Umstead
BIRTH DATE: 2.15.1972
🏠 Taos, NM
EVENT: Visually Impaired—
Downhill, Super G, Super
Combined, Giant Slalom,
Slalom

Rob Umstead
BIRTH DATE: 3.10.1970
🏠 Taos, NM
POSITION: Guide—Danelle
Umstead

Stephani Victor
BIRTH DATE: 8.29.1969
🏠 Park City, UT
EVENT: Sitting—Downhill,
Super G, Super Combined,
Giant Slalom, Slalom

Tyler Walker
BIRTH DATE: 4.10.1986
🏠 Franconia, NH
EVENT: Sitting—Downhill,
Super G, Giant Slalom,
Slalom

Alpine Skiing

Bradley Washburn
BIRTH DATE: 10.12.1986
⛰ Winter Park, CO
EVENT: Standing—Downhill, Super G, Giant Slalom, Slalom

Gwynn Watkins
BIRTH DATE: 4.3.1974
⛰ Mt. Shasta, CA
EVENT: Guide—Caitlin Sarubbi

John Whitney
BIRTH DATE: 1.13.1984
⛰ Towson, MD
EVENT: Standing—Super G, Giant Slalom, Slalom

Betty Lynn
BIRTH DATE: 12.20.2006
⛰ Taos, NM
POSITION: Off Slope Guide—Danelle Umstead

Biathlon & Cross-Country Skiing

Monica Bascio
BIRTH DATE: 9.16.1969
⛰ Evergreen, CO
EVENT: Sitting—5km, 10km, 1km Sprint

Sean Halsted
BIRTH DATE: 11.24.1970
⛰ Spokane, WA
EVENT: Sitting—10km, 15km, 1km Sprint

Chris Klebl
BIRTH DATE: 1.5.1972
⛰ Heber City, UT
EVENT: Sitting—15km, 1km Sprint

Greg Mallory
BIRTH DATE: 3.23.1968
⛰ Portland, OR
EVENT: Sitting—15km

Andy Soule
BIRTH DATE: 12.2.1980
⛰ Pearland, TX
EVENT: **Biathlon:** Sitting—12.5km, 2.4km Pursuit | **Cross-Country Skiing:** Sitting—10km, 15km, 1km Sprint

Kelly Underkofler
BIRTH DATE: 4.10.1984
⛰ St. Paul, MN
EVENT: **Biathlon:** Standing—12.5km, 3km Pursuit | **Cross-Country Skiing:** Standing—5km Classic, 15km Free, 1km Sprint

Sled Hockey

Mike Blabac
BIRTH DATE: 1.18.1794
🏛 Buffalo, NY
POSITION: Goaltender

Steve Cash
BIRTH DATE: 5.9.1989
🏛 Overland, MO
POSITION: Goaltender

Taylor Chace
BIRTH DATE: 5.9.1986
🏛 Hampton Falls, NH
POSITION: Defense

Jimmy Connelly
BIRTH DATE: 10.27.1989
🏛 Galloway, NJ
POSITION: Defense

Brad Emmerson
BIRTH DATE: 12.16.1985
🏛 Amherst, NY
POSITION: Forward

Joseph Howard
BIRTH DATE: 5.26.1966
🏛 Kingston, MA
POSITION: Forward

Tim Jones
BIRTH DATE: 12.16.1987
🏛 Mt. Ephraim
POSITION: Forward

Nikko Landeros
BIRTH DATE: 4.28.1989
🏛 Berthoud, CO
POSITION: Defense

Taylor Lipsett
BIRTH DATE: 1.20.1987
🏛 Mesquite, TX
POSITION: Forward

Adam Page
BIRTH DATE: 3.10.1982
🏛 Lancaster, NY
POSITION: Defense

Joshua Pauls
BIRTH DATE: 12.31.1992
🏛 South Plainfield, NJ
POSITION: Defense

Alexi Salamone
BIRTH DATE: 6.17.1987
🏛 Grand Island, NY
POSITION: Forward

Gregory Shaw
BIRTH DATE: 2.28.1990
🏛 Park City, UT
POSITION: Forward

Michael Torres
BIRTH DATE: 10.31.1991
🏛 Riverside, NJ
POSITION: Forward

Andy Yohe
BIRTH DATE: 7.21.1978
🏛 Bettendorf, IA
POSITION: Defense

Wheelchair Curling

James Joseph
BIRTH DATE: 9.1.1962
🏠 New Hartford, NY
POSITION: Second

Jacqui Kapinowski
BIRTH DATE: 11.28.1962
🏠 Point Pleasant, NJ
POSITION: Lead

Patrick McDonald
BIRTH DATE: 6.9.1967
🏠 Orangeville, CA
POSITION: Alternate

Augusto Perez
BIRTH DATE: 11.9.1972
🏠 East Syracuse, NY
POSITION: Skip

Jim Pierce
BIRTH DATE: 2.17.1963
🏠 North Syracuse, NY
POSITION: Vice-Skip

(PHOTO BY KEVIN C. COX/GETTY IMAGES)

2014 OLYMPIC WINTER GAMES

See you in Sochi

(Photo by Hannah Johnston/Getty Images)

USA

Table of Contents

Whistler Village. (PHOTO BY FABRICE COFFRINI/AFP/GETTY IMAGES)

2010 U.S. OLYMPIC TEAM
Chef de Mission

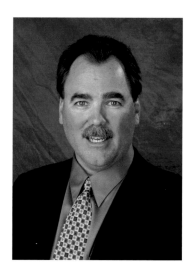

Olympic history was made during seventeen remarkable days in February, 2010, when the U.S. Olympic Team established a new record by winning 37 medals at the XXI Olympic Winter Games, the most by any nation since the inaugural Winter Games in 1924 in Chamonix, France.

The breathtaking performances by our athletes during the Games, and their conduct as representatives of the nation, their families, hometowns and their sport, were brilliant standards of achievement. But none of this came about only during the seventeen days of the Games, it began some seven years ago as Vancouver won the right to host this gathering of the greatest athletes in the world.

The men and women of the United States Olympic Committee's Sports Performance and International Games Division, working side by side with the winter sport National Governing Bodies, carefully crafted what became a marvelous blueprint for success. The plan utilized financial and operational resources and an exceptional level of support services before and during the Games, presenting every American Olympian with the opportunity to focus on reaching the podium and realizing their dreams.

The Vancouver Olympic Games Organizing Committee, its staff and leadership and its thousands of dedicated and passionate volunteers, made the Olympic Family and the IOC proud while conducting compelling and exceptional Games. VANOC was at its best, creating world class facilities, new state-of-the-art Olympic villages in Vancouver and Whistler, and generously assisting the USOC and the United States delegation with a "can do" attitude from the beginning in 2003 through the Closing Ceremony.

We are grateful and appreciative of the dedication and commitment by our Canadian hosts and colleagues for their professionalism and the production of these wonderful Games, and to the citizens of a proud Canada.

A world-wide television audience of almost four billion witnessed the majestic pageantry of British Columbia and historic performances by U.S. athletes. Bode Miller, Lindsey Vonn, Julia Mancuso, Apolo Ohno, Shani Davis, Evan Lysacek, Shaun White, Bill Demong, Johnny Spillane, Seth Wescott, Steve Holcomb's Night Train bobsled team, and the U.S. Men's and Women's Hockey Teams among so many American athletes who carried a nation's pride, hopes and honor on their shoulders as they stood on the victory podium.

Two hundred sixteen American Athletes made a country proud and inspired its youth.

These Games will define future expectations for U.S. Athletes, the National Governing Bodies, resources and Games preparation by the USOC. The historic results are attributable to a pursuit of excellence and perseverance of our Olympians, as well as the USOC's steadfast commitment to its organizational mission and values.

I was proud and honored to lead the 2010 U.S. Olympic Winter Games Team as its *Chef de Mission*, and respectful and proud of the extraordinary effort by the National Governing Bodies in preparing the athletes who served our country with passion, respect and pride.

I am deeply grateful to Larry Probst, Scott Blackmun, Mike English, Leslie Gamez and scores of others with the USOC who provided leadership and support to our delegation and its critical operations and execution. This exemplary effort achieved our historic results, the work of many behind the scenes as well.

Two hundred sixteen American Athletes made a country proud and inspired its youth. I am gratified to have been a part of their record setting Olympic Games legacy.

With admiration,

Michael P. Plant

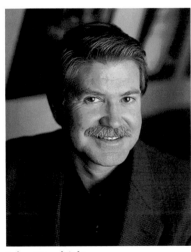

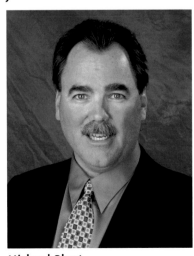

275

Executive Leadership

Scott Blackmun
Chief Executive Officer

Lisa Baird
Chief Marketing Officer

Norman Bellingham
Chief Operating Officer

Larry Buendorf
Chief Security Officer

Rana Dershowitz
General Counsel, Chief of
Legal & Government Affairs

Mike English
Chief of Sport
Performance

Robert Fasulo
Chief of International
Relations

Walt Glover
Chief Financial Officer

Charlie Huebner
Chief of U.S. Paralympics

Janine Alfano Musholt
Chief Development Officer

John Ruger
Athlete Ombudsman

Patrick Sandusky
Chief Communications
Officer

Christopher G. Sullivan
Chief Bid Officer

Alan Ashley
Managing Director,
Sport Performance

Trevor Miller
Managing Director,
Information Technology

Pam Sawyer
Managing Director,
Human Resources

Debra Yoshimura
Managing Director, Audit

2010 U.S. OLYMPIC TEAM
Support Delegation

USOC DIVISIONS

Athletes Advisory Council
Sloan DuRoss | Athlete Services Coordinator-Vancouver
Nina Kemppel | AAC Representative
Sarah Konrad | Athlete Services Coordinator-Whistler
Matt Van Houten | AAC Chairman

Board of Directors
Larry Probst | Chairman
Ursula Burns | Board of Directors Member
Anita DeFrantz | Board of Directors Member
James Easton | Board of Directors Member
Jair Lynch | Board of Directors Member
Mary McCagg | Board of Directors Member
Mike Plant | Chef de Mission

Board Liaison
Carol Brown | Board Liaison

Broadcasting
Mike Favatella | Games Broadcasting Support
Andy Goyne | Games Broadcasting Support

Communications
Keith Bryant | Press Officer
Bob Condron | Director of Media Services
Lindsay Hogan | Olympic Ambassador Program and
  Managing Victory
Erica Hutchinson | Press Conferences
Peggy Manter | Main Press Center Office Manager and
  Volunteer Coordinator
Kevin Neuendorf | Media Services Manager-Whistler
Lisa Ramsperger | USA Daily and Daily Wrap-Up Editorial
  Director
Nicole Saunches | NBC Relations
Cindy Stinger | Team Processing and USA House Store
Maureen Weekes | Chief Communications Officer Support
  and Managing Victory

Development
Janine Alfano | Donor Program
James Bjorklund | Donor Program
Sarah Cantwell | Donor Program
Gail Doyle | Donor Program
Christine Walshe | Donor Program
Jill Zeldin | Donor Program

Executive
Scott Blackmun | Secretary General
Norman Bellingham | Chief Operating Officer
Michelle Stuart | Executive Assistant to the Secretary
  General

Chris Sullivan | Board and Guest Liaison

Executive-Audit
Debra Yoshimura | Team Processing Office Manager

Executive-Communications
Patrick Sandusky | Chief Communications Officer

Executive-Finance
Walt Glover | Chief Financial Officer

Executive-Information Technology
Trevor Miller | IT-USA House

Executive-International Relations
Robert Fasulo | Chief of International Relations

Executive-Legal
Rana Dershowitz | General Counsel, Chief of Legal and
  Government Affairs
John Ruger | Ombudsman

Executive-Marketing
Lisa Baird | Chief Marketing Officer

Executive-Security
Larry Buendorf | Chief Security Officer

Executive-Sport Performance
Alan Ashley | Managing Director
Mike English | Chief of Sport Performance

Finance
Morane Kerek | Finance-Whistler
Bruce Scott | Finance-USA House

Government Relations
Desiree Filippone | Government Liaison
Karen Irish | Government Liaison

Hamilton Watches
Heather LaRocco | Team Processing

Information Technology
Richard Bittles | IT-Whistler
Mia Delumpa | IT-Team Processing
Dave McDaniel | IT-Vancouver Village
Mike Redmond | IT-General Support
Donnie Schexnayder | IT-Main Press Center and USA House
Ray Velchek | IT-Main Press Center and USA House

International Games
Lenny Abbey | Ground Transport Manager
Linda Addington | Housing Manager-Vancouver Village
Katie Clifford | Team Processing Director
Rebecca Crawford | Village Director-Vancouver Village
Lisa Elson | Team Processing-Apparel Distribution
Leslie Gamez | Games Director
Nancy Gonsalves | Tickets/VIK/Air Travel Director
Doug Ingram | Performance Services Center Director
Debbie Jacobsen | Team Processing-Housing and IT Support
Ian Jaray | Team Processing-Logistics & Shipping
Brittney Moore | Administrative Support
Charles Paddock | Airport Operations Support
Denise Thomas | Accreditation and Sport Entry

International Relations
Nancy Balty | IR Manager
Carolina Bayon | IR Director
Dragomir Cioroslan | IT Director
Sabrina Failler | IR Support
Annie Grabarsky | IR Manager

Legal
Gary Johansen | Legal Athlete Support
Laura Macaulay Peeters | Legal Athlete Support-Observer
Amy Savela | Marketing Legal Support

Marketing
Rachel Barkan | USA House Operations
Mary-Clare Brennan | USA House Operations
Jennifer Brown | Administrative Support
Chris Coleman | Athlete Marketing
Susan Goldsmith | Partner Servicing
Jim Hadley | USA House-Whistler
Tricia LaChat | USA House-Retail Store Operations
Michael O'Conor | Partner Servicing
Mallika Pereira | USA House-Whistler
John Pierce | Partner Servicing
Mitch Poll | Partner Servicing
Jordan Schlachter | Business Development
Anne Shoulders | USA House-Store Operations
Laura Sokol | USA House-Retail Store Manager
Erin Turner | USA House Operations
Chester Wheeler | Business Development
Peter Zeytoonjian | USA House-Retail Store Manager

Member & Event Services
Mayo Arties | USA House-AV/Sound/Operations
Dereck Fisher | USA House-AV/Sound/Operations
Emily Ford | USA House Manager-Whistler
Michelle Mostert | Board of Directors Support
Benecia Newhouse | USA House Operations
Jerri Roush | USA House Director
Nicole Sather | USA House Support
Blake Zink | USOC Headquarters-Transportation

New Media
Scott Cronk | USA House-Store Support
Kyle Davidson | Team Processing
Lauren Pasquale | Director of New Media

NGB Business Development
Tammie Liddie | USA House Front Desk
Guillermo Rojas | USA House Operations and NGB Support

NGB Development
Eric Parthen | Airport Operations

Nortel
Clinton Berger | IT
Mark Tsujihara | IT

OC Tanner
Sandra Christensen | Team Processing
Mary Saenz | Team Processing

Genevieve Spackman | Team Processing
Allison VanVranken | Team Processing

Olympic Training Center-Colorado Springs
Teresa McAlpin | USA House Operations
Alicia McConnell | Team Processing-Apparel distribution
Terri Moreman | Team Processing and Nutrition
Nicki Robinson | Housing Manager-Whistler
Jerry Searson | USA House and Headquarters Transportation Manager
Fred Serna Jr. | Team Processing Transport and Shipping Support
Sherry Von Riesen | Procter & Gamble Family Center

Olympic Training Center-Lake Placid
Julie Garrett | Procter & Gamble Family Center

Paralympics
Jeannine Hansen | USA House Media
Dean Nakamura | USA House-AV/Sound/Operations
Sonya Norris | USA House Operations

Polo Ralph Lauren
Kendra Bracken-Ferguson | Team Processing
Jimmy Cabailo | Team Processing
Jose Collado | Team Processing-Tailor
Karey Crowley | Team Processing
Elsa Vera | Team Processing-Tailor

Singapore 2010
Vincent Eu | Team Processing Support

Sport Performance
Laura Anderson | Dietician
Alan Ashley | Performance Services Center Director-Whistler
Jill Baker | Team Processing-Apparel distribution
Wes Barnett | Performance Services Technician
Christine Bolger | Whistler Courier and Order of Ikkos
Michelle Brown | NGB Services & Logistics
Matt Cramer | NGB Services & Logistics-Whistler Village
John Crawley | Video Technician
Joe Cygan | Athletic Trainer-Whistler PSC
Kelley Fisher | Transportation
Tammie Forster | Airport Operations Support
Jennifer Geisheker | Administrative Support-Headquarters Hotel
Tammy Hendrian | Performance Services Center Administrative Support
Margie Hunt | Athletic Trainer and USADA Advisor
Rachel Isaacs | USA House-Operations and NGB Support
Stephanie Isley | Team Processing-Apparel distribution
Jay T Kearney | Performance Services Technician
Elizabeth Klikier | USA House Support
Robyn Mason | Video Technician
Dave McCann | Courier and Order Ikkos
Charles McClinton | NGB Services & Logistics
Fiona Morrison | Executive Assistant to Chief of Sport
Susie Parker-Simmons | Nutrition
Kirsten Peterson | Sport Psychology-Figure Skating

Steve Powderly | Transportation-Whistler
Scott Riewald | Performance Specialist
Kelly Skinner | Village Director-Whistler
Stacy Struble | Athletic Trainer
Peter Vint | Performance Specialist
Randy Wilber | Physiology

Strategic Planning
Tommy O'Hare | Strategic Planning
Lisa Sweet | Strategic Planning

United Airlines
Kim Mobley | Air Travel
Cassie Preston | Air Travel

University East London
Keith Gilbert Team Processing

USOC Contractor
Aimee Berg | TeamUSA.org Senior Writer
Steve Jeffries | Security
Bob Long | Photographer
Steve Powell | Videographer
Janis Sandberg | Photographer Assistant
Peggy Shinn | TeamUSA.org Senior Writer

Volunteer
Craig Bohnert | USOC News Bureau
Dr. Robert Bray | Physician-Whistler Performance
  Services Center
Dr. Per Gunnar Brolinson | Physician-USOC Headquarters
Penny Capps | Massage Therapist
Alexandra Clark | DePaul University-USA Daily, News
  Bureau
Chris Condron | Main Press Center-Press Conferences
Jim Constandt | Main Press Center Office
Charlotte Eriksen | DePaul University-USA Daily, News
  Bureau
Bill Hancock | Media-Special Ticketing
Nicki Hancock | Main Press Center Office
Dr. Tetsuya Hasegawa | Chiropractor and Athletic Trainer-
  Whistler Village
Linda Jager | Press Officer-Short Track
Christiana Johns | DePaul University-USA Daily, News
  Bureau
Brett Johnson | USOC News Bureau

Nicole Jomantas | Press Officer-Whistler Village
Brad Jones | Physical Therapist-Snowboard
Jill Kolivoski | Massage Therapist-Hockey (W)
John Kristoff | DePaul University-USA Daily, News Bureau
Bruce Lifrieri | Massage Therapist-Hockey (M)
Karen Linhart | USOC Hometown News Bureau
David Liu | Main Press Center Office
Dr. Michelle Look | Physician-Whistler Performance
  Services Center
Ben Lydon | Main Press Center Office
Mary Jo Maffei | DePaul University-USA Daily, News Bureau
Bill Mallon | USOC News Bureau-Olympic Historian
Candice McCallie | USOC News Bureau-USA Daily
Betsy McMillan | MPC Office & Press Conferences
Barb Meendering | Main Press Center Office
Dr. Ed Merrens | Physician-Whistler Village and all
  mountain sports
Jim Moeller | Chief Medical Officer
Irv Moss | USOC News Bureau
Joe O'Donnell | DePaul University-USA Daily, News Bureau
Nick Olivier | News Bureau-Whistler
Adam Perreault | Physical Therapist-Alpine Ski (M)
Debra Price | Massage Therapist-Whistler Performance
  Service Center
Michael Reed | Medical Director-Whistler Village
Mandy Rost | USA House Front Desk
Josh Sandell | Athletic Trainer-Whistler Village
Lynn Simmons | Main Press Center Office
Tim Simmons | Main Press Center Office
Lindsey Sine | Press Officer-Skiing
Jennifer Sullivan | DePaul University-USA Daily, News
  Bureau
Kevin Sullivan | USOC News Bureau
Alan Thomas | Massage Therapist
Dr. Blase Toto | Chiropractor
Ray Tufts | Athletic Trainer-Ice Hockey (M)
Cherylyn Underwood | Main Press Center Office
Vanessa Verbitsky | Main Press Center Office
Mike Walters | Massage Therapist-Whistler Village
Rob Weekes | Press Officer
Ron Wisner | Team Processing

NATIONAL GOVERNING BODY (NGB) STAFF

Alpine Skiing

Adam Korzun | NGB Support-Food Services
Dion Agee | Parent Program-Whistler
Josh Applegate | Assistant Coach-Technical (M)
Luke Bodensteiner | Vice President-Athletics
Michael Branch | Assistant Coach-Speed (M)
Chris Brigham | Head Coach-Speed (M)
Tobie Bow | NGB Support-Food Services
Ron Cake | NGB Support-Food Services
Forest Carey | Conditioning Coach
Dave Coombs | Technical Technician (M)
Ryan Cornish | Speed Technician (W)
Jen Desmond | Parent Program-Vancouver
Miha Dolinar | Speed Technician (W)
Sarah Duffany | Team Leader (W)
Anna-Katrina Egger | Team Leader (M)
Matteo Fattor | Technical Technician (W)
Troy Flanagan | Physiologist and Sport Science Director
Tara Fontenot | Physical Therapist (W)
Heinz Haemmerle | Speed and Technical Technician (W)
Martin Hager | Coach-Special Projects (W)
Jacque Hamilton | NGB Support-Food Services
Doug Haney | Press Officer (M&W)
Keith Henschen | Sport Psychologist
Alex Hoedlmoser | Head Speed Coach (W)
Robi Horvat | Technical Technician (M)
Kazuko Ikeda | Coach-Special Projects (W)
Alex Kalamar | Technical Technician (M)
Frank Kelble | Assistant Coach-Speed (W)
Tom Kelly | Press Officer
Mike Kenney | Combined Coach (M)
Karl Klein | NGB Support-Food Services
Chris Knight | Assistant Technical Coach (W)
Pete Korfiatas | Assistant Coach-Technical (M)
Pete Lavin | Coach-Start (M)
Seth McCadam | Assistant Coach-Technical (W)
Sean McCann | Sport Psychologist
Leo Mussi | Speed Technician (M)
Dokmai (Flower) Nowicki | NGB Support-Food Services
Dr. Terry Orr | Physician (M)
Rewk Patten | Assistant Coach-Speed (M)
Adam Perrault | Physical Therapist-Technical (M)
Richard Quincy | Medical Director
Sasha Rearick | Head Coach (M)
Christa Riepe | Physical Therapist-Speed (M)
Ernie Rimer | Coach-Conditioning (W)
Oliver Saringer | Coach-Special Projects (W)
Matt Schiller | Speed and Technical Technician (M)
Lesli Shooter | Physiologist (W)
Ales Sopotnik | Speed Technician (W)
Rudi Soulard | Head Coach-Technical (M)
Dr. Bill Sterett | Physician (W)
Jim Tracy | Head Coach (W)
Robert Trenkwalder | Coach-Special Projects (W)
Bernie Trojer | Technical Technician (M)
Andrea Vianello | Technical Technician (W)

Thomas Vonn | Coach-Vonn (W)
Trevor Wagner | Head Coach-Technical (W)
Chip White | Assistant Speed Coach (W)
Brandie Yeik | Physical Therapist (W)
Sepp Zannon | Speed Technician (M)

Biathlon

Armin Auchentaller | Head Coach
Remigius Bauer | Ski Technician and Grinder
Martin Biermaier | Physiotherapist
Bernd Eisenbichler | Team Leader
Andreas Emslander | Ski Technician
Viktoria Franke | Press Officer
Petr Garabik | Ski Technician
Per Nilsson | Head Coach
Christian Sieler | Ski Technician

Bobsled

Amanda Bird | Press Officer
Frank Briglia | Sled Technician and Mechanic
Sandy Caligiore | Press Officer
Byron Craighead | Athletic Trainer
Angelo Guerrera | Sled Technician
Lenny Kasten | Equipment & Logistics Manager
Scott Novack | Team Leader
Francoise Plozza | Assistant Coach-Driving
Sepp Plozza | Head Coach
Dr. Jason Ross | Start & Speed Coach
Janis Skrastins | Assistant Coach (M)
Brian Shimer | Head Coach (M)
Darrin Steele | Team Manager
William Tavares | Assistant Coach (W)

Cross-Country Skiing

Joakim Augustsson | Technician
Margo Christiansen | Press Officer
Erik Flora | Assistant Coach
Randy Gibbs | Technician
Chris Grover | Head Sprint Coach
Jon Hammermeister | Sport Psychologist
Kurt Jepson | Physical Therapist
Peter Johansson | Technician
Peter Vordenberg | Head Coach
Justin Wadsworth | Assistant Sprint Coach

Curling

Scott Baird | Strategy & Tactics Coach
John Coumbe-Lilley | Assistant Athletic Director and Sport Psychology
Phillip Drobnick | Coach (M)
Wally Henry | Coach (W)
Scott Higgins | Assistant Team Leader (and Assistant Coach)
Terry Kolesar | Press Officer
Brian McWilliams | Physiotherapist and Athletic Trainer
Rick Patzke | Press Officer
Rodger Schmidt | Strategy & Tactics Coach
Mark Swandby | Team Leader

Figure Skating

Scottie Bibb | Press Officer

Mickey Brown | Press Officer
Frank Carroll | Personal Coach-Lysacek/Nagasu
Richard Dalley | Team Manager and Technical Advisor
Judy Holmes | Team Physical Therapist
Lyndon Johnston | Personal Coach-Evora/Ladwig
Gennadi Karponosov | Personal Coach-Belbin/Agosto
Mitch Moyer | Team Leader
Yaroslava Nechaeva | Personal Coach-Samuelson/Bates
Lorrie Parker | Team Manager and Technical Advisor
Jim Peterson | Personal Coach-Denney/Barrett
Yuka Sato | Personal Coach-Abbott
Igor Shpilband | Personal Coach-Davis/White
Dr. Joseph "Skip" Zabilski | Physician
Tom Zakrajsek | Personal Coach-Flatt
Galina Zmievskaya | Personal Coach-Weir

Freestyle Skiing
Tschana Breslin | Conditioning Coach-Aerials
Matthew Christensen | Head Coach-Aerials
Brian Currutt | Assistant Coach-Aerials
Lasse Fahlen | Coach-Moguls Top
Josh Finley | Physical Therapist and Athletic Trainer-Ski
    Cross
Garth Hager | Coach-Moguls Bottom
Mike Henderson | Press Officer
Justin Hunt | Physical Therapist and Athletic Trainer-Moguls
    and Aerials
Dmitriy Kavunov | Assistant Coach-Aerials
Alex Moore | Conditioning Coach-Moguls and Ski Cross
Cheryl Pearson | Team Leader
Scott Rawles | Head Coach-Moguls
Dr. Andreas Sauerbrey | Physician
Todd Schirman | Coach-Moguls Airs
Chris Seemann | Coach-Moguls and Aerials
Tyler Shepherd | Head Ski Cross Coach
Ryan Snow | Assistant Coach-Aerials
Jonathan Weyant | Technician-Ski Cross
Willy Wiltz | Ski Cross Technician
Jeff Wintersteen | Head Coach

Ice Hockey – Men's
Brad Aldrich | Video
Mike Aldrich | Equipment
Brian Burke | General Manager
Dave Fischer | Press Officer
Scott Gordon | Assistant Coach
Gerry Helper | Press Officer
Jim Johannson | Team Leader
Bruce Lifrieri | Massage Therapist
David Poile | Associate General Manager
Derek Settlemyre | Equipment
Dr. Michael Stuart | Physician
John Tortorella | Assistant Coach
Ray Tufts | Athletic Trainer
Ron Wilson | Head Coach
Stan Wong | Athletic Trainer

Ice Hockey – Women's
Michele Amidon | Team Leader and General Manager

Dave Flint | Assistant Coach
Cornelia Holden | Sports Psychology Consultant
Dr. Jolie Holschen | Physician
Jim Jeans | Equipment
Christy Jeffries | Press Officer
Mark Johnson | Head Coach
Jodi McKenna | Assistant Coach
Emily McKissock | Video
Teena Murray | Strength Coach
Jill Radzinski, Athletic Trainer

Luge
Amanda Bird | Press Officer
Sandy Caligiore | Press Officer
Jim Cerullo | Athletic Trainer
Klim Gatker | Assistant Coach and Sled Equipment Support
Ron Rossi | Administrator
Wolfgang Schadler | Head Coach
Miro Zayonc | Assistant Coach
Fred Zimny | Team Leader

Nordic Combined
Paolo Bernardi | Technician
Margo Christiansen | Press Officer
John Farra | Team Leader
Dr. Larry Gaul | Physician
Chris Gilbertson | Assistant Coach
Rich Gordin | Sport Psychologist
Randy Hill | Physiologist-Nordic Combined and Cross
    Country
Dave Jarrett | Head Coach
Greg Poirier | Coach
Aaron Saari | Physical Therapist
Clarke Sullivan | Technician

Short Track
Jae Su Chun | Head Coach
Laurent Daignault | Assistant Coach and Equipment
    Technician
Nicole Detling-Miller | Sport Performance Consultant
Shane Domer | Strength Coach and Video Specialist
Brent Hamula | Athletic Trainer
Linda Jager | Press Officer
Jimmy Jang | Assistant Coach
Jack Mortell | Team Leader
Dr. Mike Noyes | Physician
Eric St. Pierre | Athletic Trainer
Guy Thibault | High Performance Director

Skeleton
Amanda Bird | Press Officer
Sandy Caligiore | Press Officer
Orvie Garrett | Sled Technician
Dr. Tetsuya Hasegawa | Chiropractor and Athletic Trainer
Lenny Kasten | Equipment & Logistics Manager
Scott Novack | Team Leader
Sepp Plozza | Head Coach
Martin Rettl | Coach-Driving
Darrin Steele | Team Manager
Gregory Sand | Team Manager and Assistant Coach

Ski Jumping
Jochen Danneberg | Head Coach

Snowboarding
Jeff Archibald | Coach-Snowboardcross
Nick Alexakos | Press Officer
Curtis Bacca | Technician-Snowboardcross
Rick Bower | Coach-Halfpipe
Tschana Breslin | Conditioning Coach
Andy Buckley | Technician-Snowboardcross
Alex Deibold | Snowboardcross Wax Tech (Pilot)
Stephan Eiseneggar | Technician-Parallel Giant Slalom
Peter Foley | Head Coach-Snowboardcross
Jeremy Forster | Program Director
Dr. Tom Hackett | Physician
Gillian Honeyman | Physical Therapist
Mike Jankowski | Head Coach-Halfpipe
Brad Jones | Half Pipe Physical Therapist and Conditioning
  Coach

Bud Keene | Coach-Halfpipe
Abbi Nyberg | Team Leader
Rob Roy | Assistant Coach-Parallel Giant Slalom
Lindsey Sine | Press Officer
Stu Soars | Technician-Halfpipe
Jan Wengelin | Coach-Parallel Giant Slalom

Speedskating
Ross Flowers | Sport Psychologist
Dr. Eric Heiden | Physician
Peri Kinder | Press Officer
Mike Kooreman | Team Leader and Assistant Coach-Sprint
Derek Parra | Head Coach-Allround
Carrie Petteys Needham | Dartfish Video Specialist
Ryan Shimabukuro | Head Coach-Sprint
Guy Thibault | High Performance Director
Laura Tietjen | Athletic Trainer-Speedskating
Fikre Wondrfrash | Athletic Trainer-Sprint

Evan Lysacek joins skating greats Peggy Fleming (Grenoble 1968), Brian Boitano (Calgary 1988) and Kristi Yamaguchi (Albertville 1992) at the USA House in Vancouver. (PHOTO BY CHRISTOPHER POLK/GETTY IMAGES)

France's Ted Piccard and Daron Rahlves (right) of the United States collide during the men's ski cross 1/8 final race. (Photo by Adrian Dennis/AFP/Getty Images)

TEAM USA - MEN'S
Alpine Skiing

By Anna-Katrina Egger

Alpine skiing is an individual sport but an alpine athlete can only be successful if he has a strong team behind him, which includes coaches, supporting staff as well as other athletes who push him to his limits.

Selecting the 2010 Olympic Team consisted of an on-going evaluation process to identify top performing athletes. It was a tough decision and was only completed by Jan. 26, 2010, (two weeks before departure day). There was an extensive list of criteria which provided the guidelines for the selection process, and all the athletes were aware of it at the beginning of the season. The criteria included their performance during the whole season; e.g. one or more top three finishes in International Ski Federation (FIS) Alpine World Cups. If there were no open spots, it ultimately came down to the discretion of the head coach, with input from the assistant coaches. For 2010 our team was a mix between experienced athletes like four-time Olympian Bode Miller and young athletes like first-time Olympians Tommy Ford and Nolan Kasper, who were 20 in Vancouver.

We had a very good preparation period this past summer with several training camps including two Southern Hemisphere camps in New Zealand and Chile in addition to several conditioning and other ski camps in the United States. Those camps were very important for the athletes as that was the time they got their equipment set up, and were in race shape and spirit for the upcoming competition season. Prior to the Games, the athletes competed in numerous competitions including FIS World Cup, Europa Cup and NorAm races where they competed against the world's best racers. There also was an Olympic Test Event in Whistler in winter of 2007/08 in the form of a World Cup race. Some selected athletes were able to get their first feeling for the future Winter Games race course.

Going into the Games we wanted to have everything as "normal" as possible. Our goal was to minimize the level of excitement and distraction. Therefore, we used outside housing. This ended up to be the right thing to do for our athletes and staff. Everybody was relaxed and an environment was created to ensure the athletes had everything they needed to prepare mentally and physically for high performance. The athletes were still able to experience the "Olympic feeling" by staying at the Olympic Villages in Whistler and Vancouver for a couple of nights after they were done competing.

> For 2010 our team was a mix between experienced athletes like four-time Olympian Bode Miller and young athletes like first-time Olympians Tommy Ford and Nolan Kasper, who were 20 in Vancouver.

During the Games, we also had a United States Olympic Committee (USOC) chef cooking for us. This was a key factor as well. He was already on the road with us for our long camp in New Zealand and then again for the FIS World Cup races in December and January. The whole team really enjoys having him around and it is great to see how this supported their nutrition program prior to, as well as during the Winter Games.

Also, the use of the two school gymnasiums in Whistler was great. The athletes were able to work out there every day by playing different team games like volleyball and soccer.

Once the 2010 Olympic Games began, our team was already dialed in with the area and the race venue. After a few delays and rescheduled races (due to weather), our team started off great with a bronze medal by Bode Miller in downhill. This first medal was for sure a big motivator for the rest of the team even if the weather kept causing delays and rescheduled events.

The second event was the super-G, where we won two medals with Miller (silver medal) and young Andrew Weibrecht (bronze medal). The whole team gained momentum again.

In super combined, our third and final speed event, Miller completed his medal set by winning an inspired gold medal. The race was also highlighted by Ted Ligety, Will Brandenburg and Miller finishing 1-2-3 in the slalom portion of the race. Ultimately it was an incredible team performance with Miller's gold, Ligety finishing fifth, Brandenburg in 10th and Andrew Weibrecht in 11th.

Unfortunately, we did not win any more medals in the technical events of slalom and giant slalom, but the athletes still did a good job and kept fighting.

By Closing Ceremony, it had become the most successful Olympic Winter Games in the history of the U.S. Alpine Ski Team. We won eight medals in total, four by men's alpine and four by women's alpine. Everybody had a great time, and the team proved its tightness once again.

TOP / *Marco Sullivan, who started in bib 26 in the super G, battles soft snow and deteriorating conditions to finish 23rd at Whistler Creekside.* (Photo by Olivier Morin/AFP/Getty Images)

BOTTOM / *First-time Olympian Will Brandenburg shook off a serious downhill training crash the day before the super combined to post the second fastest slalom run on the day for an incredible 10th place finish landing three American men in the top 10.* (Photo by Clive Rose/Getty Images)

Alpine Skiing

By Sarah Duffany

Kaylin Richardson sliced her way to 17th in the super combined to cap her career with a second trip to the Olympic Winter Games. Richardson retired from ski racing following the 2010 season. (PHOTO BY FABRICE COFFRINI/AFP/GETTY IMAGES)

To have this opportunity to be so involved with the women's alpine ski team in Vancouver was such an honor and incredible experience.

Olympic preparation began back in the 2008/2009 season when a World Cup event was held in Whistler.

The women's U.S. Ski Team training schedule for May through October consisted of conditioning and testing in Park City, Utah, on-hill ski training in Mammoth, Calif., New Zealand, Chile, and the glaciers of Europe. With last season's poor snow year in Europe, our best quality training happened during August and September in Chile and New Zealand.

The women's alpine team was selected based on World Cup results from the 2009/2010 in addition to coaches' discretion for the third and fourth athletes slated to the disciplines of downhill, super-G, super combined, giant slalom, and slalom. Athletes were selected in late January at a World Cup in Europe. With the alpine schedule, I do not see a way to move this date up. It was a time crunch for those athletes that were right on the edge of making the team. Athletes continued to train in Europe and some in Jackson Hole, Wyo., prior to the Games, with some rest days at home. It was very helpful for athletes to have a few days at home to recoup and prepare for the Games.

"Games-time" training was great. Multiple courses were set on the hill and athletes had options each day. We also set up our own gym which worked great for the athletes.

We are very pleased with women's alpine performance. We earned four medals with Lindsey Vonn earning gold in the downhill and bronze in the super-G, while Julia Mancuso boosted her career Olympic medal total to three by earning silver in both downhill and super combined.

With her giant slalom gold from 2006, Mancuso is now the most decorated Olympic alpine skier for American women.

None of this would have been possible without a solid athletic plan. The most important factor was our off-site housing with meals cooked by a USOC chef. This set-up provided us with our own personal space, removed the hassles of village entry and exit, and provided us with high quality meals. We were also able to create a relaxing and comfortable environment for the entire team to prepare for competition at the highest level, where their every need was taken care of.

Finally, I would like to thank USSA and the USOC for this incredible experience. I look forward to future challenges working in the athletic and Olympic Winter Games world. Confucius said, "Find a job you love and you'll never work a day in your life." I find myself very lucky to have done this. Skiing is my passion and it's incredible that my passion has brought me to be part of the winningest women's alpine team.

First-time Olympians Leanne Smith (opposite, top) and Megan McJames (opposite, bottom) gained valuable big event experience in their disciplines and are already gunning for Sochi 2014. The 22-year-old Smith competed in the super-G and McJames, also 22, raced in the slalom and giant slalom events.

Bode Miller claimed his first Olympic gold medal in the super combined event. He left Vancouver as the most decorated American male Olympic alpine skier. (PHOTO BY ALBERTO PIZZOLI/AFP/GETTY IMAGES)

Lindsey Vonn at the start of the first official training for the Olympic downhill.(Photo by Olivier Morin/AFP/Getty Images)

Not to be outdone, a lynx majestically crosses the finish line during the first official training for the men's Olympic downhill at Whistler Creekside. (PHOTO BY MICHAEL KAPPELER/AFP/GETTY IMAGES)

TEAM USA
Biathlon

By Bernard Eisenbichler

One lesson we learned is that it is important, even at the Games, to stick to routines.

I am a member of the National Governing Body staff. I served as a Team Leader at the 2009 World Championships in Pyeongchang, Korea, and the 2008 World Championship in Ostersund, Sweden. I was notified early of my role as Team Leader which provided a lot of time to prepare for the Games. I attended the May 2008 Key Decision Maker meeting which was very good for getting an inside view of United States Olympic Committee (USOC) and the Vancouver Organizing Committee (VANOC) operations. The Team Leadership Kick-Off meeting was good for reviewing our plans with the USOC, and the Final Countdown meeting in Vancouver was very helpful in becoming familiar with the Olympic Village, specifically the housing situations.

Biathlon is the combination of a time-based ski performance with a time- and precision-based shooting performance. This makes it hard on the one hand to run as fast as possible while on the other to stand still (with a racing pulse), and hit a very small target as quickly as possible.

We trained two weeks in May at the Olympic Games venue in Whistler. After that, we trained until August at Lake Placid. We had a long European camp of more than seven weeks in Germany and Sweden. In October, we prepared for three weeks at altitude in Salt Lake City at the 2002 Olympic Winter Games site. Our preparation also included a snow camp in Sweden. The final pre-Games training took place at Mount Washington on Vancouver Island. The only suggested change I would make is to give the athletes more time at home prior to the start of the Games.

We had a prequalification system that allowed up to 50 percent of each gender to qualify for the Games the season before with excellent international results. The next chance to prequalify for an additional spot for each gender was at the December World Cup. The last spots were given out in a trials situation at the European Cup in Altenburg, Germany. This is where the best athletes from the NorAm Cup met with those who had not yet prequalified from the December World Championships to race for the two available spots for men and three open spots for women. Therefore, most of the team members were selected through the prequalification opportunities, while the last ones were named on Jan. 11, 2010. We believe the selection process produced the best athletes for the team. Through our filter process, we made sure to get the top athletes with the strongest performances with the total highest levels over a longer period

of time before the Games, and who demonstrated the ability to compete at the international level. The only possible change we might have made would be to allow for more coaches' discretion.

As mentioned, the selected team participated in two World Cups in Europe, spent a week at home and then met for final preparation at Mount Washington on Vancouver Island for a 10-day camp. There are no changes I would make in this area concerning the time frame and activities. Prior to the Olympic Winter Games our athletes participated in two events held at the official Games site: the Canadian Champs in April 2008 and the February 2009 World Cup. This experience was beneficial for the team because the courses in Whistler are very technical. In addition to these two competitive events, we held three skiing camps there to adjust the running technique to the course, and this worked very well. However, some of the course prep for training could have been a little better. Overall, the facilities did not cause us any problems.

As a team, 50 percent of the athletes did their season- or, in some cases, lifetime-best at the Games. Jeremy Teela's ninth place at the sprint event was the best result ever at the Olympic Winter Games for an American biathlete. Nonetheless, the sprint was a big disappointment as three of the four men starting had no chance to perform well due to weather conditions. Heavy snowfall made the chance of a good performance impossible following Bib No. 15. Two of the athletes shot clean, but still had no chance of getting credit. It was also too bad that the pursuit race is counted after the sprint result; consequently, we had two races ruined for three of our four male athletes. In the long individual races we had a top result by Lanny Barnes with a 23rd place. The biggest disappointment of the entire Games was in the two relays where our athletes were not able to perform at their normal level.

Overall, we had a very good experience at the Games, even though we wished for better results. The staff with the coaches, wax technicians, grinder, doctor and physical therapist did an extraordinary job. All the athletes were very

professional giving it their all. One of the best experiences for us was that the ski grinding project with Muck Bauer from Germany worked so well. We went to Whistler five times in the three years before the Games and tested more than 120 different grinds. We had great skis at the Games and, with the tested grind, won this testing marathon. In fact, the nordic combined athletes won all their four medals on our grind which showed that this time, money and intense testing program worked superbly! An even more intense and USOC-supported relationship with nordic combined should be the goal as we move towards Sochi 2014!

We did not experience any programs or procedures that did not work well. Although, maybe a little more down time at home prior to the Games would have been good. Having the ski grinding machine nearer to the venue would be helpful. This time we had it in Vancouver, which worked but was a huge logistical and time consuming job. One lesson we learned is that it is important, even at the Games, to stick to routines. We did that and that worked very well.

We also learned, as a team, to better deal with more media interest. We got a lot through Tim Burkes' success prior to the Games. We handled it well, I think, but learned some lessons how to do it better.

The support and direction we got from USOC prior to and at the Games was superb. We feel very thankful for that. The support with cell phones for staff and athletes was very helpful for easy and constant communication! Team Processing was organized perfectly. Also, transportation to Whistler Village was organized very well. The USOC Whistler Village staff was there for us and helped out with everything at any time. It was very important and good for us that the whole staff could stay in the Village. This made all logistics, meeting organization, and communication much easier. It also helped to build a real team feeling for us. The USOC preparation meetings starting so early before the Games were very important; they should be kept the same in preparation for Sochi 2014.

Wynn Roberts (left) and Lowell Bailey pause during a training session at Whistler Olympic Park. (Photo by Alberto Pizzoli/ AFP/Getty Images)

Bobsled | Skeleton

By Scott Novack

In bobsleigh and skeleton, the four pillars which are required to reach the medal stand include equipment, athletes, coaching, and technology.

I am the High Performance Director for U.S. Bobsled and Skeleton Federation. I was notified in October 2008 that I had been selected as Team Leader. There was ample time to prepare. I was also Team Leader at the 2008 Beijing Olympic Games, the 2007 Pan American Games, the 2005 Summer World University Games, and various World Championships and World Cups since 2000 for numerous other Olympic sports. I did not attend the May 2008 Key Decision Maker meeting in Vancouver. However, I did participate in the Team Leadership Kick-Off meeting/conference call (May/June 2009) and the Team Leadership Final Countdown meeting (November 2009 in Vancouver).

Speed is essential to success in bobsleigh and skeleton. The difference between medaling and not medaling is measured by one-hundredth of a second. Our teams' training programs are very individualistic during the off-season. In-season, we do have a "start" coach who helps with the strength training of the athletes. One change to help better prepare the sport in the future is to develop a greater depth of quality pilots. This would require more funding for the lower tier tours so pilots could develop their driving skills.

The athlete selection procedures are very complicated. Bobsleigh selection is both qualitative and quantitative. Pilots are selected via their ranking from the Team Trials. Push athletes are selected via a team selection committee through quantitative criteria. Skeleton's selection is based upon rankings from the Team Trials. However, for the Olympic Winter Games, skeleton athletes and bobsleigh pilots are selected via their Federation Internationale de Bobsleigh et de Tobogganing (FIBT) Ranking, after a quota position is secured. The athletes were selected in St. Moritz after the final FIBT Olympic Qualifying race on Jan. 18, 2010.

The selection process did identify and allow us to select the best athletes for the team. The goal was to put the fastest teams together. In the past, that was not always the case and the pilots selected their teams. The Team Selection Committee selected the teams and put the bobsleigh team combinations together. There is nothing we would change in this process. We published our criteria, and we had a mandatory team meeting in June to review the selection criteria and process. We followed the selection procedures and selected the fastest and best combinations available.

We implemented a comprehensive Olympic Winter Games Training Plan. Initially, the team trained at Park City, Utah, and Lake Placid, N.Y. This was followed by the first series of international training opportunities including Whistler; Cesana, Italy; and two additional World Cups in Germany: Winterberg and Altenberg. After the Christmas holidays, the team returned to Europe to Konigssee, Germany; St. Moritz, Switzerland; and Igls, Austria. The teams came from their different locations to Park City for five days for a final Winter Games tune up. The only change we would make is to allow for more down time in Park City with fewer activities. Each day was packed with different functions and training runs.

Part of our training plan included competing in the 2009 World Cup in Whistler. It was absolutely beneficial for the team, which is reflected in the top three medal finishes. Further, the United States had a total of 11 teams/athletes in the top 10 of each competition.

Our Games time training was a major project that required two years worth of planning. In Vancouver, we trained at Vancouver College for both sprint and strength training. In Whistler we had three available options for training: a speed board from Colorado Springs was brought to Whistler Village; indoor training at a local school; and sprint training outdoors in the village and at Whistler Sliding Centre. For strength training we used the facilities in the village. The facilities were accessible and appropriate. We had no major problems and everything ran very smoothly.

In the men's four-man bobsleigh, USA I "Night Train" (Steven Holcomb, Justin Olsen, Steve Mesler and Curt Tomasevicz) cruised to first place winning by a margin of .45 seconds ahead of Germany 1, thus ending a 62-year gold-medal drought. USA II (John Napier, Jamie Langton, Steven Berkley and Christopher Fogt) was in seventh after the first heat. Due to minor injuries, USA II was unable to finish the competition. Having only driven the Whistler track a total of 17 times before the four-man competition, USA III pilot Mike Kohn and the crew of Jamie Moriarty,

Billy Schuffenhauer and Nick Cunningham finished 13th.

The men's two-man bobsleigh competition was a small disappointment with USA I "Night Hawk" (Holcomb/Tomasevicz) finishing sixth. USA II (Napier/Langton) was 10th, and USA III (Kohn/Cunningham) was 12th. More than a dozen crashes occurred during two-man training on an extremely fast Whistler track.

Start times and getting through critical curves played vital roles in final finishes and medaling for the women's teams. USA 2 (Erin Pac and Elana Meyers) had competitive push times, but ended with a bronze medal. USA 3 (Bree Schaaf and Emily Azevedo) was consistent and finished in fifth place with USA 1 (Shauna Rohbock and Michelle Rzepka) ending in sixth.

Despite qualifying the maximum quota for men's skeleton at the 2010 Vancouver Olympic Winter Games, the results were considered a disappointment. The trend of the fastest push times correlating with final down times and finishes played out in men's skeleton. Zach Lund was the highest U.S. finisher with fifth place. Eric Bernotas came in 14th and John Daly 17th. To win a medal, an athlete needs a combination of being a good pilot as well as a fast pusher.

Noelle Pikus-Pace finished fourth in the women's skeleton. She missed out on a bronze medal by .04 seconds. Katie Uhlaender finished in 11th place.

In bobsleigh and skeleton, the four pillars which are required to reach the medal stand include equipment, athletes, coaching, and technology. With all four of these components combined, a team has a legitimate chance at reaching the podium as proven in Whistler. The equipment and the Bo-Dyn Bobsled Project are among the main contributors to the success of the men's and women's bobsleigh teams. The athlete pool for men's and women's bobsleigh is the deepest it has ever been with quality world class athletes. Almost all of the athletes have Division I athletics background in track and field, football, softball, and/or weight lifting. These athletes had strong continuity with the coaching staff that focused on the starts and helped the pilots learn each track.

The teams that had the fastest push times in Whistler correlated with the fastest down times and ended up on the medal stand. There was also a correlation with start times and finishes from the Whistler World Cup in 2009 and the Winter Games. Knowing this data, and with the support of the United States Olympic Committee (USOC), a start coach was brought on board to work with specific athletes on their start times and technique.

Skeleton was a disappointment, and this is something that needs to be reviewed. A skeleton sled program should be developed. The biggest lesson learned is that athletes and coaches must trust each other, the process, and the equipment so performance goals can be reached. When there is a lack of trust, and individuals work on an island, the chances for reaching the podium are minimal.

Emily Azvedo (left) and pilot Bree Schaaf of USA 3 celebrate their fourth run, which placed them fifth overall in the bobsleigh competition. (PHOTO BY ALEXANDER HASSENSTEIN/BONGARTS/GETTY IMAGES)

TEAM USA
Curling

By Mark Swandby

"Curlers play to win,
but never to humble their opponents.
A true curler would prefer to lose
rather than to win unfairly....."

I am a volunteer for the United States Curling Association (USA Curling), and Team Leader for the men's and women's teams. In January 2010, I retired after a long career as a department administrator at the University of Wisconsin-Madison. Much of my UW career included duties similar to those of a Team Leader. I was named Team Leader for Vancouver in December 2008. This gave me a long lead time to prepare. Prior to the Olympic Winter Games, I was a Team Leader for the 2008 World Junior Curling Championships in Ostersund, Sweden, and for the 2009 World Men's Curling Championships in Moncton, Canada. I was a timing official at the Salt Lake City 2002 Winter Olympic Games and in 2006 represented USA Curling as National Governing Body president at the Torino Games.

Curling is a team sport with winners determined objectively by outscoring the opposing team. Like golf, it requires excellent physical technique combined with great nerves, the will to win, and mental toughness. Curling strategy is fascinating to experienced players as well as to those viewing it on TV. The unique "Spirit of Curling" states that "Curlers play to win, but never to humble their opponents. A true curler would prefer to lose rather than to win unfairly....." Thus, curlers largely police themselves so that officials, while present, rarely interact with the game and then only when a ruling is requested by the players.

I attended the Key Decision Maker meeting in Vancouver in May 2008, before I was selected as Team Leader. I attended curling's Team Leadership Kickoff meeting via telephone in late April, 2009 and finally the Team Leadership Final Countdown meeting in Vancouver in November 2009. These meetings were very comprehensive and helpful. Virtually all the information presented was pertinent and useful at the Games.

The men's and women's Olympic Teams were selected through a playdown process during the 2008-09 season. The final event of this process was the Olympic Trials in Broomfield, Colo., at the end of February 2009. The Trials format was a 10-team round- robin followed by a Page-playoff to determine the men's and the women's winners. The winning teams competed in the 2009 Men's and Women's World Championships in Canada and Korea, respectively.

This early selection of the teams enabled a comprehensive training program prior to the Games. Historically, U.S. curling teams have not practiced during the summer due to the unavailability of on-ice training facilities. However, throughout the summer of 2009 curling ice was made available at the Green Bay Curling Club in Green Bay, Wis. Seven summer training camps were held in Green Bay and one in Park City, Utah. In August the teams traveled to Switzerland for an extended training trip and competition. During the fall cash bonspiel season, and into January 2010, both teams competed in numerous bonspiels in Canada, Europe and the United States. Many of these competitions included the Olympic Teams from other countries. One final training camp was held in December 2009 in Green Bay. The teams traveled to Vancouver 10 days before the start of the Games competition. Ice time was rented at the Richmond Curling Club and training continued there until the beginning of the Games.

This was without a doubt the most extensive pre-Olympic Training Program undertaken by any U.S. curling teams since curling again became a medal sport in 1998. Despite some press reports to the contrary, this training and competition program created optimism on behalf of USA Curling that the teams would do well in Vancouver. The women's team, especially, had the most success on the cash bonspiel circuit of any US team to date, men's or women's.

Thus, each team winning just two games and finishing in last place was disappointing. Both teams played competitive, close games in the early going. Unfortunately, missed key shots at critical moments resulted in losses. The men's team lost three straight games on the last rock in an extra end. The women also had opportunities to score, but could not convert. As happens so often in curling, when a team gets off to a bad start it is difficult to maintain the confidence required to turn things around. The teams tried hard, even going so far as to change the person throwing last rocks, a move very rare in world-level curling. As in other sports, regardless of preparation and training, there comes a time when athletes must perform. In these Games, the wins did not happen for curling. USA Curling has undertaken an independent review of its high performance plan

as part of its commitment to reaching the performance level required to medal at the World and Games level.

Despite the poor competitive performance, there were many positive experiences in Vancouver for our teams and for curling. The Canadians were excellent hosts, continuously upbeat and welcoming. The village was outstanding with the U.S. curling teams occupying the penthouse in our building. The food service was excellent and the security, while active, was friendly and efficient. Our teams participated in the Opening and Closing Ceremonies and were privileged to meet Vice President Joe Biden. The teams had the opportunity to interact with many national TV news and sports personalities.

Canada is the number one curling country in participation, and this was reflected in the curling competition. The venue facilities were top notch, from the individual locker rooms through the Games-themed arena. Ice conditions are critical to top-level curling, and these were excellent. The seats were filled for virtually every draw and spectators were enthusiastic. There was a great deal of American support for our curling teams. Both Olympian

Carl Lewis and San Francisco 49er Vernon Davis met with our teams to show their support. Every game was televised and there was much TV coverage in the US. Many U.S. curling clubs took advantage of this exposure by holding open houses which attracted thousands of attendees across the country. Many acquaintances have expressed their enjoyment of watching curling on TV regardless of the performance of the U.S. teams.

The United States Olympic Committee's (USOC) support of the Olympic Teams provided them with the opportunity to succeed. The USOC staff in Vancouver was ever-present and helpful in managing the logistics of the Games. The security provided was greatly appreciated. Accreditation was provided for coaching staff in each of the areas critical to curling performance. The teams had the resources to train and compete to prepare for their Games experience. Going forward, the U.S. Curling Association and its athletes must commit to using these resources to establish a culture of excellence that will achieve international performance at the highest level.

Skip Debbie McCormick (facing), Nicole Joraanstad, Allison Pottinger and Natalie Nicholson (right) discuss strategy against Canada in the women's curling round robin session match. (PHOTO BY SAEED KHAN/AFP/GETTY IMAGES)

Figure Skating

By Mitch Moyer

The U.S. skaters narrowly missed two other podium placements by finishing fourth in ladies and ice dancing.

I have served as the senior director of athlete high performance for U.S. Figure Skating since 2006. Based on the results of the 2009 International Skating Union (ISU) World Figure Skating Championships in Los Angeles, Calif., the United States qualified three men, three ice dancing teams, two ladies and two pairs teams to compete at the 2010 Olympic Winter Games in Vancouver, British Columbia.

The 2010 AT&T U.S. Figure Skating Championships, held in Spokane, Wash., was the last of the six competition criteria used for the nomination of the 2010 U.S. Olympic Figure Skating Team. The six qualifying events, in priority order, were the 2010 AT&T U.S. Figure Skating Championships, 2009 ISU Grand Prix of Figure Skating Final, 2009 ISU World Figure Skating Championships, 2009 Four Continents Figure Skating Championships, 2009 World Junior Figure Skating Championships and 2009 ISU Junior Grand Prix of Figure Skating Final. At the conclusion of each event at the U.S. Championships, the International Committee Management Subcommittee (ICMS), a nine-member committee, nominated the athletes to be approved by the 35-member International Committee for the Olympic Winter Games.

One suggestion for the selection criteria for 2014 is to add the Grand Prix Series competitions to the criteria. The 2010 U.S. Figure Skating Championships were held over the course of two weekends, with the pairs and men on the first weekend, and the ladies and ice dancing over the second.

The two pairs teams (Amanda Evora and Mark Ladwig; Caydee Denney and Jeremy Barrett) nominated to the U.S. Olympic Team remained in Spokane to train and participate in the Smucker's Skating Spectacular the following weekend. The three nominated men (Evan Lysacek, Jeremy Abbott and Johnny Weir) went home to train. They returned for the Smucker's Skating Spectacular the following weekend.

The ladies and ice dancing events were held the second weekend. Mirai Nagasu and Rachael Flatt were the nominees for the ladies; nominees for ice dancing were Meryl Davis and Charlie White; Tanith Belbin and Ben Agosto; and Emily Samuelson and Evan Bates.

The athletes returned home after the conclusion of the U.S. Championships to train for three weeks before the Olympic Games. The athletes' training before the Games was productive, and all the skaters arrived in top form for the Games.

The pairs arrived in Vancouver on Feb. 8. The men were scheduled to arrive Feb. 10, and the ladies and ice dancing teams were scheduled for Feb. 11. Due to a significant snowstorm in the east, Weir and the ice dancing team of Belbin and Agosto were forced to change their original arrival days. Instead of arriving Feb. 10, Weir came to Vancouver on Feb. 9 to beat the storm's arrival. Belbin and Agosto decided to stay with their original plans but were unable to arrive on their scheduled day due to multiple flight cancellations.

Belbin and Agosto made it to Vancouver on the day of the Opening Ceremonies, just in time to participate in the ceremony. The pairs competition was the first event, and there was a day between Opening Ceremonies and the pairs short program. Therefore, all the figure skating athletes were able to participate in the Opening Ceremonies.

Keeping up with reporting the whereabouts of the team while processing, helping the athletes get settled in the village and changes in flight plans because of the weather all proved to be challenging. Several of the athletes and coaches went in many different directions during the first two weeks of the Games. Once the processing was completed and the athletes were in the village, the schedule became significantly easier. Richard Dalley, the team manager/technical advisor for ice dancing, focused on housing and the dance teams, while Lorrie Parker, the team manager/technical advisor for singles and pairs, focused on the pairs and singles skaters. I was able to float to various practices and work with the USOC on reporting issues that arose during the Games pertaining to the U.S. Figure Skating Team.

Processing went very smoothly, and the delegation loved all the gear. Sizing became an issue for the figure skaters arriving Feb. 11, as many of the athletes had already been through team processing, and most of the very small sizes were no longer available for the ladies contingent. The athletes really liked the official clothing, and Nike and Ralph Lauren should be applauded for a job well done.

Providing the coaches with the Opening Ceremonies

apparel made it possible for the coaches to participate, and Frank Carroll and Igor Shpilband became the first U.S. figure skating coaches to march in the Opening Ceremonies with the U.S. delegation. These two coaches were selected based on having coached athletes who medaled at previous Olympic Games.

U.S. Figure Skating, working with Skate Canada, was able to secure practice ice in nearby Port Moody, which also served as the practice ice for the Canadian figure skaters during the Games. This enabled the U.S. skaters to remain in Vancouver to train after the Opening Ceremonies.

The ice dancing teams were able to train for four days in Port Moody prior to skating on the official practice ice. Nagasu practiced for two days in Vancouver prior to returning to Los Angeles to train, and Flatt practiced for three days in Vancouver before returning to Colorado Springs. Both athletes returned to the Games on Feb. 19.

Port Moody was a first-rate facility, and the athletes were welcomed with open arms by the staff and the city of Port Moody. The private ice obtained in Port Moody proved to be very beneficial for the team.

The Olympic Village provided first-class accommodations. The rooms were large and offered a home-like atmosphere. Other than the beating drums during the first week, the rooms were quiet most of the day. The village in Vancouver set a standard that will be difficult for any nation to top in future Olympic Games. The athletes competing for the first time in an Olympic Games will realize that they were spoiled in Vancouver. The waterfront view, along with the spacious rooms, provided a relaxing atmosphere and an opportunity to escape from the other athletes when needed. The main living space in our condo was large enough to host meetings for our delegation and provide an additional room for the athletes to congregate.

U.S. Figure Skating maintained an office across the street from the athlete entrance at the Pacific Coliseum. The athletes had easy access to the office, which served as a meeting place for the athletes to meet family and friends. In addition, the office was used for family and friends to pick up tickets, watch the events, access the Internet and acquire information from U.S. Teams Manager Julie Schmitz and Bob Dunlop, U.S. Figure Skating's senior director of events.

In May 2009, U.S. Figure Skating acquired the services of Mike Cunningham. One of the top experts in the field of skating equipment and maintenance, his presence at the Games was an important factor in the success of the team.

Lysacek's skate was damaged after his short program

Fourth-place finishers in ice dancing, Tanith Belbin and Ben Agosto of the United States perform during the exhibition gala held after the Olympic figure skating competition. (Photo by Vincenzo Pinto/AFP/Getty Images)

vancouver
20

Johnny Weir, who rode horses competitively as a child, was inspired watching 1994 Olympic champion Oksana Baiul. Weir taught himself roller skating in the family basement and then ventured outside on ice skates when a nearby cornfield froze over. The 25-year-old two-time Olympian skated two solid programs to finish sixth in the men's competition. (PHOTO BY MATTHEW STOCKMAN/GETTY IMAGES)

The atmosphere on the figure skating floor
was a daily reminder of the pride
each member of the team felt
in representing the United States.

performance, and Cunningham was able to fix the blade without making a major adjustment that could have disrupted Evan's confidence in his equipment. What started out as an "insurance policy" by having a skate technician at the Games proved to be a substantial asset for U.S. Figure Skating and most likely saved a gold medal for the United States.

U.S. Figure Skating's "safe house" was used primarily for the staff that worked out of the U.S. Figure Skating office. The house was also used to accommodate two coaches, Gennadi Karponosov and Natalia Linichuk, for several nights. In addition, the house provided some of the athletes a quiet place to escape during the day.

As was the case at the 2006 Olympic Winter Games in Torino, Italy, the coaches were able to stay in the Olympic Village. Having easy access to the athletes has proven to be quite practical and essential for the athlete's peak performance. The coaches are able to communicate more efficiently with their athletes by residing in the Olympic Village.

The venue at the Pacific Coliseum was nice, and the athletes mentioned numerous times how much they liked the ice, and how pleasant and helpful the staff was.

The mixed zone presented problems for the athletes and the coaches. Coaches were not allowed to go through the mixed zone with their athletes, yet were called back for interviews while their athletes were in the mixed zone. Lysacek's skates were damaged after the short program because the VANOC representative accompanying him did not know how to handle his skates and accidentally banged the blades together. Nagasu was challenged by difficult questions when she was informed of the passing of Joannie Rochette's mother. Shaken by the bad news of Joannie's mother, the questions shifted onto the topic of Mirai's mother's bout with cancer this past year. The IOC should reconsider the policy of not having coaches or a press officer from the national governing body accompanying these athletes through the mixed zone.

The dynamics of the U.S. Figure Skating Team was fascinating to observe prior to and during the Games. As expected, those athletes that had competed in Torino gained experience in 2006 and entered Vancouver with a more business-like approach. These athletes wanted to experience the Games but not at the cost of becoming distracted and having their performance be affected. The athletes that arrived in Vancouver as first-time Olympians barely had their feet on the ground until after the Opening Ceremonies. Many of these first-time Olympians developed very close relationships with one another in the junior circuit and brought with them a team spirit that became contagious within the whole team. The staff, coaches and athletes bonded to further enhance the team spirit. Lorrie Parker, in particular, spent many hours fostering a unified atmosphere, adorning the floor in the hallways with USA banners and decorations that could compete with any Fourth of July parade. The atmosphere on the figure skating floor was a daily reminder of the pride each member of the team felt in representing the United States. The athletes appreciated the support, expertise and enthusiasm that each member of the team (athletes, coaches and staff) brought to the Games. The U.S. Figure Skating Team became a very close-knit group prior to and continuing throughout the 2010 Olympic Winter Games.

ABOVE / *Ice dance skaters Emily Samuelson, 19, and Evan Bates, 20, both students at the University of Michigan, skated to an American country dance theme in the original dance program.* (PHOTO BY MATTHEW STOCKMAN/GETTY IMAGES)

Freestyle Skiing

By Cheryl Pearson

In all of our disciplines
we had a great combination of veteran
and rookie athletes competing.

I was honored to be the Team Leader for USA Freestyle Skiing, of the U.S. Ski and Snowboard Association. This was my very first experience at an Olympic Winter Games. It was a surreal experience from the beginning. I knew there were going to be many tasks that needed to be accomplished prior to and during the Games. I was up for the challenge because of my role with the freestyle team on a day-to-day basis as the Program Manager for the national team and USSA Freestyle.

Freestyle skiing disciplines in the Winter Games consists of aerials, moguls, and ski cross. Aerials and moguls are judged sports, while ski cross is a head-to-head sport. In all of our disciplines we had a great combination of veteran and rookie athletes competing. We had 18 athletes representing USA Freestyle Skiing: eight aerials skiers (four men/four women), eight moguls skiers (four men/four women) and two male ski cross skiers.

The 18 athletes qualified for the Winter Games through early season World Cup events. Aerials and moguls athletes also had an Olympic Trials event held in Steamboat Springs, Colo., in which the winners earned an automatic spot on the Olympic Team.

Aerials are similar to gymnastics or diving, but with skis connected to the athletes' feet. Some of the athletes are launched upwards of 50 feet into the air. Athletes have the choice to perform a single, double, or triple flip. The degree of difficulty of the trick performed changes by the number of flips and twists an athlete adds to the jump. American Jeret "Speedy" Peterson won the silver medal and performed his signature maneuver, the "Hurricane," which is a jump that consists of three flips and five twists. The "Hurricane" is the most difficult trick being executed in competition at this time. Ryan St. Onge just missed the podium and earned fourth place. We had two male athletes and three female athletes in finals. This was the first time that three of our female athletes qualified for finals since the Nagano Games, where only two qualified for finals. This was a huge success for our ladies.

Moguls was the event in which the United States had the most success, collecting three medals: a gold and two bronze. Moguls skiing, to the novice, seems very jarring and painful to the athlete's body, but when done correctly it is as smooth as riding a bike. The competition course consists of three mogul sections divided by two aerial jumps. The two jumps enable athletes to demonstrate their aerial skills.

All aerial maneuvers have a certain degree of difficulty which is 25 percent of the athletes' score. The U.S. team opened the Games with two medals in the ladies moguls competition. During the women's finals, the rain was blowing sideways across the hill, but that didn't stop Shannon Bahrke from skiing with amazing determination. Her run was fast, clean, and earned her a bronze medal. She was so excited for her medal, that those watching would have thought that she won a gold. Hannah Kearney was last to ski in finals as she had the best qualifying run. From the jumbo screen Kearney looked poised and confident knowing what she was about to accomplish. She ended up dominating the ladies field by nearly a full point, a huge margin in moguls, with a near flawless run. Bahrke and Kearney set the tone for the United States at the Winter Games. After that evening's competition the vice president of athletics at USSA asked me "Aren't you excited? Our team just won the gold medal!" At that point I was still in shock by the entire experience, but I looked at him and said very calmly as a smile spread across my face, "No, we didn't just win the gold, we won gold and bronze." The next day, American athlete Bryon Wilson performed the most difficult aerial maneuver to date in moguls competition. He performed a double full, which is a single flip with two twists. By landing that jump and with his fast dynamic skiing skills, Wilson won a bronze medal. The U.S. ladies and men's moguls teams won three of the six Olympic medals.

Ski cross was the new, highly-anticipated sport added to the 2010 Winter Games. Ski cross is mix of traditional alpine racing and motocross. Each athlete gets one qualification run that seeds him or her into brackets. Athletes are grouped into heats of four, and the first two athletes crossing the finish line move on to the next round. They ski head-to-head down a slope with varying terrain consisting of rollers, bank turns, table tops, step downs, and large pro jumps. What makes this sport exciting for the viewer is the limited space the athletes have to share while flying down the course. It is inevitable that athletes will collide with each other and spectators will end up seeing big crashes. We were very lucky to have had two extremely decorated

> Moguls skiing, to the novice,
> seems very jarring and painful
> to the athlete's body,
> but when done correctly
> it is as smooth as riding a bike.

former alpine athletes competing for the United States in the debut of this new sport. Unfortunately, the athletes were unable to win medals in this discipline.

Cypress Mountain, site for the freestyle events, had its challenges due to the low altitude of the venue with very wet and warm weather conditions. There was an Olympic Test Event hosted one year prior to the Games at Cypress. During that event, the organizers were challenged with warm rainy weather that didn't allow for the jumps on the aerials and moguls site to ever set up completely. The Games event organizers took this challenge head on and came up with a creative solution. They placed plastic tubes into the primary section of each jump and filled the tubes with dry ice, then blasted the entire jump with fire extinguishers. This process solidified the jumps completely. It was a brilliant concept by the organizers that can be mimicked and used in the future.

Cypress was hit with heavy rain before the Games. The organizers knew they were going to be limited by the amount of snow on the venues. Another concept they developed was to use hay in the building of the features on the ski cross course. Barrels of snow and hay were air lifted into the venue by helicopters. By doing this, enough of the larger features were built with the hay and packed in snow over the top. The result was spectacular!

I was very fortunate to have been able to attend the Team Leadership meeting in Vancouver in November prior to the start of the Games. I found this experience extremely valuable to be able to understand the layout of the city. In addition, it was very helpful to be able to put names of all the wonderful United States Olympic Committee (USOC) staff to their faces. I was able to connect and understand what each staff person of the USOC role would be during the Olympic Winter Games.

Upon my arrival in Vancouver in February, I was greeted by the USOC staff I had met the previous October. For the first five days of the Games, I assisted the freestyle team through processing at the Delta. All staff and athletes were outfitted by Nike and Polo apparel.

When our teams and I moved into the Village, we again were greeted by more USOC staff. The staff helped assist with the check-in process through security and into our rooms. This was the same when we checked out. Team members with flights were able to check luggage the day before travel from the Village to make airport check-in extremely simple.

I was the USSA staff member designated to live in the Village during the entire Winter Games. I'm happy to say that by being there I met so many wonderful people from the USOC and other sports. I had many laughs in the USOC work space and I really felt that they adopted me into their family.

This entire experience was surreal and very fulfilling for me. As a child I had always watched the Winter Games on TV. Growing up, I became a competitive moguls skier and my dream was to compete in the Games. Many knee surgeries later, I knew that my dream was not going to come true. I realized this past winter that my dream did come true. I am very proud to have been able to assist the freestyle athletes from the United States to accomplish their Winter Games dreams. I learned, as a staff member, that you can't keep the athletes in a protective bubble but you can shield them from the extra chaos that forms from the excitement of the Olympic Winter Games.

Heather McPhie of United States competes in the women's moguls qualifications. She finished 18th overall. (PHOTO BY JAMIE SQUIRE/GETTY IMAGES)

TEAM USA - MEN'S
Ice Hockey

By Jim Johannson

The little things matter like meals, family plans, communication to players, consistency in management, and the player evaluation process.

I have been an employee at USA Hockey, Inc., for the past 10 years and Vancouver 2010 was my fifth Olympic Winter Games overall and third Games (2002 and 2006) serving as the Team Leader. The men's ice hockey competition has had the shared cooperation and player access of NHL players since the 1998 Olympic Winter Games. The previous three Winter Games with NHL players featured six different countries in the gold-medal game (USA in 2002), so it has been a very competitive and balanced tournament with NHL player involvement.

I was able to attend all of the United States Olympic Committee planned preparation meetings and these were of valuable assistance in our overall preparation. I think equally important was my knowledge of the venue and the venue management group because I have been associated with them from several past events.

The biggest change I have seen over the course of the past three Olympic Winter Games is the utilization of online forms and overall email communication methods. I think there are some definite benefits to this, but also feel it is an area that can be better streamlined and made more user friendly.

Starting with our management group, we had a well-planned player evaluation process with game reports and a few competitions (World Championships) to directly evaluate the players. We were able to have the head coach behind the bench with several players at the 2009 World Championships, and it led to a core leadership group that was identified and brought in to discuss our planning. The August Olympic Orientation Camp, which included 34 players and our entire Games staff, was a key phase of our preparation and set the tone for our identity as a team. We maintained good communication throughout the fall and had regular meetings with our management group to evaluate and rate the players. The head coach was brought into the process for feedback and understanding of the direction and shape that the team was taking, as well as giving his feedback on specific players. I think our association with Operation Homefront (Wounded Warriors) was a key element to our team identity and purpose throughout the Olympic Winter Games. We had the staff we needed to serve our team in all areas, including management, coaching, medical, communications, equipment, and identity

with Chris Chelios (four-time Olympian), and Operation Homefront. We catered meals to the arena and arranged a restaurant for night-before-game meals which was also very critical to our success and overall operation.

Specifically with the USOC, I would say the core and support staff, mainly in the Village and airport arrivals/departures at the Games, did a fantastic job. We had good communication in most areas and had great support throughout the Games. Our players all arrived the day before our first game and we had one practice prior to playing our first game against Switzerland at noon on February 16th. The NHL had nine games on Feb. 14, so it was obviously a very quick turnaround to get the players to Vancouver. The USOC was very helpful in the pre-packing of all our apparel and assisting to make sure all our needs in the village were ready upon the player and staff arrivals.

In the end, we played in the gold-medal game and came out on the wrong side, but that is sports and we fully appreciate and respect the opponents we faced at the Winter Games. We never trailed in the entire tournament until the gold-medal contest, and in that we came back from a two-goal deficit to go into overtime. I am hard pressed to come up with areas that did not go well or work. The four-on-four overtime format changed the dynamic of how you have to play (it becomes a less physical and more cautious game). My only comment on that is that the last 10-12 minutes of the game (played five-on-five) was carried by Team USA. Who knows if the result would have changed if overtime was played the same as regulation? This is just an observation, not an excuse or complaint. In these events the formula for success is a simple statement: Score big goals and get better goaltending than your opponent! Sounds simple, but that is what separated teams in Vancouver.

The little things matter like meals, family plans, communication to players, consistency in management, and the player evaluation process. We did all of these things very well in Vancouver and in most cases did not have as many obstacles to get this done. We learned in Torino it is

an energy tournament, and you need depth in the roster to play all situations, while at same time having players for specific roles addressing penalty killing, face-offs, power plays, defending, size and grit. We had a much better defined team for the roles guys fill and it is a direct result of a deeper talent pool in all aspects of the game.

As we prepare for Sochi 2014, there will be some factors that by location and venue will be different than Vancouver. Travel, logistics, family arrangements and nutrition/meals are the current concerns. The unknown looms again with no NHL agreement in place for participation in Sochi. That does not change or alter any planning in the near future. Our programs are working at all levels. We had seven National Team Development Program alumni on a team with an average age of 26.6 years old (the youngest team in the tournament). We continue to develop more players capable of playing at this level. We have a great environment with our core players and need to build on this as we prepare for Sochi.

Silver medalists (from left to right) David Backes, Brooks Orpik and Bobby Ryan of Team USA gaze at the scoreboard during the medals ceremony. Canada defeated the United States, 3-2, in overtime. (Photo by Bruce Bennett/Getty Images)

TEAM USA - WOMEN'S
Ice Hockey

By Michele Amidon

> In Vancouver we were very young with an average age of 24.2 years old. We only had six returning Olympians out of the 21 rostered players.

I have been the director of women's ice hockey at USA Hockey, Inc., for the past four years and Vancouver 2010 was my first Olympic Winter Games as the general manager.

In our sport, the NCAA women's collegiate program is the highest level of women's ice hockey in the world. The Olympic women's hockey competition has had shared cooperation and player access from the NCAA since the 1998 Winter Games.

I was able to attend all of the United States Olympic Committee Team Leader meetings held in Colorado Springs, Colo. and Vancouver, B.C. My diligent work with the USOC's Sport Partnership Division, in particular Kelley Fisher and Michelle Brown, over the past three years was invaluable during our team's overall preparation. In addition, members of USA Hockey had previously worked with the venue and venue management. In September, the International Ice Hockey Federation and Vancouver Organizing Committee hosted a women's ice hockey test event with the top four nations. This served extremely beneficial for all teams, the IIHF and VANOC.

I think there must be one point person between the USOC and the National Governing Body in the lead-up to the Games. This will help eliminate confusion and frustration. I also feel strongly that the USOC needs to provide top-notch medical providers to all the NGBs. The health of our athletes can determine how well we perform at the Olympics.

Our entire Games staff had been involved with our women's elite programs since August 2006. They were involved in world championships, off-ice training camps, international tournaments, coaching education, selection processes and elite development camps. We had a semi-resident program two years out from the Games and a full-time resident program in Blaine, Minn., six months out from the Games. Throughout the quad, Randy Wilber and John Crawley from the USOC's Sports Performance Division assisted our team in testing lactate threshold, power and strength. Our team participated in an intense off-ice training camp in June in Colorado Springs. The Manitou Springs Incline became one of the team's most feared and favorite competitions. These opportunities helped prepare our players and staff for Vancouver. Having credentials for all the staff who worked with the players during the quad was essential to our success.

The biggest challenge for our sport is keeping the players fit and engaged at the elite level during the first two years of the Olympic training quad.

USA Hockey has the athletes compete at camps and international events approximately 10 weeks of the year. With half of our top pool of players finishing out their NCAA eligibility, it makes it hard for the post-NCAA players to train. They can train on their own at home or move to Canada to play in a semi-pro women's league. The lack of strong established professional leagues makes it difficult for all federations to keep their players in top hockey shape. During our preparation for Sochi we will add 12-14 more boys'/junior games to prepare our team at a higher intensity.

I thought our selection procedures were flawless. We had been scouting, coaching and evaluating the players for four years. Our final tryout occurred in Blaine right before our test event in Vancouver. We invited 41 players to tryout for 23 spots. Our selection committee was made up of six people.

The set-up of the Village was outstanding. Having the USOC in the same building and accessible at all hours of the day was important. Team processing, the Olympic Ambassador Program and transportation all ran very smoothly for our group.

We played in the gold-medal game and came out with the silver medal. We fell just short of our goal, not by capturing the silver but by not performing to our best in that one game. We had to perform in front of a sellout crowd in Canada against the home team. There were about 1,000 U.S. fans scattered throughout 15,000+ loud and enthusiastic Canadians. The loss was heartbreaking, but our women gave it their all. I believe we only need to tweak a few minor things in our plan for Sochi.

All the little things can add up to what matters most when dealing with elite athletes and sport. We have learned a lot from Nagano, Salt Lake and Torino. Our players and staff recognize that the vision and goals for the program have changed drastically since Torino. All these little things

brought us gold at two IIHF World Women's Championships and two IIHF World Women's U18 Championships in a recent years. We are proud of what we have accomplished.

As we prepare for Sochi 2014, we will roll out an extension of our Vancouver vision and goals. We will build off our success and learn from our missteps. It will be interesting to see how many veterans retire and how many try to make the 2014 Olympic Team. In Vancouver, we were very young with an average age of 24.2 years old. We only had six returning Olympians out of the 21 rostered players. We have some great young talent coming up the ranks and our current young Vancouver players will be wiser and more-seasoned for Sochi.

Hilary Knight (#21) of the United States is challenged by Gina Kingsbury (#27) of Canada during the women's gold-medal game.
(PHOTO BY BRUCE BENNETT/GETTY IMAGES)

Luge

By Fred Zimny

Luge is also the fastest
of the sledding sports
with speeds in Vancouver reaching
95 mph from the men's start
and 90 mph from the women's start.

Luge is unique among the three sliding disciplines (luge/bobsleigh/skeleton) in that it is the only sliding sport timed to the 1/1000th of a second. It is not uncommon to see races won, lost, or even tied to the 1/1000th of a second in international competitions. The Olympic Winter Games consists of four runs (two for doubles) with all run times combined to determine the winner. Racing can be so competitive that athletes must complete four virtually perfect runs in order to become Winter Games champions. Never would you see an athlete skid, hit a wall or experience other major problems and still be able to win the race.

Luge is also the fastest of the sledding sports with speeds in Vancouver reaching 95 mph from the men's start and 90 mph from the women's start. It is not a sport for the faint of heart and requires the ability to relax and work as one with the sled under extreme speeds and G-forces. It requires an athlete to anticipate the unexpected and react to sudden changes in a split second when the sled is not on the correct line. The top athletes know where their sled is and what it is doing at every moment. Being "soft" on each entry and exit of a 16-curve track could gain athletes a tenth of a second by the time they reach the bottom of the track; that's an eternity in luge terms.

The first step in the selection process for the 2010 Olympic Luge Team began with selection to the 2009-2010 National Team. Once selected to the National Team, athletes participated in four race-off competitions in fall 2009 designed to reduce the number of athletes down to World Cup team size (there were two races in Lake Placid, one in Park City and one in Whistler). After the final race-off, the remaining athletes participated in the four World Cup races scheduled in fall 2009 prior to the Christmas break. Through their results in each of these four races, athletes aspired to achieve pre-determined Tier levels. At the conclusion of the fourth race on approx. Dec. 13, the three men, three women and two doubles teams with the highest tier levels qualified for the Olympic Team.

Between the end of the Olympic Team selections and the Games, the athletes participated in the entire second half of the World Cup season (four races) and one week of training in Park City immediately prior to departing for Vancouver. This format worked well as the entire Olympic Team traveled together creating a positive team bonding environment.

The team participated in a test competition event on the Games track during the winter of 2008-2009 as well as an International Training Week in November 2009. Naturally, participation in both these events was beneficial to the athletes as it was an opportunity to gain valuable training experience on the Winter Games venue that otherwise had limited access.

Games time training on the Games track was, of course, strictly monitored with every athlete receiving the same number of training run opportunities. The biggest issue was the tragic death of Republic of Georgia athlete Nodar Kumaritashvili. This occurred during men's singles training on the morning of Feb. 12, just hours before the Opening Ceremonies. Training was halted and cancelled for the rest of the day. Obviously, this was a terrible loss to the entire Winter Games movement, in particular to the close knit luge community. Knowing that their competition was scheduled to begin only 24 hours later, the athletes on the U.S. Luge Team, though shaken, handled the incident in a very professional and respectful manner. Upon returning to the Olympic Village, the team had a meeting to discuss what had happened, and the services of Sean McCann were made available to our athletes if needed. During the Opening Ceremonies, each member of the U.S. Luge delegation wore a black ribbon and Republic of Georgia Winter Games pin on the lapel of their jackets. This was thanks to the quick work of Athlete Ombudsman John Ruger, who was able to secure the pins from the Georgian delegation at the Vancouver Olympic Village.

Following the crash, the organizers decided to lower the start heights with the men sliding from the women's start, and women and doubles sliding from the junior start. When training commenced the next day, additional training runs were added so athletes could familiarize themselves with the new start positions. Thanks to the luck of the draw, Tony Benshoof of the United States was the first athlete down the track. Despite being the first sled following the fatality, he was able to stay composed, focused and lead the sport back to its purpose for being in Vancouver: Winter Games competition. The lowered start heights forced all athletes to scramble to learn the new start curves and track lengths.

Although the competition began under a dark cloud, the day after the Opening Ceremonies there was still a race to be run and medals to be awarded. In the men's competition, Benshoof completed four solid runs and finished in eighth place despite reoccurring back problems that hindered his start. He was somewhat disappointed, hoping for something closer to a top five finish. Chris Mazdzer finished 13th, a strong performance for his first Winter Games and Bengt Walden, hoping for more consistent runs and a top 10 finish, completed the competition in 15th after experiencing problems on his first run.

In the women's competition, the lowered start height proved challenging for the U.S. team. The first curve had a very difficult entrance and the U.S. women and coaches struggled to find the correct sled set up, driving style, and line through the curve. Erin Hamlin, after finishing fifth the year before in the Vancouver test race had high hopes for a podium finish at the Winter Games, but finished 16th. Julia Clukey was one spot behind in 17th. Megan Sweeney fought hard but finished 22nd. It was the first Games for both Clukey and Sweeney.

In the days before the competition, doubles looked promising as the experienced teams of Mark Grimmette and Brian Martin, and Christian Niccum and Dan Joye both posted very impressive training times. Come race day Grimmette and Martin experienced problems on the start curve on both runs and finished in 13th place. Niccum and Joye fared much better completing two consistent runs for a final sixth-place finish.

In terms of planning, I don't believe there is much that would be done differently in the months and years preceding the 2010 Winter Games. A great deal of thought and planning went into the selection process and the Games themselves. Regarding the actual races, it is easy to second guess decisions made in the heat of Winter Games training and competition after the fact. Significant challenges presented themselves that required the staff to make quick decisions on the fly, and all were based on what would have the most positive impact on performance. These decisions will be assessed for future impacts on the American teams, although in one sense or another, such an event affects all competitors.

American Chris Mazdzer prepares for take-off. Mazdzer finished 13th in the men's luge competition. (Photo by Leon Neal/AFP/Getty Images)

Nordic

By John Farra

Our athletes competed in test events which proved beneficial. By Games time, they were comfortable and confident with the venues.

I am the Nordic Director of U.S. Ski and Snowboard Association and a past Olympic team member. This was my first time at the Olympic Winter Games as a Team Leader. I was leader in 2009 for the Nordic World Championships which seemed like a complicated event to plan, but in retrospect it was not even close to complicated compared to the Winter Games. I was a cross-country skier and 1992 Olympian.

With more than a year in advance to plan, there was plenty of time to prepare for the craziness that is part of the Games. I attended all of the strategic planning meetings, including the key decision maker gathering in May 2008 and the November 2009 Team Leadership Final Countdown, which were both held in Vancouver. I also participated in the Team Leadership Kick-Off meeting in spring 2009. It was important to have deadlines for following up on details, and a chance to review progress towards achieving final plans. These meetings provided opportunities to force me to focus on just the Games planning instead of all the other responsibilities that present themselves in my position.

Cross-country makes it a priority to get on-snow training, and chose New Zealand as the site for that training. Nordic combined uses two trips to Europe and Scandinavia to jump with other national teams on their ski jumps. Ski training on roller skis is done at those locations. Each ski jumping athlete spent time during the summer competing in Europe on plastic. I am not sure we would change anything, but we'll review our procedures this spring (the season is not even over yet). We have planned many years in advance to create the optimum preparation strategies for the Games. We followed our plans perfectly, which worked well for nordic combined. The jury is still out for cross-country. The ski jumpers had a solid international competition schedule in advance of the Games.

Our team selection was based on season-long performances in Continental Cup and World Cup competitions. In the case of cross-country, we utilize the USSA National Ranking List points system. We did have one Olympic Trials event for one spot of the nordic combined Team, however, as predicted, that event selected someone who was already qualified via World Cup performance criteria. We typically don't utilize trials events for major championship selection. Generally, we choose athletes who are performing well in the months leading up to the event rather than just consid-

ering results at trials. We use coaches' discretion if the objective criteria fails to identify the right people. Yet, we are cautious of using it for the Winter Games. Athletes were selected as late as Jan. 21, 2010. This allowed us more time to include more events during the selection period. Consequently, we feel the best athletes were selected for the team, so I would not make any changes to the selection process. Between the trials period and start of the Games, we held a pre-Olympic camp for nordic combined and ski jumping. A camp and World Cup were also held for cross-country, and I would not make any changes to the activities or schedule of this time period.

Our athletes competed in test events which proved beneficial. By Games time, they were comfortable and confident with the venues. We sent the nordic combined team home for five days during an eight-day break between events. This was very effective for us, providing quality training and maybe even a psychological advantage to our team, while the other teams stayed at the Olympic Winter Games venue.

The ski jumpers were not expected to contend for medals at these Games, but they gave us all a thrill when all three performed well enough to qualify in the top 50 to compete for the normal hill event. Two out of the three qualified for the large hill event later in the Games. They borrowed a nordic combined athlete, Taylor Fletcher, to be able to complete a team of four jumpers in the large hill team event and finished in 11th place.

Cross-country had a relatively disappointing Games for most of the participants. That was a challenge for the staff to keep things light and positive, but we had a few highlights: Kikkan Randall's eighth in the sprint, and with Caitlin Compton, sixth place in the team sprint.

The nordic combined team had success for the first time in the first event when Johnny Spillane won a silver medal breaking the seal for the team. His teammates Todd Lodwick and Billy Demong took fourth and sixth, respectively, showing the strength of the whole team. The nordic combined team won the silver medal in the team event,

which was an awesome accomplishment. This was followed by Billy Demong's first-ever gold medal in any nordic sport for the United States! Spillane took another silver medal to complete the sweep: three events and three silver medals!

Living in the Village was a good choice. It was simple and close to our venue. I can't think of any changes or processes that should be changed. Lessons learned include being prepared for everything, but knowing I should not try to do everything myself. It's important to know the United States Olympic Committee (USOC) staff who can help because they are there to be called. There are so many resources available, it's important to use them.

I am honored to have been able to serve my small role in the whole puzzle. I am now grateful that I will have three years recovery before the next one!

Billy Demong is congratulated by American teammates Todd Lodwick (center), Johnny Spillane (right) and Brett Camerota (left) after claiming the silver medal in the nordic combined team event. (Photo by Don Emmert/AFP/Getty Images)

Short Track Speedskating

By Jack Mortell

Our benchmarks were readiness to perform, minimize distractions, proper focus, execution during races and admirable behavior following either victory or defeat.

Being a former U.S. Speedskating staff member, where I was variously employed as Short Track National Team coach, Short Track 1992 Olympic Winter Games head coach, 1994 and 2002 Winter Games Team Leader I was comfortable accepting my role. My name was in play in the fall of 2008 for the 2010 Team Leader, so I had plenty of time to prepare. I also have experience as a Team Leader at the World University Games, World Championship and international competition levels.

Short track (ST) is contested on an 111m-oval placed on a traditional International size figure skating/hockey rink. ST is a mass start, head-to-head sport that involves qualifying through placement heats. Speeds can reach 30 mph, spills are often spectacular and the cunning required to advance from round to round to reach the finals are often compared to NASCAR. Fitness, pack sense, and the ability to change speeds on a dime are key. Olympic Winter Games events are 500m, 1000m, 1500m, for women and men, 3000m relay for women and 5000m relay for men. These are relays only in the sense that each of the four skaters must skate at least one segment. In reality, the relay is more akin to a track cycling team race with racers being exchanged in and out, but not every participant covers the same distance as everyone else. In all events there are no lanes once the gun goes off. The correct skating pattern is judged by five referees and video replay is used. Some of the disqualifications (DQs) called or not called can be confusing to the viewing public. Generally, the DQs calls follow the guidelines.

The United States Olympic Committee (USOC) was great in providing heads-up info. I attended Team Leadership Kick-off Meeting May 2009 in Colorado Springs and the Team Leadership Final Countdown meeting in Vancouver in October 2009. I am a fan of face-to-face meetings, and I would have preferred more face-to-face Team Leaders meetings during the Games.

Our intense off-season training started in April 2009 with our 2009/10 National Racing Team Program. Nine of the 10 ST Olympians emerged from this Program and the 10th skater trained in a sister program in Salt Lake City. Training was primarily held in and around the Utah Olympic Oval, a week-long summer camp at the Olympic Training Center in Colorado Springs, and a nearly two-week ice and dryland camp in Marquette, Mich. These camps were helpful in building teamwork, spirit and a sense of mission. The camps indicated to key staff which adjustments had to be made for the Games, especially with regards to support staff.

Communication can always be improved no matter how well it is covered. Head coach Jae Su Chun and his role required better support from the assistant coaches, the U.S.S. High Performance Director and the U.S.S Executive Director to get his coaching philosophy and Program understood. Ultimately, Jae Su and I were able to get that headed in the right direction. The role of the head coach will be clear in 2014.

Performance/results at the ST Olympic Trials determined a place on the Olympic Team or not. The Olympic Trials were held in Marquette, Sept 8-12, 2009. All Winter Games distance were contested twice in the same fashion as they would be at the Games. The Trials were held on a level playing field and I feel that the skaters/results established the correct ST Olympic Team. The team selected had three Winter Games veterans in Apolo Ohno, Allison Baver and Kimberly Derrick, plus seven first timers, four of whom were still in their teens. However, each newcomer had a reasonable amount of international racing experience. With the Games being in Vancouver we had an advantage of skating on our own continent.

The Olympic Team trained and competed as a unit from the Trials through the Games, including four World Cups, two in Asia, and two in North America. These determined not only ranking at the Games, but start positions per each distance for each country and which eight teams would compete in either the women's or men's relays.

We instituted a well-balanced meal plan at our base site in mid-December 2009. These nutritionally-balanced meals were placed between the morning and afternoon workouts at the Utah Olympic Oval. In retrospect, we should have had a well-balanced meal plan during the entire training year.

For venue familiarization we competed in a World Cup in Vancouver in the fall of 2008. This Olympic test event was held at the Pacific Coliseum which was the Games venue for ST and figure skating. We skated well at the test event and were immediately comfortable with the site.

Olympic Games ice training was split between the Pacific Coliseum and the Killarney Ice Rink located 25 minutes away. To be fair to each competing country, the times and locations varied by day and by venue. This was to ensure that no team had an edge as far as ice practice was

concerned. This still resulted in some scheduling problems for us during Team Processing and one medal ceremony.

Apolo Ohno tied Bonnie Blair's record as the most decorated Winter Olympian with his sixth Olympic Medal, a silver in the 1500m, his bronze in the 1000m broke the record and gave Apolo the title of the most decorated. He added an eighth Olympic medal as a member of the bronze medal 5000m relay team.

Katherine Reutter became the first US women's ST individual medalist since 1994 with her strong silver medal finish in the women's 1000m. Kimberly Derrick and Allison Baver finished 20th and 29th in the same event. Reutter finished in 4th in the women's 1500m with Baver and Derrick ending up 15th and 21st. The 500m saw Reutter finishing 7th with Alyson Dudek in 13th. The women's 3000m Relay team of Reutter, Dudek, Derrick and Lana Gehring skated a terrific semi-final to qualify for the A Final. Baver substituted for Derrick in the Medal event with the team finishing 4th but moving up to a Bronze Medal when the Korean team was DQ'd. This was the first women's relay medal since 1994.

Ohno and J.R. Celski both showed great racing skills in the men's 1500m. They crossed the line for silver and bronze medals respectively! This is the first time the U.S. has had two male Olympic Medalists in the same Games race. (Cathy Turner and Amy Peterson were the only other U.S. short trackers to achieve this prior. Turner's gold medal and Peterson's bronze medal came in the 500m in Lilliham-mer in 1994.) unfortunately Jordan Malone was DQd in the 1500 and finished last. Ohno captured a Bronze in the 1000m with Celski and Travis Jayner finishing 8th and 23rd. The men's 500m saw Ohno cross the line in 2nd in the medal round but the silver medal was taken away by a DQ. Simon Cho finished 11th with Malone in 29th. The men's 5000m relay team of Ohno, Celski, Jayner and Cho had a solid semi final race to advance to the final where Malone substituted for Cho and the U.S. men won bronze behind Canada and Korea.

I talked to other key staff and our skaters before, throughout and after the Games to ask what should or could we change? Our benchmarks were readiness to perform, minimize distractions, proper focus, execution during races and admirable behavior following either victory or defeat. We represent the entire population of the United States. If everything has been done to win, it is important to hold your head high after every race no matter the outcome. We were proud to be the only short track Olympic Team in Vancouver where all 10 members went home with Olympic Medals.

In a four-year cycle, the U.S. Speedskating Short Track Team competes on the road all over North America, Europe and Asia as a self contained autonomous entity. Our goal is to put together a staff that works well in concert with the vision of a head coach, and to have a system for selecting athletes that is fair. Teamwork is fostered among our athletes and we become a well-oiled unit traveling, preparing and competing at the highest level of competition. We are successful and our staff manages every aspect of the process. But during that one month at the end of the cycle, our most critical time for results, we must deal with all the distractions—good and bad—at the Games. Nonetheless, our chief ally and sponsor, the USOC, has a presence and needs that must be dovetailed into the rhythm of an estab-lished successful autonomous team. We were very pleased with this relationship in Vancouver and the vast majority of the USOC worked overtime for our team's benefit. It was apparent that the USOC embraces the partnering approach more each cycle. There is a fine line between help and hindrance, and the USOC is the model for the help side of the line. Thanks to all the cheerful, helpful, understanding, tireless hardworking USOC staff and volunteers that pulled hard for the success of the U.S. Short Track Team. Our success would not have happened without the hard work, dedication and support of the entire U.S. short track staff.

Coach Jimmy Jang, Jordan Malone, J.R. Celski, Simon Cho, Katherine Reutter, Travis Jayner, Apolo Anton Ohno and coaches Jae Su Chun and Laurent Daignault pose together at USA House. (PHOTO BY ALEX GRIMM/GETTY IMAGES)

Snowboarding

By Abbi Nyberg

The selection process was very intense, almost more so than the actual Winter Olympic Games. We have a very strong team with multiple people vying for those few spots.

I am program manager for U.S. Ski and Snowboard Association (USSA) Snowboarding and was notified in June 2006 of my role as Team Leader. This gave me enough time to prepare for the Winter Olympic Games. I have also been involved in the 2007 World Championships, and the 2007, 2008, 2009 Junior World Championships. Snowboarding has several elements of competition. Snowboarding halfpipe is a judged sport. Snowboardcross (SBX) features four racers on course at one time, and the first one down wins. Parallel giant slalom (PGS) is time-based with two athletes racing each other.

I attended the May 2008 Key Decision Maker meeting in Vancouver, the Team Leadership Kick-Off meeting in spring 2009, and the Team Leadership Final Countdown meeting, also in Vancouver in November 2009.

The SBX team spent August in Argentina. Additional training took place in Telluride, Colo., in November and December. The team also trained in Park City, Utah, at the Center of Excellence for three months in the fall. The half-pipe team spent September in New Zealand, January in Park City, and February in Aspen, Colo. The PGS team was at Mount Hood, Ore., June to August. In October, the team trained in Holland and Switzerland. Oregon's Mount Bachelor and Mount Washington, British Columbia, were training sites in February. We felt we prepared very well for the Games.

In 2008, we drafted and adopted the selection criteria for the 2010 Snowboarding Winter Olympic Team. During the 2008-09 season, the U.S. Snowboarding athletes worked very hard for the United States to send a full quota of 18 athletes. In order to do this, athletes had to travel to multiple World Cup events around the world. Our team did a great job. In the fall of 2009 we determined we would secure the full quota, and moved into selecting those 18 athletes.

The selection process was very intense, almost more so than the actual Winter Olympic Games. We have a very strong team with multiple people vying for those few spots. The United States has the strongest men's halfpipe team in the world, but during a training camp in January one of the top contenders sustained a major concussion that put him in a coma for three weeks this resulted in career ending injuries. Two weeks later another one of the top competitors broke his back which took him out of Winter Games contention. These were major blows to the snowboarding community and affected everyone. The men's SBX selections

were just as intense, with the final team selection coming down to the last event in Stoneham, Canada. We selected a best-in-the-world team on Jan. 24, 2010.

Once the team was selected, most of the athletes went to the X-Games and then to training camps. Our teams had staggered arrivals in Vancouver. As Team Leader, I arrived on Feb. 5. The SBX team arrived first on Feb. 9 and we went through Team Processing. They moved directly into our off-site housing in West Vancouver. The halfpipe team arrived on Feb. 10 and after processing they moved into the athletes village for three nights. The PGS Team arrived last on Feb. 11 and stayed in the village until the 14th before going to Mt Washington on Vancouver Island for training.

Opening Ceremonies was a great event and our team really came together; you could feel the excitement. The team had a great time meeting Vice President Joe Biden. We have a tradition of trying to walk last in Opening Ceremonies. This year, as in years past, we had to fight off the women's hockey team for the last spot. Unfortunately, they held out longer than we did and we ended up walking second to last. Next time, we will walk last!

Our athletes did participate in test events held at the Games venue. This was beneficial for us because it showed us Cypress had very unpredictable weather. This was a factor for the athletes since the weather was a major threat to our training and cut several days of training for the athletes. The facilities were accessible and appropriate, and the weather was only the major problem. We overcame weather-related issues with good attitudes and umbrellas!

Leading up to the start of the events, it rained for five days at Cypress Mountain. The venues were in rough condition. We had a lot of events ahead of us and luckily the weather started to clear up a little. The first event was men's SBX and we had four guys looking to take medals. All of the men made finals, and in the final heat of the day Nate Holland and Seth Wescott were both vying for the gold. Wescott made some amazing passes and with a little magic he took the gold medal! He is the only man to win the SBX gold medal (2006 and 2010). We had hoped for better re-

sults from our SBX women, but that is the nature of the sport. Lindsey Jacobellis was looking for redemption after the 2006 Winter Games. But it was not her day. In the semi-finals she was disqualified as she went for a pass and cut on the inside of a gate. It was one of the most depressing moments of the Games. Jacobellis went on to finish fifth.

Up next was the men's halfpipe event. This is the main attraction and Shaun White was out to win a gold medal again. He didn't disappoint, going bigger and with more technical tricks than anyone else. Once again, White proved he is the best halfpipe rider in the world. Women's Halfpipe was the final event in the four-day stretch. With the combination of rain and so many people riding the pipe, it was not in good condition. The women were up to the challenge and they came through with Hannah Teter taking a silver medal and Kelly Clark the bronze medal.

There was a gap of six days until the PGS competitions, during this time the athletes went on a full media tour, we had won five medals in four days. It was also amazing to see how many athletes took full advantage of being at the 2010 Winter Games and enjoying the experience. The SBX and halfpipe team athletes moved in to the village. There was a lot of movement during this time trying to get luggage, athletes, and coaches into the village or on flights home.

The PGS team returned to Vancouver on Feb. 21 and tried to train at Cypress, but the weather was so terrible they only got in two days of training out of a possible seven. First up was the women's PGS and the weather was miserable. We only had one competitor, so the staff did our best to keep her dry and happy. It was raining buckets and soaking everyone to the bone. Michelle Gorgone stayed positive and finished 12th. The next day it was raining harder than the day before, which I didn't think was possible. Men's PGS is an exciting event to watch, but with the pouring rain it was tough to enjoy the competition. Tyler Jewell and Chris Klug advanced to finals, but did not make it to the final round. I was impressed by their positive attitudes; neither of them complained once and did their very best under the challenging circumstances.

Overall it was a great experience. It worked very well to have offsite housing for our athletes to stay in while competing. Transportation was tough, and with very few parking passes made it hard to get to where we needed to go easily. It was an amazing experience. There were a lot of moving pieces, but I felt our team worked well together and provided the athletes with the best possible support to bring home the medals. It was really nice to have the huge support staff at the United States Olympic Committee (USOC) help us achieve our goals!

The media deemed American Snowboardcross athlete Graham Watanabe the most quotable Olympian. When asked by a reporter what it feels like to be in the Olympic Games, he responded, "Try to imagine Pegasus mating with a unicorn and the creature that they birth. I somehow tame it and ride it into the sky in the clouds and sunshine and rainbows. That's what it feels like." (PHOTO BY JAMIE SQUIRE/GETTY IMAGES)

TEAM USA
Speedskating

By Michael Kooreman

After the Olympic Team was finalized, the athletes had one month to recuperate from the difficult World Cup racing season and prepare themselves for the Games.

I was selected as the Team Leader for the Long Track Speedskating Team in April 2009. I was chosen because I have been a coach and Team Leader at international events (World Cups and World Championships) over the last two seasons. I was humbled and honored to serve in such an important role. While fulfilling my Team Leader duties I was also the Long Track Program Coordinator, the Assistant Coach for the National Sprint Team, and our National Team Equipment Technician.

In May 2009, I attended the Team Leadership Kick-Off meeting where we began working on the initial stages of our Olympic Winter Games Preparations. I also attended the Team Leader Final Countdown Meeting in Vancouver in October. This was key in providing essential information for the final preparations leading into the Winter Games season.

It was a busy summer of National Team Training Camps and Team Pursuit Training Camps. This was the first year that we had Team Pursuit specific camps. One reason for having these camps is so that all of our potential Team Pursuit members had the opportunity to train and practice together. Unfortunately, our Allround Program has been inconsistent due to not having a constant coach in place and therefore a majority of our distance skaters train outside of our National Team Program.

The sport of long track speedskating is the fastest human-propelled sport without the help of gravity or mechanical devices. The skaters race on a 400m track against the clock in distances ranging from the 500m to 5000m for women and 10,000m for men. Additionally, there is also a Team Pursuit competition where three skaters race together as a team and work their way through two qualifying rounds and a medal round.

In order to have the best skaters competing at the Winter Games, U.S. Speedskating along with the United States Olympic Committee (USOC) created a very sound and detailed qualification system. The best part about the qualification system was that it was all based on the performance of the athletes. In October 2009, the skaters competed in the U.S. Single Distance Championships, which doubled as a qualifier for the Fall World Cup. After five World Cups/Olympic Qualifying Competitions (OQCs), the top ranked skaters in each distance had earned their places on the Olympic Team. The final spot in each distance was raced for at the U.S. Championships in late

December. This allowed skaters who may have been sick or injured in the fall, and those who were coming on stronger later in the season, an additional opportunity to make the team. The Team Pursuit teams were named from the skaters who qualified for individual distances based on performances at the Team Pursuit Camps combined with their performance in races throughout the season.

After the Olympic Team was finalized, the athletes had one month to recuperate from the difficult World Cup racing season and prepare themselves for the Games. We had hoped to have our Team Pursuit skaters train together that month. Unfortunately, this did not happen. All of the athletes had been on the road for most of the year and no one would consider doing Games preparation away from home. The skaters who train in the same location did their Team Pursuit-specific training together, but half of the women's team was in Salt Lake City while the other half was in Milwaukee. Three of the four men were in Milwaukee. With a solid Allround National Team Program this would not have happened, so we did the best we could.

Other than the Team Pursuit issue, the preparations for the Games went very well that month. Everyone got in a solid training block and, other than Maria Lamb, no one got sick or injured. The team went into Vancouver a little early (Feb. 3) which was very beneficial. We were the only team in processing, which made it a very relaxed atmosphere. Everyone had a good time and was comfortable with everything. The USOC staff made us feel very welcome and was extremely helpful.

The competition structure at the Winter Games for long track speedskating is different from most sports. Other sports compete in multiple events/distances in a day and then have some time off to prepare for the next event. In long track there is only one distance contested per day, which stretches the sport over the entire length of the Games. With races and multiple practice sessions everyday, the staff was at the venue all day, every day throughout the Games.

The first event on the first day of the Games was the men's 5000m. Americans competing in the event were

Chad Hedrick, Shani Davis, and Trevor Marsicano. Hedrick finished in 11th place, followed by Davis in 12th and Marsicano in 14th.

On the following day, the women began competition with the 3000m event. The United States has not won a medal in the women's 3000m event since Beth Heiden won a bronze medal in 1980. Nancy Swider-Peltz Jr. had the best performance of her career to-date finishing ninth. Jilleanne Rookard was 12th and Catherine Raney-Norman was 17th.

After two of the distance events we moved onto the sprints. In the 500m, skaters race the distance twice and the results come from the fastest combined time. It isn't necessarily who skates the fastest 500m, it is who puts two perfectly executed races together.

The day the men raced the 500m was a strange day. Both of the ice resurfacing machines broke down during the competition and the top competitors were made to wait 2.5 hours from the time that they warmed up to the time that they raced. In an event where consistency is key, the athletes' preparation is vital to a good performance. Due to this unforeseen problem a lot of mistakes came from nor-

mally very consistent skaters. American Tucker Fredricks, arguably one of the most consistent 500m skaters (he won the overall World Cup Title), made a few mistakes in his races and ended up in 12th place. The other Americans in the event were Nick Pearson who ended up in 26th, newcomer Mitch Whitmore was 37th, and Davis had to pull out of the event due to a concern with his groin.

The ice-crew at the Richmond Olympic Oval took care of the resurfacing machine issues and the women's 500m event got underway with no delays. This Winter Games was one year too early for rising star Heather Richardson. She narrowly missed earning her first Winter Games medal finishing in 6th place. Also in the event were Americans Elli Ochowicz 17th, Jennifer Rodriguez 21st, and Lauren Cholewinski 30th.

Next up was the men's 1000m. Competing in the event was a strong contingency of American skaters including Davis, Hedrick, Marsicano, and Pearson. Davis stepped up to the challenge and skated an incredible race winning the gold medal and posting a track record time. This marked the first time that anyone has ever repeated Winter Games

Americans (from left to right) Brian Hansen, Jonathan Kuck and Chad Hedrick celebrate their victory over the powerful Dutch team in the semifinals of team pursuit. (PHOTO BY DAVID HECKER/AFP/GETTY IMAGES)

gold medals in the 1000m! Hedrick won the bronze medal, and Pearson finished seventh. Marsicano ended up in 10th. Four Americans in the top 10 was a huge accomplishment for our team.

In the women's 1000m there were no American medal contenders, but there were medal hopes in Rodriguez and Richardson. The summer before the Games, Rodriguez lost her mother, her number one supporter, to cancer. Rodriguez skated a race that her mother would have been proud of but ended up missing a medal by only 0.3 of a second. Richardson skated a great race and finished ninth. The other Americans in the race were Ochowicz who finished 26th and Rebekah Bradford who finished 28th.

Next up was the men's 1500m. The United States had three medal contenders in Olympians Davis (silver medalist), Hedrick (bronze medalist), and Marsicano. The other American in the event was Brian Hansen. Davis won the silver medal matching his performance in the Torino Games. Hedrick finished in sixth place. Marsicano finished 15th and Hansen skated to 18th place.

In the women's 1500m Richardson finished in 16th place and Rodriguez came in 18th. Other Americans in the event were Rookard, who finished 24th, and Catherine Raney-Norman who finished 31st.

The final individual distances at the Games were the men's 10,000m and the women's 5000m. The United States had no medal contenders in these events but saw some great performances from Jonathan Kuck who placed eighth in his first Winter Games. Ryan Bedford ended up in 12th. The 5000m is Rookard's specialty event. But, like Rodriguez, she has struggled with events outside of sport. She lost father years ago and then her mother to a battle with cancer shortly before the Games. She fought hard and her 5000m was an incredible race to watch earning her an eighth place finish. Maria Lamb competed with an injury but still pulled off a 15th place finish.

In long track speedskating the Team Pursuit is an entirely different event than the races that the athletes are used to. Normally it is just them against the clock. In the Team Pursuit they have to work as a perfectly synchronized team.

Only three skaters race each Team Pursuit but each country is allowed to have four skaters listed on the team pursuit roster. Following a series of qualifying races, the team of Hansen, Hedrick, Kuck and Marsicano skated to a silver medal. The women's pursuit team of Rodriguez, Rookard, Raney-Norman and Swider-Peltz Jr. finished in fourth place.

While at the Games we received a lot of great support from the USOC, Vancouver Olympic Committee (VANOC), and its volunteers. The transportation system worked out really well as did the location of all of the resources in the Village. There was never a moment during then Games when a situation arose that could not be handled.

> One thing I would highly recommend to all future Team Leaders is designate a friends and family liaison. This is a person who all of the friends and family can turn to for answers.

I cannot say enough about how awesome the Proctor & Gamble U.S.A. Family House was for the athletes to celebrate their victories. Having a place where family and friends could go and be taken care of is extremely important to the success of our athletes. Eliminating distraction is a key element to success, and the P&G House played a huge role!

One thing I would highly recommend to all future Team Leaders is designate a friends and family liaison. This is a person who all of the friends and family can turn to for answers. They connect everyone and can communicate amongst themselves about tickets, places to stay, pins, events, etc. This lifts a huge burden off of the athlete.

One issue we faced was accreditation for personal coaches. We obviously cannot get credentials for every personal coach, and this caused a problem. We dealt with it the best we could on the spot, but this area will need better planning in the future.

Derek Parra was our Allround Coach this year and did a great job. He and I worked very hard to facilitate a cohesive team atmosphere. The Team Pursuit Camps definitely had a positive impact. However, since this was our first year, there were a few kinks to work out if we do them again. If not for those camps, our skaters would not have skated together other than at the World Cups.

Ryan Shimabukuro was our sprint team coach. After the Games in Torino, the sprint team went back to the drawing board to bring in younger skaters who had not made it on the international scene. Other than Tucker Fredricks, the team did not have many international performances. I became Shimabukuro's assistant (and program coordinator), and we hired Shane Domer as our strength and condition coach. One thing that we really lacked in the last quad was junior/development programs. We really need to focus our attention on building these programs. We need an 8-12-year plan rather than focusing on four years at a time.

Our medical staff at the Games consisted of Dr. Eric Heiden, Fikre Wondafrash, and Laura Tietjen. Just having Dr. Heiden present with the team was very important. His

medical expertise far exceeds what a team needs in its medical staff. What he brings to the team is a feeling that they are part of something great. Wondafrash and Tietjen are not only great at what they do but have also become like team psychologists. Tietjen even received the Order of Ikkos from the men's team pursuit team! The Order of Ikkos was a great opportunity for the athletes to reward the person who really helped them get to where they are. This award should be engrained into the Olympic Movement for years to some.

The other staff members who were absolutely irreplaceable were Carrie Needham (video specialist), Ross Flowers and Nicole Detling-Miller (Sports Psych), Guy Thibault (High Performance Director), and Peri Kinder (Media/PR). Our entire staff worked as a solid cohesive team and helped to improve every aspect of our team's performance.

The USOC has a good job description for the Team Leader. Here are a few responsibilities to pass along to future Team Leaders:

1) Athletes first. No matter what, the athletes and their needs come before anything else;

2) Don't plan on sleeping;

3) Be prepared to fight for the athletes when priority of performance may be overlooked;

4) Have a game plan for everything and make sure everyone associated with the team has a game plan;

5) Plan on random and unforeseen events;

6) Manage the stresses of the athletes, coaches, media/PR personal, staff, and NGB management then turn them into positive situations; and

7) Remember to take a couple of moments to step back and just appreciate how awesome the Olympic Winter Games are.

Jilleanne Rookard of United States finished eighth in the 5000m. (Photo by Jasper Juinen/Getty Images)

Accreditation

By Denise Thomas and Rebecca Crawford, International Games

T he United States qualified and entered 216 athletes in the 2010 Olympic Winter Games in Vancouver, British Columbia, Canada. Based on 216 athletes, the United States Olympic Committee (USOC) was awarded (by the International Olympic Committee) a quota of approximately 213 Ao and 22 National Olympic Committee (NOC) accreditations, of which approximately 106 and 66, respectively, were transferable and able to be used by a second (Ao) or third (NOC) person.

There are two (2) primary types of accreditation: "A" (Aa, Ao, Ac), and "NOC" as noted in the accreditation summary below.

The USOC mission drives the Olympic Winter Games accreditation strategy, which is to maximize opportunities to win medals by identifying the appropriate number of qualified performance support staff needed to serve U.S. athletes/teams. Lessons learned from a 2008 Beijing Olympic Games debrief enabled the USOC to streamline the accreditation strategy and process for Vancouver. Direct input from individual NGBs resulted in an earlier (18 months out) and more customized accreditation allocation process. The primary accreditation takeaway from the Olympic Winter Games in Vancouver is to continue the strong and early collaboration with NGBs to ensure a strategic and timely process that has the most positive impact on sport performance.

2010 OLYMPIC WINTER GAMES ACCREDITATION SUMMARY

TYPE	POPULATION	NUMBER
Aa	Athletes	216
Ac	Chef de Mission	1
Ac	Deputy Chef de Mission	2
Ac	Attaché	1
Ao	Team Officials *(Coaches, Team Leaders, Performance Staff –* *technicians, medical, media, security,* *Olympic village)*	247
NOC	USOC President and Secretary General and Guests	4
NOC	Transferable Guests *National Governing Body Executive Directors/Presidents,* *USOC Board of Directors/Executives, Sponsors)*	44
TOTAL ACCREDITED USA DELEGATION		**515**

Air Travel

By Nancy Gonsalves, Associate Director, International Games

Booking air travel is like a slow dance— a lot of back and forth!

The United States Olympic Committee (USOC) coordinates air travel for athletes, coaches, administrators, staff and other delegation members. For the Vancouver Olympic Winter Games, we created and tracked reservations for more than 600 people. We are extremely fortunate to have an excellent sponsor in United Airlines. We were also fortunate that Vancouver was directly serviced by more than 15 daily flights on United (versus having to go with other carriers or private charters), although we predominantly used three specific flights: the early afternoon arrivals from Chicago, Denver and San Francisco. These particular flights were chosen to coincide with the Team Processing schedule, which occurred immediately upon arrival in Vancouver at an airport hotel location.

The process began at least one year out from the start of the Winter Games with the seat block request to United Revenue Management. We reviewed the specific schedules as they were known at that time and determined the best flight options for our teams. Critical things to consider were departure and arrival times, connection options, and type and size of aircraft (necessary to accommodate the sports equipment and luggage). United then confirmed our block request, ideally at the lowest booking class available to help lower ticket costs. These seats were then reserved specifically for the delegation unless we released them.

The next step was determining what each individual sport discipline would like in terms of routings (from camp or hometowns), dates and times. This information was gathered during the initial surveys and at the Team Leadership Kick-off and Final Countdown meetings. Booking air travel is like a slow dance—a lot of back and forth! With the National Governing Bodies' (NGBs) agreement, we mutually decided on dates of travel and set aside a specific number from the block for each sport team. As plans solidified, requests for changes were made and accommodated if at all possible (most were). Once the team was named, actual itineraries were created, agreed upon and ticketed. Since many team trials were very late [in relation to the start of the Games], we were issuing tickets from mid-October (USOC staff and some NGB team staff) all the way thru Feb. 12—Opening Ceremony day!

Most teams were able to fly on United flights, although exceptions were granted to fly other carriers. While a direct flight on Delta might have seemed more advantageous, in the end, Delta's excess baggage fees and assistance from the

on-site, USOC-dedicated United customer service staff clearly outweighed using off-line carriers. A few of the more well-known athletes were flown first class by sponsors or even on private planes.

In order to assist the Team Leaders, as well as their assigned United Winter Games desk agents, I developed a travel template, capturing required information for each discipline. This proved to be very helpful and streamlined the ticketing process. I pre-populated key fields with information downloaded from the Games records database (legal passport name, date of birth and United Mileage Plus number). All the Team Leaders had to do was fill in the proper date and origination and return destinations.

I had more interaction with the organizing committee, Vancouver Olympic Committee (VANOC), than at previous Games and provided them with arrival and departure information to support their ground transport movements. Similarly, we met often to develop the plan for off-site check-in at the conclusion of the Games and that worked extremely well. Like all other organizing committees, their timeline and forms were much too restrictive for a National Olympic Committee (NOC) that had about 600 people to consider. However, they were very appreciative of the spreadsheet format and detailed content I provided via the travel manifest.

The travel manifest is a detailed Excel spreadsheet that captures each individual passenger, sport, role, arrival and departure date, flight number and airport. The manifest supported ground transportation foremost but was also used extensively for accreditation and housing. It was absolutely critical that the data entered was checked and double checked for accuracy and that all flight changes that occurred were kept up to date. United agents on-site at the Games confirmed each passenger at least 24 hours in advance and also tracked the flights on a daily basis for any weather or mechanical delays that may have caused rerouting. In turn, they radioed any last minute updates to the staff working at the airport. As a result, we were able to efficiently meet and greet every passenger affiliated with

the delegation, including NGB VIPs, hand off their accreditation card for validation in the baggage claim area, and help guide them to the proper ground transportation option.

Needless to say, I worked extremely close with United Airlines. All the agents on the United Desk were assigned specific sports so I spoke to all of them almost daily. I also worked with their supervisors on the seat block. Even though I was very involved, I think there was still a lot that went on that I did not even know—like the supervisors sending itineraries to the rate desk to be fared at a lower cost or pulling seats that weren't available and giving them to the USOC. United really puts the USOC and our athletes first!

In addition to the United Desk, we met several times with the United airport personnel at Vancouver International Airport (YVR). Nigel Newsome is the station manager and he has a long tenure with YVR Airport. He, in turn, introduced us to YVR Airport operations and the core VANOC airport logistics team whom we met with on several occasions in the year leading up to the Games. In fact, they commented that we were the most organized and forthcoming NOC with data and they used our stats for their modeling and projections!

The Salt Lake City (SLC) United Airlines personnel also proved to be great partners. Due to Park City training camps and U.S. Speedskating based in nearby Kearns,

approximately 65 percent of our delegation flew to/from SLC to Vancouver. I flew out to meet with the station manager and operations supervisor five months before the Games to review each of our teams' plans. Over the course of the next two months, United met with Team Leaders at their respective camps, evaluated their equipment size and loads, and developed creative solutions in order to accommodate their needs. As a result, all equipment made it to Vancouver either with or ahead of the team! One incredible example of going above and beyond for our team is that United was able to schedule a diversion of a Denver to Vancouver non-stop flight to SLC to pick up three alpine ski coaches and 165 ski bags in advance of the 10 athletes flying the next day. Even the YVR Airport personnel were impressed!

The airline industry as a whole is in a constant flux; fuel prices, security concerns and even volcano eruptions can happen at any time. The USOC was prepared to look at each Games location and determine the best possible solution to meet the performance needs for each team. For the Vancouver 2010 Olympic Winter Games, air travel was mostly problem free. A large part was due to the unseasonably warm weather for all mountain and West coast locations. While Washington, D.C., and the mid-Atlantic were hit with a string of blizzards, 99 percent of our delegation was unaffected and arrived on-time or early!

American Lacy Schnoor reserves a place in the finals with her high-flying skills. She finished ninth overall in the ladies' aerials.
(Photo by Adrian Dennis/AFP/Getty Images)

OLYMPIC EXECUTIVE REPORTS
Athletes Villages
Vancouver & Whistler

By Rebecca Crawford, Director, International Games
& Kelly Skinner, Team Leader, Sport Performance

The Athlete Village is "home" for athletes during the Olympic Winter Games. The Village is designed, developed and maintained by the organizing committee for the respective Games; for 2010 this was the Vancouver Organizing Committee (VANOC). The United States Olympic Committee (USOC) is responsible for daily operations for the U.S. delegation, including setup and tear-down of offices, a medical clinic, and an athlete services center, as well as providing the equipment, supplies and dedicated services for Team USA members. Our primary mission is to provide a world class environment that eliminates distraction so athletes can focus on medal-winning performances.

Following the setup of past Olympic Winter Games, VANOC utilized a two Village system in order to provide the best possible environment for the athletes. The main Village was located in Vancouver and housed athletes from the sports of curling, figure skating, freestyle skiing, ice hockey, snowboarding, speedskating, and short track speed-skating. The secondary Village was located in Whistler and accommodated biathlon, bobsleigh and skeleton, luge and the alpine and nordic skiing sports.

The USOC had a very good working relationship with VANOC, in particular with Andre Bourgeois, National Olympic Committee (NOC) Relations Manager. He was very helpful to our delegation in a variety of ways by helping us manage the logistics associated with a team of approximately 475 delegation members. Our relationship with the Village Logistics team was critical to our plan of minimizing distractions so that we could put the athletes' needs first and therefore assist in fantastic performances. We were able to build effective relationships in a short period of time that enabled us to perform our duties and provide very good customer service to the National Governing Bodies (NGBs).

Looking ahead to the 2014 Olympic Winter Games in Sochi, Russia, there are a few things we need to consider:

- Change and/or enhance plan for provision of cell phones/phone plan for athletes and possibly NGB staff (coaches, Team Leaders).

- Develop and execute a more effective and efficient Village Guest Pass system.

- Minimize/eliminate martyr syndrome among staff while, at the same time, recognizing that people are "wired" differently and flexibility is key.

- More and earlier pre-Games integrated planning of Village roles between staff from non-International Games and International Games divisions.

- More and earlier interaction/planning between Village and NGB staf. Primary goals would be to ensure the most effective use of human resources and time and a thorough understanding and agreement of systems and roles.

The staff members identified to work in the Villages were carefully chosen with an eye toward maximizing sport relationships and performance. An absolutely fantastic staff was assembled for these Games. There is no doubt that the same people can't keep serving in the same role for every Games—it is important that we prepare others for these roles—but the staff members who worked in either Vancouver or Whistler were excellent and they would be great teams to reassemble in part or in whole for any future Games.

A view of the Vancouver Athletes Village. (Photo by Kevork Djansezian/Getty Images)

Media Services

By Bob Condron, Director of Media Services

The volunteers were like the sunshine in a meadow. You just relaxed when you saw them.

The United States Olympic Committee (USOC) Media Services was responsible for all planning, staffing and implementation of media and communications areas for Team USA and the delegation at the Olympic Winter Games.

This included the following tasks:

- Assign USOC staff responsibilities for Games
- Assign press officers for sport support, Village duty
- Oversee selection, training and equipping of press officers
- Oversee credentials, housing and transportation for press officers
- Select, design and equip USOC office in the Main Press Center (MPC)
- Plan and oversee media services at Team Processing, Athlete Villages
- Cultivate, establish relationships with the Vancouver Olympic Committee (VANOC) and International Olympic Committee (IOC) staff
- Oversee budget planning and oversight
- Oversee recruiting and training of office staff
- Oversee relationships with national, international media at Games
- Responsible for planning, oversight of U.S. Olympic Team Media Summit, the preview of the U.S. Olympic Team
- Responsible for the accreditation allotment for U.S. Media covering the Olympic Winter Games
- Oversee special ticketing for USOC-accredited media at Games

Press Operations and Services for the 2010 Olympic Winter Games may have been the best in Olympic history. The MPC, the venues, the transportation system, photo services, wireless data transmission, and the knowledgeable and excellent staff made these Games efficient and enjoyable. Being in Canada and enjoying the Canadian hospitality made the 2010 Olympic Winter Games something special.

From a USOC perspective, here's a look at what we did and how we did it:

MEDIA ACCREDITATION

Media accreditation for Vancouver went exceptionally well. The USOC was awarded 480 credentials by the International Olympic Committee for the U.S. media and went through a fair and equitable process for awarding these credentials. The Associated Press Sports Editors Association was the group that made final recommendations to the USOC. The group met in Chicago at the O'Hare Hilton Hotel. Peggy Manter and I coordinated this system for U.S. media. I was also a member of the IOC-selected group that awarded accreditation to the 205 National Olympic Committees.

CD MEDIA GUIDE

The USOC went to a CD format for its media guide for the third Games in a row. This time, however, it was the only format. In the past we've done a combination of hard copies, CDs and flash drives. The result was mainly positive and there were only a few complaints about the format. One was that a few computers are still left that don't have disc drives. Lisa Ramsperger compiled and edited the media guide.

PERFORMANCE OF PRESS OFFICERS, STAFF

The Media Services staff was outstanding. A combination of USOC staff, National Governing Body (NGB) staff, professionals from the field and volunteers made up a knowledgeable and professional group who provided valuable assistance to media, athletes and the USOC delegation at the Games.

RELATIONSHIP WITH MEDIA, VANOC, IOC

In a survey taken midway through the Games, the media gave the USOC Media Services staff a 94 percent satisfaction rate. The best part of our team was the relationships we have with the media, VANOC and the IOC. It was nurtured over many years and it is a friendship blended with a large amount of respect. It is a two-way street and we are constantly working to help make these Games better and make the role of the media easier and more productive.

USOC NEWS BUREAU, INFORMATION DISTRIBUTION

Very efficient in telling the stories of our athletes and teams. Headed by Lisa Ramsperger.

BREAKING NEWS BUREAU

Continued to be one of the best areas in our Media Services program. It kept the media and Olympic Family up to date and was always popular with every recipient. It's an email program and more than 1,000 were on the Games list for late-breaking news. Craig Bohnert was the editor of the service.

USA DAILY

The delegation newsletter and preview went online-only for the first time and was well received by everyone. We made the decision to do it online for several reasons and let everyone know if they wanted copies they had to coordinate their own printing. USA House did this and the results were very popular. We do the basic service and whoever wants it can make it happen on their end. Lisa Ramsperger was the editor of the Daily.

USA WRAPUP

This day-end compilation of results of all U.S. athletes and teams was put together by the interns in Colorado Springs under the guidance of Kevin Sullivan from our Vancouver office. It was a good breakfast publication to see how we did the day before. This also was online-only.

HOMETOWN NEWS BUREAU

This was our first attempt at a Hometown News Bureau. Because of the downturn in the media industry and the turn-back of about 100 credentials from newspapers, we made a specific effort to target the hometown media of our Olympic athletes. We alerted media about teleconferences in Vancouver and Whistler, we lined up more than 50 interviews between athletes and hometowns, and we took advantage of this program to work with a very important media: the athlete's hometown media. Karen Linhart managed this service for the USOC.

HISTORICAL ASPECT, RECORDS INFORMATION

Another new program in the Media Services for the Games was the addition of historian Dr. Bill Mallon who provided a mass of details about records, updates, Games bests and information about the day's activities. Having him there also spawned some stories on their own.

MANAGING VICTORY

Managing Victory is a program that features a media plan after winning a medal. This program was a huge

success in Vancouver and Whistler. Lindsay Hogan coordinated the program in Vancouver and Kevin Neuendorf did the same in Whistler. This program featured more than 30 athletes during the Games and provided millions of viewers a night in extra coverage with the non rights holding broadcasters such as ESPN, CNN, AP TV, Reuters TV, Yahoo, AOL and other websites throughout the United States.

PRESS CONFERENCES

The USOC organized and hosted 60 press conferences in Vancouver and Whistler, including 29 pre-competition press conferences involving every team and discipline competing at the Games. Team USA averaged three major press conferences a day for the 21 days of pre-Games and competition featuring about 190 athletes. This did not include the press conferences that were held at the venues post competition. The bulk of the press conferences were held at the Main Press Center in Vancouver and the Whistler Media Center and the non-accredited media center in Whistler. Others were held at Media Days at the venues, Athlete Villages and other places. Erica Hutchinson coordinated all the details of USA press conferences in Vancouver.

WHISTLER MEDIA SERVICES OPERATION

The USOC had two bases of operations at the 2010 Olympic Winter Games—one in Vancouver and one in Whistler. Neuendorf was the USOC's Media Services Director in Whistler with a full staff of press officers, its own Managing Victory Program, an Athlete Village press officer and operation and an office at the Whistler Media Center. Many of the press conferences and the Managing Victory program were held at Whistler Media House, the non-accredited media center that was adjacent to the Medals Plaza and had a tremendous logistical advantage over the Whistler Media Center as far as athlete drop-off and pickup. USA House in Whistler was the culmination of the Managing Victory Program and the attitude and operation of the staff in Whistler provided the final media opportunity for our medal-winning athletes.

PRESS OFFICER TRAINING, EDUCATION

A special effort went into training and educating the press officers and media service staff. This involved the writing and distribution of "The Press Officer's Guidebook for the Olympics," three specific teleconferences with the full staff, a two-day meeting with the Media Services staff as part of the Games Staff meeting in Colorado Springs, and individual visits with every sport on the program. Eight members of the NGB PR staff were first-time Olympic staff members. This education and training program was mandatory from that standpoint. It was vital that we, as a full team, were prepared and knowledgeable about our athletes, our teams and the way we treat our athletes and media at these Games. The point was made that this is not a World Championship, a

World Cup or a National Championship. The Olympic Winter Games are vastly different and it was our job to get that message to every member of our staff. With a 94 percent rating by a survey taken with the national and international media, this goal was very successfully reached.

U.S. OLYMPIC TEAM MEDIA SUMMIT

The U.S. Olympic Team Media Summit, held in Chicago, Sept. 9-11, set the stage for successful media coverage of the U.S. Team in Vancouver and Whistler. More than 500 media attended the three-day event at the Palmer Hilton Hotel to learn in advance the stories of our Olympians. This premier USOC event gives the nation's media a chance to sit face to face with about 90 Olympic athletes and fill their notebooks and video tape library with notes, quotes and story ideas that await the Games. The U.S. media was the most prepared group of media in the world as far as knowing the stories of the Olympic Team. This event helps provide that wealth of knowledge, details and personal relationships with Team USA.

VOLUNTEER OFFICE STAFF, DEPAUL STUDENTS

Once again our volunteer office staff took us from great to sensational with their spirit, drive and eagerness to be affiliated with the Olympic Winter Games and with our staff. They paid their own way to the Games, including housing, airfare and meals to be able to work 12-14 hour days at the Main Press Center in Vancouver. DePaul University's school of Sport Management and Communications brought seven students who filled roles ranging from Newsletter editors to writers to helping with media services at USA House and the morning shows. They added a wealth of talents to the staff and were a vital part of the New Media strategy involving Twitter, blogs and our website material. The USOC provided a small stipend to each of the volunteers to help defray the cost of meals. These stipends ranged from $200 to $500 depending on the situation. Peggy Manter coordinated the office and volunteer staff for the USOC.

OFFICE SETUP, MPC

The USOC had a 300-square meter office located in the Main Press Center in Vancouver and a 50-square meter office in the Whistler Media Center. These were our bases of operation for the Games. These offices served as workrooms for the staff, our special ticketing operation, USOC News Bureau, Hometown News Bureau, Breaking News Bureau, USA Daily, USA Wrapup and the offices for the USOC and NGB staff during the Games. These offices were equipped with faxes, telephones, a wi-fi setup, INFO2010 system, printers and supplied with refreshments such as Cokes, water and snacks. The office in Vancouver was located adjacent to USA Today and near other U.S. media organizations. In Whistler, the USOC office was the first one in the hallway near the VANOC welcome center.

ATHLETE VILLAGE MEDIA SERVICES

The USOC had media services operations in two villages. Keith Bryant was the USOC press officer for the Vancouver Village and Nicole Jomantas was the press officer in Whistler. This was an important element of our media services because it was the point where we touch athletes more than any other place at the Games. We supported hometown media here, we arranged interviews with national and international media and we had two NBC cameras and crews that set up in our residential area. One of the cameras was termed the "Disaster Cam" and the other was for the NBC website and local affiliates of athletes who volunteered for interviews in a specially located room away from the USOC daily business centers.

USA HOUSE MEDIA SERVICES

The Vancouver USA House had a lively Media Services operation staffed by two DePaul University students and was overseen by Maureen Weekes and Lindsay Hogan. There was a media workroom and interview space on the ground floor, next to the gift shop. This location was advantageous because it offered an area not secured at the top levels for staff, sponsors and invited guests. Media who wanted to access the top floors for tours or business reasons needed to apply for accreditation 24 hours in advance and were escorted.

UPDATED HTTP://USOCPRESSBOX.ORG

This website was critically important to our media services information distribution. It was our main vehicle to disseminate stories, quotes, advisories and results of our athletes and programs. With the upgrading and design by Microsoft, the 2010 version of press box was the best ever. It was easy to navigate, contained more information and was more user-friendly than anything we've done in the past at the Olympic Games. Media gave it a 90 percent approval rating and it provided a service for those media and fans not at the Games. It was a great improvement, managed by Kevin Neuendorf.

TRANSPORTATION

● Transportation for the Media Services staff was as good as it was going to get with the limitations of very slow and very crowded streets in Vancouver and a two-hour trip from Vancouver to Whistler. There were some inbred problems that we seemed to overcome to get our work done. The railway system was a great part of this system mainly because it didn't have to negotiate the Vancouver city traffic. It was connected to shuttles and other services but the rail line was the backbone of travel for these Games in Vancouver.

- The trip to Whistler was tough, especially coming back because it was usually in rainy and wet conditions with bright lights and orange cones making travel difficult.

- VANOC showed some flexibility in granting a request from the USOC to provide a direct shuttle from the nordic events in the Olympic Park to Cypress Mountain for certain freestyle events. VANOC changed the time and added a larger shuttle capacity for those journalists who wanted to cover events such as nordic combined in the morning and freestyle halfpipe at night.

- Supplying our own dedicated drivers was a huge benefit for our press conferences and Managing Victory program. It would have been impossible for us to host the numerous press conferences with athletes who needed transportation from the Village or the Medals Plaza or to USA House. It was crucial to have a pool of about five drivers to make this happen each day.

- Having the correct VAPP passes was crucial to our ability to get athletes to press conferences at the MPC. These passes enabled us to park a few feet from the elevator that took the athletes to the Green Room and press conference areas.

- The "Clean to Clean" setup from the MPC to Canada Hockey Place and BC Place was outstanding. It eliminated standing in line outside the security entrances, sometimes for more than an hour.

MIXED ZONE ACCESS

The special armband issued by the IOC to NOCs was a huge addition to the ability to assist athletes in the difficult area of the Mixed Zone at the Games. The armband enabled NOC press attaches to walk with the athlete in the press area. Press attaches still can't get into the broadcast area of the Mixed Zone but this was a solid step in the right direction.

SPECIAL MEDIA DAYS

The USOC organized and hosted special media days at the Athletes' Village, at the U.S. Team Flag Raising and at Team Processing at Delta Hotel. The Village tour involved the team's residence areas, the medical areas and the USOC working areas for the international media. Reuters and AP did an international story on our delegation, interviewed about five athletes, Chief Medical Officer of Team USA Dr. Jim Moeller and delegation director Leslie Gamez. A variety of photos were captured by the world media. I coordinated the media day at the Village with assistance from Village Press Officer Keith Bryant. Bryant also coordinated the media at the U.S. Team Flag raising in the Village and arranged interviews with a variety of U.S. athletes at the occasion. Team Processing media day was organized to coordinate the requested interviews with U.S. athletes as they got their apparel at the Delta Hotel. In addition to NBC coverage, a wide variety of media were on hand to detail the clothing, watches and rings at the event. Lindsay DeWall and Maureen Weeks coordinated the media day at Team Processing.

A LOOK AT OUR HOSTS: THE IOC AND VANOC

IOC

The press operations of the IOC continued to be outstanding. Under Anthony Edgar, there are a variety of experts such as Richard Palfreyman, Susan Polakoff-Shaw, Gary Kemper, Hugo, Gabbie Steinneger, and Sue Graham who add a huge dimension to the success of the press operations of the Games. With this staff, under Olympic Games Director Gilbert Felli, the press operations will always be good and professional. Journalists will be able to count on a certain standard for every Games.

The media relations staff was more visible for these Games than in past Games. Mark Adams and his staff were available, they were present at the daily briefings and the work area in the media workroom was a great service to journalists needing information. The main staff headquarters was at the IOC headquarters at the Westin, but there was sufficient assistance at the MPC so questions could be answered.

VANOC

One of the lasting memories of these Games will be the VANOC staff and their professionalism, their efficiency and attention to detail. More than that, what made these Games sensational was the attitude they carried around 24 hours a day. Their smiles in dark and far away places, away from the spotlight, brought a bit of warmth to those of us who worked 16-hour days for almost a month. It was a sense of humor when it was needed the most, that will linger for years from these Games. A laugh, many times at themselves brought an aura of goodness to this event.

The press operation staff was amazing. Everything worked. If it didn't, it soon did. If something needed to be changed, or tweaked, it was. The right people were in the right place and they knew what they were doing. And, they always had time for whatever problem you thought you had. This was a family and you always felt like you were loved.

The volunteers were like the sunshine in a meadow. You just relaxed when you saw them. There was never a question "too stupid." It could be the Canadian mindset but you always felt like somebody cared. That care went on for a long time, it never wavered.

Performance Service Centers

By Doug Ingram & Alan Ashley

The United States Olympic Committee (USOC) Sport Performance Division has set up versions of Performance Service Centers (PSCs) for our Teams at each Olympic Games since 2000 in Sydney, Australia. The PSCs are created to give our athletes, coaches and sport teams performance opportunities that enhance Team USA's success at the Games. At the PSCs in 2010, we provided video technology feedback using the international live broadcast feed of all venues. In addition, we provided supplementary support to the village operations in the areas of medicine, psychology, nutrition and physiology. Also, the centers served as meeting points for National Governing Bodies (NGBs) with non-accredited Performance personnel to connect with their accredited teammates.

The centers were set up just outside the Athlete Villages in Whistler and Vancouver in space leased from local businesses beginning two weeks prior to the Opening Ceremony until three days after the Closing Ceremony. Being close to the Athlete Villages was a critical success factor for those athletes, coaches and sports using the PSCs. The Games Organizing Committee understood the purpose of these centers and was supportive in their functionality,, particularly in allowing us to purchase the international broadcast feed for each location.

The initial intention was for the PSCs to serve also as Operation Centers for many logistical areas. However, the dynamics of the Games environment led us to a hybrid situation at the Vancouver site. The function of air travel (which once again was very well supported by the loan of two United Airlines desk agents) stayed at the Delta Hotel, the site of Team Processing once that event ended. This allowed them to be closer to the airport arrival/departures operations. By default, the sport transportation personnel also stayed at the Delta as their work aligned nicely with the air travel and airport personnel. The Delta became the de facto Operations Center with the above functions as well as ticket ops, the launching point for our courier service and the petty cash point of service. Since all the PSC and Ops personnel were living at the Delta, this became a very workable situation. The Vancouver PSC then served as a mini Ops center supporting a few logistical functions primarily event tickets and courier drops. In Whistler, the PSCs/Ops

coexisted as intended, since there was no air travel component at that site. An additional calibration was made on site in medical services. At both PSCs, we were over-staffed in this area, so we shifted some providers to the respective Villages. We need to review this for future Olympic Winter Games and adjust the number of medical providers accordingly, without allowing the pendulum to swing so far that our coverage is compromised.

The PSCs were very successful, particularly in performance technology. Not only did we exceed in this area on every deliverable committed to the NGBs, we were able to introduce some new technologies into the world of U.S. Olympic Sport. In addition to providing video recordings for post-event analysis, the USOC Sport Performance team effectively used revolutionary video technology, which enhanced our performance on the field play. Wireless air cards, netbooks, and video enabled devices allowed coaches and Sport Performance staff to communicate and share video in ways never experienced in previous Games. This gave us a distinct competitive advantage over our competitors.

There was outstanding teamwork at the PSCs. The camaraderie displayed by all team members was spectacular. Everyone was focused on performance and never worried about who got credit for any of the work. The most important bullet in the job descriptions was "other duties as assigned." The careful staff selection process and a combination of technical skills with the ability to work in the "Games mode" environment were the foremost factors we sought when putting this team together.

The search for the optimum location for the PSCs began more than four years prior to the Games. A very thorough search was done before settling on the two locations used in 2010. The space (between 1500 and 2000 square feet) was ideal for a Winter Games. The negotiation process was not as challenging as in past Games, most likely due to the lack of any language or business culture differences. Once we had the locations selected, we collected information from the NGBs through surveys, phone calls and face-to-face meetings on the key services they required at the PSCs to enhance their athletic performance. All this data was complied as a section of the Games Deliverables document. It proved an invaluable tool. We also held several meetings with key personnel to plan the details of what was needed to optimally deliver our various services in the two years prior to the Games. Plus, these key staff joined the NGBs on walk-throughs of the spaces during site visits to ensure we had a sound strategy to contribute to high performance. Once on site at the Games, we had nightly meetings and/or touched base with key individuals to ensure the execution of our plan stayed on track.

Overall, the USOC can be proud of the role the PSCs played in assisting Team USA to the all-time medal count record (37) for any nation at an Olympic Winter Games!

Security

By Larry Buendorf

Security at the Vancouver 2010 Olympic Winter Games was the responsibility of the host country. All venues, including the Village were secured by Vancouver Organizing Committee (VANOC) in partnership with local authorities. The primary security coordination was controlled by the Royal Canadian Mounted Police. Local authorities managed a Command Center that provided up-to-date information to the appropriate sources.

The U.S. State Department Diplomatic Security had a representative in the Vancouver Command Center. In addition, the U.S. State Department Diplomatic Security established its own Coordination Center that was occupied by many of the U.S. Federal Agencies including FBI, Transportation Security Administration (TSA), Postal Inspectors, Department of Defense and others. Representatives from the U.S. Coordination Center were present at most venues to establish a working relationship with local authorities and the venue managers. The United States Olympic Committee (USOC) Chief Security Officer (CSO) maintained contact with the U.S. representatives and appropriate authorities in Vancouver and visited all venues on a daily basis. Daily briefings were conducted at the U.S. State Department Diplomatic Security Coordination Center for updates on demonstrations, traffic issues and other intelligence related issues.

A temporary USOC employee was assigned security responsibilities in Whistler and performed similar duties as the CSO. There were no serious security related incidents in Vancouver or Whistler.

The view from the Olympic Village in Vancouver. Over 15,000 highly-trained security personnel provided protection during the Games. (PHOTO BY STEPHANIE LAMY/AFP/GETTY IMAGES)

Team Processing

By Katie Clifford

> The biggest challenge at Team Processing continues to be sizing. Teams who came through last were often left with the awkward sizing choices.

One of the very first stops on the Olympic Winter Games journey was Team Processing. At the Team Processing Center, athletes and members of the delegation collected all their Team USA apparel and commemorative items, had their individual and team photos taken, and received their final Olympic Ambassador Program (OAP) briefing.

Team Processing for 2010 was held at the Delta Hotel, conveniently located about five minutes from the Vancouver Airport. Teams arrived at the hotel directly from the airport, had lunch and then went through processing.

Teams began processing by getting their head shots taken by Long Photography. They then proceeded to the Commemorative room where they had the opportunity to select rings from OC Tanner, watches from Hamilton and to purchase leather jackets from Nike. Nike and OC Tanner both sent representatives from their corporate offices to help coordinate their stations. This was the first year we provided the athletes the opportunity to choose their watches. Hamilton was not sure how involved they wanted to be so they sent a rep for the first day that was able to train one of our volunteers on the product offering. Hamilton had a very good experience and would like to join us for the entire time in London.

The next stop for the team was the Apparel Distribution room. The distribution room was broken into two distinct sections: half for Polo Ralph Lauren (PRL) and half for Nike. The athletes received a clipboard with a list of all the items they should receive and a cart to carry everything. They then proceeded to the PRL side of the room where they collected their Opening and Closing Ceremonies items as well as a generous gifting package. The Nike side of the room consisted of Podium wear, Village wear and Training wear. Everyone had the opportunity to try on all the items. They then checked out and went to the Ralph Lauren alterations room where the PRL tailors and stylists made sure their Ceremonies and Podium items fit perfectly. We were very lucky to have extremely talented tailors who were able to make some miracles happen as our sizing became a challenge near the end of Team Processing.

After the aforementioned steps were complete, teams had dinner and the opportunity to ship any unnecessary items home. The following morning, all athletes were required to participate in the OAP. The primary purpose of this program was to help build excitement for the upcoming Games in addition to discussing the responsibility each athlete shared being a member of Team USA. This hour and a half program also included doping and medical information. Presenters included former Olympians Nikki Stone, Dan O'Brien, Vonetta Flowers, Bonnie Blair, and Picabo Street. Following the OAP, the teams boarded buses and headed to either the Villages in Whistler and Vancouver, or private housing.

Despite mostly consistent scheduling, a few teams needed to make adjustments. For example, a few of the OAP presentations were held in the evenings to allow those athletes to get to the Villages earlier. A couple of athletes came at odd hours and we did one-on-one processing with them. The men's hockey team was not able to come through processing due to NHL schedules so we pre-packed all their bags and sent them directly to the Village. There were a few other athletes and staff members whose schedules forced us to pre-pack and send their apparel packages directly to them.

The United States Olympic Committee (USOC) staff arrived five days early to set up for Team Processing. Three trucks arrived on our first day and two trucks arrived on our second day. We were lucky to have quite a bit of help from all USOC staff who had down time before their Games role began. Despite a small ballroom and upstairs storage, the energetic and creative staff built an impressive "store" in only a matter of days.

Team Processing could not have been as successful without an incredibly strong volunteer force. After contacting local schools and sports commissions in Vancouver, we ended up using a club called "Democrats Abroad" to fill the majority of our volunteer staff. They were mostly Americans who were so excited to be part of Team USA. We also had a number of volunteers travel to Vancouver from the United States to work at Team Processing. Many volunteers arrived early and helped with the initial unloading and setup. This experience was extremely helpful as they were primarily responsible for training the daily volunteers upon

arrival. We also assigned a volunteer team captain to both Nike and PRL and those team captains were responsible for dealing with any issues that arose to a level where it was necessary for a USOC staff member to be involved.

On Feb. 9 and 10 we invited the media to participate and film Team Processing. We had a high level of interest from national and international media outlets. While the cameras and extra bodies slowed things down, and we occasionally had to remind media members to give the athletes adequate space, it was great to have the media involved in this portion of the Games experience.

The biggest challenge at Team Processing continues to be sizing. Teams who came through last were often left with the awkward sizing choices. It was also frustrating for the volunteers to have to continually tell athletes we were out of their sizes. We tried our best to take care of everyone through alterations or offering items they could use as gifts but there were definitely some disappointed athletes. Two months after the Games we are still in the midst of making

up for sizing issues. We will be addressing this concern with our sponsors as we prepare for future Games.

The Delta Hotel was an ideal venue for Team Processing. Our Event Managers worked diligently to do as much advanced preparation as possible so upon arrival everything was ready. The staff was incredibly accommodating and took care of all of our requests in a timely and efficient manner. It was really nice to be staying on location as it allowed Team Processing staff to have sufficient down time. The teams also really appreciated not having to shuffle around too much since everything was in one place. The hotel was clean and comfortable, the food was great and the location was practically unbeatable.

Overall, Team Processing was a success that we can use as a building block for the future. Athletes and team staff were generally happy with the process and excited about the apparel. Looking forward, our two main priorities for future Games are to minimize the impact on sport performance while maximizing exposure for our sponsors.

Luger Megan Sweeney receives the official gear during the Team USA processing at the Delta Hotel. (PHOTO BY MATTHEW STOCKMAN/GETTY IMAGES)

USA House Business & Hospitality Center

By Jerri Roush

The purpose of the USA House Business and Hospitality Center (USA House) for the United States Olympic Committee (USOC) is to provide an umbrella program for all our key constituents at the Games; these include sponsors, suppliers, licensees, donors, National Governing Bodies (NGBs), International Relations, Olympians and 2010 Olympic Winter Games Team Members.

The process for developing the plan for USA House started approximately two and a half years out from the Games when we began getting the layout from USOC to understand the plans for the venues, accommodations, transportation, live sites, medals plaza and other pertinent operational details. For Vancouver, after learning of all these details, the analysis was made that it would be important to have two USA Houses: one in Vancouver and one in Whistler. This was due to the fact that the Vancouver Olympic Committee (VANOC) had set up separate operations for both of these areas including the Athlete Village, media center and medals plaza. With that in mind, we set out looking for two properties. It was the first time we had ever done two official USA Houses at any Olympic Games. In previous summer Games we have participated in sponsoring hospitality villages. These were within the fence lines and controlled by the host organizing committee. The USOC had programs in both Sydney and Athens. Overall, we looked at approximately 25-30 venues between Whistler and Vancouver. In Whistler we decided rather quickly upon a 4,000 square foot private home that could/would accommodate our needs. We negotiated the deal and signed the agreement on June 15, 2009, thus giving us six months, not a year, to build out. As for the Vancouver USA House, we found a location that appeared to be the perfect fit for the USOC. However, after almost a year of negotiations, new property management and failing to come to an agreement, we decided we were just not finding common ground that would meet both parties' needs. In late 2008 we began searching again for an alternative location. With a little bit of luck we found two locations that could meet our needs. One of the locations was a historic building that hadn't been in use for more than four years, and it was located very close to the Main Media Center. These all posed different challenges. We decided on 1022 LEVEL Furnished Living, an apartment complex, commercial building space under construction on the perimeter of Yaletown, centrally located to our other USOC operations. We agreed on renting three floors of commercial space of 25,000 square feet to build out as we needed for the Vancouver USA House.

The last time we did a full construction build out was in Salt Lake City when we first started this integrated hospitality approach. The number one benefit is that it could be built-out to meet the needs of our guests, and we could determine electrical, phone and plumbing configurations based on our needs. Once the contract was signed in January 2009, we then had a big construction project on our hands to finish in a year! We hired an architect to help design the interior so that we could provide the following services for our USOC team and our guests:

- Work space for USA House staff, marketing, broadcasting, IR, Development, Executive Team and offices for the President, CEO, CMO, COO and CFO

- Storage for the gift closet and the store, coat and baggage check, kitchen and back of house space for caterers

  - Dining and private event space
  - Media work room
  - U.S. Olympic Team Store
  - Live feed
  - AT&T All Access Internet Lounge
  - Allstate Hall of Fame Tribute Wall
  - Bud Lounge
  - Deloitte meeting and conference rooms
  - Hilton Concierge Service
  - Acer Laptop Check-out
  - United Transportation kiosk
  - McDonald's McCafe

Upon completion of the architectural drawings we had regular meetings with the builder, Onni. In this instance, like Salt Lake City, proximity to Colorado Springs was key because we could make regular trips to Vancouver to check on construction, pick out fixtures, answer questions and adjust accordingly as things came up. The USOC officially took over the building on Jan. 1 and construction was completed around Jan. 15th, just in time to begin moving in furniture, Panasonic equipment, catering equipment, the store merchandise and more.

Each Games bring their own unique challenges depending where you are in the world. With the Games

Short track speedskating bronze medalist J.R. Celski signed the wall at USA House. (PHOTO BY SCOTT HALLERAN/GETTY IMAGES)

being in North America, and no language barriers involved, we felt it would be a smooth Games logistically. Overall it was, but our biggest hurdles as it related to the USA House operations were the permitting processes for liquor, building, temporary use and catering in Vancouver and Whistler. There were different and separate rules for both houses regarding processes, fees and paperwork. VANOC didn't have a point person to go to for help walking through the process. A tremendous amount of time and energy was spent on the processes between both properties.

While building and dealing with permits, we were also working to arrange contracts for parking, security, cleaning, laundry, snow removal, garbage/recycling pick up and other services in order to manage the house on a day-to-day basis. Typically we would use the service providers the building already had contracted but in both of these instances we went out and found our own providers. Our catering company from New York City, Framboise, worked diligently on the food and beverage side to secure all necessary kitchen needs, staff and vendors to execute the project. Due to the rules and regulations with venting hoods and grease traps, we couldn't afford to put in a full kitchen on-site, so they acquired another catering company that was going out of business and utilized those facilities for the core work. Consequently, we had a substantial prep kitchen and walk-in cooler on-site in Vancouver. In Whistler we were able to utilize the extensive kitchen within the home to do more of the open kitchen concept with the chef preparing the food in front of USA House guests. The remaining back of house for the kitchen was set up in the three-car garage.

All of these preparations, plus putting the right configuration of staffing together for both USA Houses was a critical part of the overall execution. The staff for the USA Houses was pulled from Lake Placid, Chula Vista and other departments outside of Marketing (Sport Performance, Paralympics, NGB Business Development, Athlete Services and others) in order to compose a strong team to manage the needs during hours of operation: 10 a.m. to 1 a.m. in Vancouver; and 11 a.m. to 11p.m. in Whistler; and pre/post Games setup and teardown. In Vancouver we had two shifts of six plus three staff to manage the store operations; in Whistler we had one shift of eight. The staff dynamics for both Houses turned out very positive, which tends to be one of the hardest components but we had assembled excellent teams.

The USA Houses hosted more than 18,000 guests between the two locations, 27 Managing Victory tours, 25 Order of Ikkos presentations and 120 meetings /special events. We had a number of visiting VIPs, celebrities and dignitaries, including Vice President Joe Biden, Gov. Arnold Schwarzenegger, Brian Williams, Prince Albert of Monaco, Cuba Gooding Jr., Vera Wang, Mike Eruzione, Wayne Gretzky, Michael Phelps, and Peggy Fleming to name a few. The U.S. Olympic Team Shop in Vancouver was our largest

store to date with sales of more than $850,000, and we had more sponsors activate around the USA Houses than in years past (activation noted above in house services). The key to the success of the USA Houses is based on a combination of factors:

- Location, location, location

- Services offered to guest
- Food and beverage program
- Access for partners
- Registration process
- Costs for additional guests
- Parking
- Comfortable environment

We were able to execute well in all of these areas in Vancouver and had a largely successful Games Hospitality Program.

The U.S. Olympic Hall of Fame sponsored by Allstate showcased past Olympians in the USA House. (GETTY IMAGES)

Pairs figure skater Caydee Denney tries on the official Polo Ralph Lauren team wear. (Photo by Matthew Stockman/Getty Images)

Shaun White beams as Bud Keene, halfpipe coach, sports the Order of Ikkos medal presented to coaches whose athletes medal during the Olympic Games. (PHOTO BY CHRISTOPHER POLK/GETTY IMAGES)

Short track speedskater Kimberly Derrick— and bronze medalist—signs the wall at the USA House.

(PHOTO BY WARREN LITTLE/GETTY IMAGES)

P&G Family Home

Hadley Hedrick, flanked by her mother, Lynsey, and her father, Chad, strikes a pose wearing her Dad's silver and bronze medals. The speedskater was one of the many athletes honored at a special medal ceremony at the P&G Family Home attended by family members. (PHOTO BY CHRIS GRAYTHEN/GETTY IMAGES)

As a sponsor of the 2010 U.S. Olympic Team, Procter & Gamble Company launched its creative "Thanks Mom" program during the Vancouver Olympic Winter Games, giving millions of television viewers an inside look at the importance of Mom in an athlete's life.

But the 173-year-old company went a step further as a proud sponsor of Team USA and created the P&G Family Home to serve as a home-away-from-home for U.S. Olympians and their families.

Located in downtown Vancouver in close proximity to the city's major hotels, shopping districts and transportation, the P&G Family Home provided an inviting and convenient environment for family members and athletes to come together and unwind during the 17 days of competition.

Team USA families enjoyed lunches, dinners and beverages, 24-7 coverage of the Games, an Internet cafe and an opportunity to meet other families. There was a Pampers play area for toddlers, Tide laundry service and, of course, pampering for Moms at the in-house salon and spa.

Another area housed the Crest/Oral B "Smile with U.S.!" room, where guests could have their picture taken in a Vancouver setting with various Team USA winter props or have their head inserted on a Team USA athlete's body in action.

The popular Pringles snack lounge gave everyone a chance to sample the 21 flavors of P&G's potato chips while playing video and board games.

In addition to hosting medal celebrations for athletes and families, the P&G Family Home hosted informal birthday celebrations. Gold medalist Hannah Kearney was honored in a ceremony that included her Mom and Dad while bronze medalist Scotty Lago presented his Mom, Christine, with a birthday cake.

Miriam Chu, mother of ice hockey player Julie Chu, summed it up well: "P&G has just gone above and beyond."

A special thank-you to our P&G partners:

Marc Pritchard, *Global Marketing and Brand Building Officer* | Melanie Healey, *Group President North America* | Kirk Perry, *VP North America* | David Palmer, *Sports Marketing* | Michelle Sims, *Sports Marketing* | Jim Kandil, *Purchasing* | Jim Leish, *Corporate Marketing* | Alexis Katz, *Corporate Design* | Dave McCracken, *External Relations* | Janet Fletcher, *Corporate Marketing* | Cheri McMaster, *External Relations* | Rick Kotwa, *Corporate Security* | Sam Minardi, *Corporate Marketing* | Nick Higgins, *Corporate Marketing* | Cheryl Hudgins, *External Relations* | Jennifer Blauvelt, *Corporate Marketing* | Randall Smith, *Corporate Communications* | Karen Tlucek, *Corporate Marketing* | Greg Via, *Sports Marketing* | Amy White, *GMR* | Jeff Handler, *GMR* | Tony Swegle, *GMR* | Cameron Wagner, *GMR* | Greg Busch, *GMR* | Corinne Holman-Martin, *GMR* | Eric Gabrielson, *W+K*

Chef de Mission

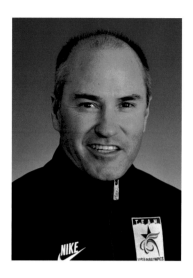

I was honored to part of Team USA as the *Chef de Mission* of the Winter Paralympic Team. I have been a long time supporter of adaptive sports and the Paralympic movement and to have the opportunity to play one role in helping the athletes and staff prepare for these games was truly humbling. I have watched many of our Paralympic athletes compete for years to prepare for these few moments in time. It is hard to describe my emotions as they gave everything they had for their country, families and friends. They were all amazing ambassadors for our country and their sport.

I had a front row seat along with thousands of Paralympic fans to witness amazing individual and team performances. Alana Nichols dominated the alpine skiing women's sitting division by winning four medals. Andy Soule became the first US athlete to win a medal in biathlon. Our US Sled Hockey team posted a 5-0 record and did not allow a single goal on their way to the gold medal. The common thread in all these performances is the athletes unwavering dedication to their sport and their commitment to excellence.

In addition to supporting the athletes, the men and women of US Paralympics , USOC Sports Performance and the International Games Division, did a terrific job supporting the families, friends and sponsors making the Paralympic experience truly memorable. I personally want to thank Larry Probst, Scott Blackmun, Norman Bellingham, Charlie Huebner, Joe Walsh and Leslie Gamez for their leadership and support. They provided the resources and performance plan for all our athletes to achieve their Paralympic dreams.

The Vancouver Olympic Games Organizing Committee provided the IPC and Paralympic fans with world class

I encourage everyone to carry forward the Paralympic Spirit.

facilities and the athletes enjoyed new state-of-the-art Olympic villages in Vancouver and Whistler. The Blue Coated Volunteers were everywhere and always ready with a smile and advice. I congratulate them on all of their efforts and know they made all Canadians proud.

As I look ahead to Sochi in 2014, I know we will build on the success of the 13 medals earned by Team USA. The commitment to provide a platform for adaptive athletes to compete at the highest levels will continue and I encourage everyone to carry forward the Paralympic Spirit.

Sincerely,

Steve Raymond

Alana Nichols dominated the alpine skiing women's sitting division by winning four medals. (PHOTO BY QUINN ROONEY/GETTY IMAGES)

2010 PARALYMPIC TEAM

Support Delegation

BOARD OF DIRECTORS
Larry Probst | Chairman
John Hendricks | Board of Directors Member
Mary McCagg | Board of Directors Member

TEAM STAFF

Alpine Skiing
Robert Lischer | Team Leader
Ray Watkins | Head Coach
Jessica Tidswell | Coach
Ian Gardner | Coach
Brad Alire | Coach
Erik Leirfallom | Coach
Kevin Jardine | Coach
Bryan Peterson | Coach
Jared Hawn | Head Wax Technician
Rick Ascher | Wax Technician
Luke Byers | Wax Technician
Ryan McDermott | Wax Technician
Dr. Ron Olson | Medical/Physician
Richard Quincy | Medical/Trainer
Kevin Pillifant | Medical/Trainer

Biathlon and Cross-Country Skiing
Sandy Metzger | Team Leader
Greg Rawlings | Head Coach
Dave Mark | Cross-Country Skiing Coach
Jon Kreamelmyer | Cross-Country Skiing Coach
James Upham | Biathlon Coach
Shawn Sholl | Wax Technician
Jeremiah Beach | Wax Technician
Dr. Jon Mulholland | Medical/Chiropractor

Sled Hockey
Dan Brennan | Team Leader
Ray Maluta | Head Coach
Bill Corbo | Assistant Coach
Bill Sandberg | Equipment Manager
JJ O'Connor | General Manager
Jim Smith | Assistant to General Manager
Brian Brewster | Medical/Trainer
Dr. Peter Donaldson | Medical/Physician

Wheelchair Curling
Marc Deperno | Team Leader
Steve Brown | Head Coach
Rusty Schieber | Assistant Coach
Harry Kapinowski | Equipment Manager
Linda Owens-Eisenhut | Medical/Massage

USOC STAFF

Communications
Jeannine Hansen | Chief Communications Officer
Beth Bourgeois | Lead Press Officer
Susan Katz | Online Media Lead
Keely Ames | Press Officer-Alpine Skiing
Jamie Blanchard | Press Officer-Online Media
Alex Clark | Press Officer-Sled Hockey
Allison Frederick | Press Officer-Biathlon & Cross Country Skiing
Josh George | Press Officer-Features
Terry Kolesar | Press Officer-Curling
Caroline Williams | Press Officer Alpine Skiing
Craig Renaud | Videography
Mami Renaud | Videography
Joe Kusumoto | Photography
Ian Lawless | Photography
Richard Lam | Photography
Randy Richardson | Photography

Headquarters
Steve Raymond | Chef De Mission
Scott Blackmun | Chief Executive Officer
Norman Bellingham | Chief Operating Officer
Charlie Huebner | Chief of Paralympics
Chris Sullivan | Chief of Bid Administration
Mike English | Chief of Sport Performance
Larry Buendorf | Chief of Security
Joe Walsh | Deputy Chef De Mission
Alan Ashley | Managing Director Sport Performance
Peter Zeytoonjian | Managing Director Marketing
Laura Macaulay-Peeters | Legal
Tommy O'Hare | Athlete Ombudsman
Abigail Tompkins | Headquarters/Protocol Manager
Benecia Newhouse | Sponsor/Hartford Support
Barbara Butler | Executive Admin Support
Jon McCullough | AAC Chair/Designee

Paralympic Experience
John Register | Paralympic Experience Director
Dean Nakamura | Paralympic Experience
Julie Minahan | Paralympic Experience
Nick Rengel | Paralympic Experience

Team Processing

Katie Clifford | Director
Lisa Elson | Housing Manager
Bridget Toelle | Finance
Mia Delumpa | IT Manager
Jamie Martin | Transportation Manager
Kallie Quinn | Transportation Manager
Carol Fritz | Food Service Manager
Rick Miner | Logistics
Pam Sawyer | Apparel Distribution
Lucy Denley | Apparel Distribution
Mike Beagley | Apparel Distribution
Justin Rogers | Apparel Distribution

Vancouver Operations

Leslie Gamez | Games Director
Doug Ingram | Games Director
Mike Mushett | Operations Director
Dawna Callahan | Operations Manager
Keri Schindler | Operations Manager
Lenny Abbey | Transportation Manager
Charlie Paddock | Transportation
Carlee Wolfe | Friends and Family
Richard Bittles | IT Lead
Desiree Filippone | Government Relations
Aundre Clinton | United Air Support

Vancouver Village

Julie O'Neill | Village Director
Janine DiSalvatore | Village Manager
Terris Tiller | Airport Operations

Jared Steenberge | Transport/NGB Services
Mike Levine | IT/Logistics/Operations
Candace Cable | Athlete Services Coordinator
Chris Schroer | Clinic Director
Dr. Shana Miskovsky | Clinic Physician

Veterans Service Organization Program

Roger Neppl | Military Programs Director
Heidi Grimm | Veterans Program
Jeff Steffen | Veterans Program
Shannon Whiteway | Veterans Program Support

Whistler Operations

Elaine Marin | Operations Director/Finance
Anna Miller | Operations Manager
Jason Delpr | Transportation/Logistics
Julie Gawronski | Friends and Family
Ruby Haddock | Operations Admin. Support
Sandy Weeks | IT Setup
Steve Jeffries | Security

Whistler Village

Laura Ryan | Village Director
Glen Werner-Roseboom | Village Manager
Tommy O'Hare | Athlete Ombudsman
John Carlock | Transport/NGB Services
Scott Riewald | Performance Technology
Dave McDaniel | IT/Logistics/Operations
Amber Jordan | Athlete Services Coordinator
Peter Toohey | Medical Director
Eugene Byrne | Chief Medical Officer
Lori-Ann Heilborn | Massage Therapist

A Lil'wat Nation hoop dancer performs during the Closing Ceremony of the Paralympic Winter Games. (PHOTO BY HANNAH JOHNSTON/GETTY IMAGES)

TEAM USA
Alpine Skiing

By Robert Lischer

I am the U.S. Adaptive Ski Team Program Manager, which is part of the U.S. Ski and Snowboard Association. I believe I had enough time to prepare for my first time as a Team Leader.

Adaptive alpine has five skiing events which include downhill, super-G, giant slalom, slalom and super combined. Skiers with blindness/visual impairment are guided through the course by sighted guides who use voice signals to indicate the course to follow. Athletes with physical disabilities use equipment that is adapted to their needs including single ski, sit-ski or orthopedic aids. Many different people with different disabilities participate at an elite level of competition. Key performances include having Alana Nichols, one of our development athletes, win four medals.

I attended the Team Leadership Final Countdown meeting in Vancouver, which helped with the process and planning for the Paralympic Winter Games. I learned what we needed to do to be as prepared as we could.

As a sport, we need to expose more athletes to an international stage to compete against the best skiers that are out there. Our athletes compete in World Cups, and team selection was based on monthly updates of points and start rights. The alpine Paralympic team was selected at the end of February. The selection processed allowed us to identify and select the best athletes for the team. The best procedure would be to pick the athletes that best suit the team and can have a great chance of getting medals. There wasn't much time between trials/selections because the team was named and then went directly to World Cup Finals in Aspen. I think the athletes need somewhat of a break between World Cup Finals and the Paralympics.

Our alpine team trains in Mt. Hood, Ore., on the glacier out there for two weeks in June and July. The athletes/team competed in a test event at the official Games site/venue prior to the Paralympic Games last year. I wasn't with the team at that point, but from what I heard, they should have had more time to train on the Paralympic race hill.

The facilities were fine for the most part. One problem arose during the last couple of days when the athletes had medals ceremonies at the venue. At first it was hard to figure out how to get them and their equipment down the hill since nothing was provided to assist or transport. There was transportation for coaches, but that did not help the athletes. Overall, the only problems we had were just the weather and not enough time for the athletes to train on the hill. The athletes made with what they were given.

Many of our athletes had great success. Stephani Victor won a gold medal in the super combined, and a silver medal in slalom. Nichols won gold medals in giant slalom and downhill, a silver medal in the super-G and a bronze medal in the super combined. Mark Bathum took the silver in downhill. Danelle Umstead won bronze medals in downhill and super combined. Rounding out the list of medalists was Laurie Stephens with a silver medal in downhill. We had a couple of athletes that should have medaled but they missed the podium by a short margin.

The transportation worked really well in getting athletes/staff to and from the venue from the Village. The athletes and staff enjoyed the accommodations that were given to the team.

Vancouver was a great experience for the team. I learned it is a tough job to be Team Leader but it was a very enjoyable experience and a great opportunity. I am very glad I got to experience it all.

American Christopher Devlin-Young competes in the men's sitting super-G. He finished fourth. (PHOTO BY QUINN ROONEY/GETTY IMAGES)

Nordic Skiing

By Sandy Metzger (Team Leader prior to the Games)

I am employed full-time by U.S. Ski and Snowboard Association as the Program Director for Adaptive Sports, and was named as the Team Leader more than one year out. I feel I had ample time to prepare. I was a Team Leader for the 2002 and 2006 Paralympic Winter Games.

Cross-country skiing is a sport based solely on time. Athletes are placed in categories determined by their level of disability. Biathlon is also timed-based, but the athletes shoot and must either ski penalty laps if they miss or have time added on their final score for any misses.

I attended the Key Decision Maker Meeting in May 2008 in Vancouver. This meeting was helpful, and the tour of the venues was good, and I attended the Team Leadership Kick-Off Meeting/Conference Call (May/June 2009). I actually attended this meeting in person in Colorado Springs. It was a great chance to meet all of the players and to go over the deliverables. I also attended the Final Countdown meeting in November. I felt well prepared going into the 2010 Paralympic Winter Games because I had all the information I needed to do the job.

All of our training camps were held in the United States. We tried to offer the athletes ample time for preparation. They were each given a prescribed strength and conditioning program to follow. The only thing I would change is to have more on-snow training time.

Selection procedures were based upon results from International Paralympic Committee (IPC) sanctioned World Cups and World Championships. The procedures were objective. The team was named Feb. 22, 2010. We named the teams as late as possible so we could include all competitions from this season. The selection procedures were fair and named the most qualified athletes to the team. In retrospect, there are no changes we would make. We would use the same selection going forward. There was no training time between selections until the Games.

The athletes did have the opportunity to compete in test events held at the official Games site prior to the Paralympic Winter Games. The test event was a great opportunity for the athletes to ski on the actual race courses. It was a beneficial event.

The following is from coach Jon Kreamelmeyer, Team Leader during Games time

The cross-country team's performance can be broken down into individual events throughout the season. The following camps/competitions were preparation for the Paralympic Winter Games.

At fall camp in November we had a time trial at the base of Howelsen Hill in Steamboat Springs, Colo. Chris Klebl was in great shape and skiing strong as usual. Sean Halsted skied well, too. Andy Soule was very slow for the amount and quality of training he had done. For Greg Mallory, and Monica Bascio it seemed apparent that their lifestyles really hampered their off season training. The coaching staff devised conditioning plans for all athletes to improve based on their performance at the fall camp.

Nationals in Anchorage were good for Klebl and Halsted in the distance events. In the sprints, Mallory did a great job as did Soule and Halsted. Klebl's non-participation in the sprint event was very unfortunate in his development as an athlete.

At World Cup in Norway, Klebl was strong but still off from where he needed to be in a Paralympic Winter Games year. His speed was not where it needed to be. Soule skied much better in all of his events than in Steamboat and Anchorage, and really fed off of the improvement. His performances would feed the rest of his season. Halsted, Bascio, and Mallory did not attend the event due to budget constraints.

In the Europe World Cups (Germany and France) the athletes were given several opportunities to ski against the same competitors they would face in the Paralympic Winter Games. The athletes learned what they needed to do to be competitive at the Games.

At the Paralympics Winter Games, Soule was a rock star, he skied great in the shorter events, and was improving in the distance events. Klebl skied solid in the sprint event. Halsted, Soule and Klebl should have had the opportunity to advance in the sprints. I think in a different format we could have won another medal. The IPC only advanced eight athletes to the finals. During the World Cup Sprints we advanced 16.

In conclusion, Soule and Halsted had some solid performances and showed great improvement as we continue on a new training program with them. They should do very well in the future and they are already looking toward Sochi. Klebl needs to change his plan; he is strong but not fast. Klebl can get away with strength in the early part of the season, but needs to ramp it up to get results throughout the season. Bascio and Mallory have had great careers and, unfortunately, this season was not their best.

There was a good program in place leading to the Paralympic Winter Games. The athletes who followed the program improved. Everything we needed to be successful at the Games was provided. The Vancouver Olympic Committee (VANOC) did a great job with all aspects of the Paralympic Winter Games. The staff we had at the Paralympic Winter Games did an excellent job with the team.

TEAM USA
Sled Hockey

By Dan Brennan

I am a member of the National Governing Body for USA Hockey, Inc., sled hockey. I was selected as Team Leader in 2009 and had enough preparation time. I have served many times as a Team Leader at the World Inline Hockey Championships.

Sled hockey is an incredible brand of hockey where disabled players all become equal playing in a sled. The players on our team are incredible people.

I attended the Key Decision Maker meeting in May 2008 in Vancouver, and the Team Leadership Kick-Off meeting/conference call in May/June 2009. I also attended the Team Leadership Final Countdown meeting in November 2009 in Vancouver. All of the meetings were very helpful.

Our team trained in the United States and was given three months off prior to training camp /tryouts in July. There is nothing of our overall program that I would change concerning our preparation for the Paralympic Winter Games. Our staff was excellent and our training methods were solid.

Initially at a tryout of 42 players we selected 18 players. We carried 18 players until Jan. 1 and cut down to 15 prior to a tune-up tournament in Japan, then on to Vancouver. The selection process absolutely identified and allowed us to select the best athletes for the team. There are no changes we would make in the selection procedures. We had a very intense schedule and full season of games, events and camps prior to Vancouver. This worked well for us.

The team played in a four-team tournament in Vancouver a year prior to the Paralympic Winter Games. This was highly beneficial.

We had a good balanced schedule with pre-game skates and staff-led days off. The facilities were accessible and appropriate. In fact, they were excellent! We did not have any problems.

The team played extremely well outscoring our five opponents 19-0 on the way to winning the gold medal.

The balanced schedule was key for us. As much as we were at the rink we also took the team away from the village a few times and allowed our players time with family members. We did not encounter any programs or procedures that caused any problems. I have no suggestions for changes to make things work better. I would say, that this was an incredible ride. However, without our prior camp in Rochester and solid team preparation by our coaches we would not have been as successful as we were.

I have been overseeing our U.S. National Sled Team for three years now and I always cringe when I hear the word disabled. Our team, from top to bottom, consists of the most able-bodied athletes I have ever been around in my 40 years in hockey both as a player and now an administrator. Our coaches were tremendous in getting the absolute most out of our players both on and off the ice. I'm beyond proud of all the players and staff. It was the best hockey experience I have ever been a part of.

(From left to right) Mike Blabac, Bubba Torres, Joe Howard (#23) and Alexi Salamone react after defeating Japan, 2-0, to win the gold medal. (Photo by Martin Rose/Bongarts/Getty Images)

Wheelchair Curling

By Marc DePerno

The Paralympic process is both mentally and physically grueling. Having a rigid daily regimen both prior to and during the Games is critical to guarantee optimal performance and outcome.

I have experience as the director of outreach and development for wheelchair curling for USA Curling. I also work as an occupational therapist at the Charles T. Sitrin Health Care Center in New Hartford, N.Y., where I direct a Paralympic Sport Club, so I have a vested interest in the sport of wheelchair curling.

I applied for the position of Paralympic Team Leader in 2008 and was notified of my selection in early 2009. This proved to be a sufficient amount of time to address the issues associated with this role.

Prior to the Games, I participated in the Team Leadership Kick-Off conference call as well as the Final Countdown meeting which provided critical information regarding scheduling, processes, points of contact, and problem solving tactics. Serving as the Team Leader at the 2007, 2008 and 2009 World Wheelchair Curling Championships gave me a keen insight as to the process associated with this position as well as the intricacies of the sport.

Unlike most wheelchair sports, wheelchair curling can be played by athletes with a wide range of ability levels. This team sport is played from a stationary position; it requires only moderate upper body strength and upper extremity range of motion to compete. Additionally, the International Federation rules mandate that teams be of mixed gender to compete, which is a unique characteristic not found in most sports. The sport is played on a sheet of ice with an objective of sliding 42-pound stones more than 100 feet towards a scoring zone. Teams, which consist of four members, "throw" a total of eight stones per end. A game consists of eight ends. Each team has 68 minutes to complete the game. Should a team's time expire before the game is concluded, that team automatically loses. Performance is based largely on team strategy and shot execution.

In 2009, USA Curling designated the 2008 U.S. National Champions as the core of the Paralympic Team as a means to best execute a plan to develop the National Team with a focus on winning a gold medal at the 2009 World Championships and 2010 Paralympic Winter Games. Additional athletes were selected for the National Team via an open process involving three try-out events prior to mid-December 2008. A panel of USA Curling judges selected the top four athletes and one alternate. This process was not only validated but proved to be most successful as the core of the National Team outperformed all other competitors at the try-out events and eventually placed fourth at the 2009 World Championships. The elite-level experience accrued by these core athletes was invaluable and ensured sound game strategy and team cohesiveness at the Paralympic Winter Games.

Considering there is limited curling ice availability throughout the summer off-season, the team took advantage of all potential opportunities in preparation for the Games. The team participated in an able-bodied bonspiel held in Cape Cod, Mass., in July and practiced in high performance camps held in Green Bay, Wis., in August, and Lake Placid, N.Y., in September. Additionally, the team communicated regularly via telephone and e-mail, and routinely reviewed game footage from previous competitions to analyze strategy. The athletes also engaged in personalized exercise routines to maintain strength and endurance.

Having the ability to practice throughout the summer and participate in additional international wheelchair bonspiels would provide our team with increased elite level competition experience. Of course, the team's ability to participate is contingent on available funding.

During the season, Team USA trained and competed extensively in preparation for the Games with sessions occurring primarily in Utica, N.Y., and Madison, Wis. The team competed in several major international bonspiels including the 4th Annual U.S. Open in Utica in which they placed first; the Norwegian Open held in Oslo, Norway, where they placed sixth; the 2nd Annual Kinross International Bonspiel in Kinross, Scotland, in which they placed third; and the 5th Annual Cathy Kerr Memorial Bonspiel held in Ottawa, where they placed first. Additionally, the team competed in several able-bodied bonspiels held in Utica; Madison; Wauwatosa, Wis.; and Cape Cod.

Coming into the Games, the team had valuable experience competing at the Paralympic venue as they were competitors in the 2009 World Wheelchair Curling Championships which served as the official test event. The familiarity with the venue proved beneficial as it ensured less questioning and potential confusion associated with location of key areas and processes.

Prior to and during the Games, the Team utilized practice ice at nearby Vancouver curling clubs to maintain the highest level of performance.

Throughout the week of competition, Team USA performed strongly finishing the round robin with a record of 7-2 and a No. 2 ranking heading into the semi-finals. Unfortunately, losses to Korea (7-5) in the semi-finals and Sweden (7-5) in the bronze medal game resulted in a fourth-place finish.

During the Games, the venue proved to be superb and the volunteer staff was exceptional. The only concern was related to the meal selection at the venue as a more neutral menu (ie., pasta, sandwiches, chicken) would have been ideal. The Paralympic Village and staff, and the transportation and wheelchair repair service staff were exceptional. The dining hall provided a vast variety of meals that exceeded our expectations. The only area of concern was related to the lack of curtains on the bedroom windows which made it difficult to sleep for many of the athletes.

Our entire delegation of United States Olympic Committee (USOC) support staff did an outstanding job and played a vital role with ensuring positive outcomes at the Games.

The Paralympic process is both mentally and physically grueling. Having a rigid daily regimen both prior to and during the Games is critical to guarantee optimal performance and outcome.

It has been an absolute honor to assist my country with the Paralympic process. The overall experience was one which I will keep close to my heart forever. I look forward to the future and assisting our nation's talented athletes achieve success at the highest level.

Jacqui Kapinowski releases the stone during the wheelchair curling round robin game between Korea and the United States. Team USA won 9-6. (PHOTO BY MARTIN ROSE/BONGARTS/GETTY IMAGES)